The Gender and Media Diversity Journal is an output of the Gender and Media Diversity Centre (GMDC). The GMDC is a physical and virtual resource centre based in Southern Africa, with linkages in Africa and across the globe. The centre envisages media that are diverse, representative, responsive, and professional, and a citizenry, women and men, who are empowered to engage critically with their media. It facilitates the collection, connection and diseemination of information resources relating to gender, media and diversity. The centre also collaborates on research, education and training.

The GMDC is a consortium of media NGOs and tertiary institutions. Working with an advisory group, Gender Links manages the centre. The advisory group includes:
- National University of Science and Technology, Zimbabwe (Kathy Matsika)
- Polytechnic of Namibia, Namibia (Emily Brown)
- Zambia Institute of Mass Communication, Zambia (Justina Phiri)
- University of Botswana, Botswana (David Kerr)
- University of Antananarivo, Madagascar (Hary Razafinmpiasa)
- Media Institute of Journalism, Malawi (Dalitso Nkunika)
- African Women and Child Feature Service, East Africa (Rosemary Okello)
- International Women's Media Federation (Liza Gross)
- African Fathers Initiative, (Trevor Davies)

Members in academic institutions

- Institut Facultaire des Sciences de I' Informationet de la (IFASCIC), (A. Obul Okwess)
- University of Lesotho, Institute of Extra Mural Studies, (Sabiie Ntoanyane)
- Eduardo Mondlane University, (Eduardo Namburete)
- Sol Plaatjie Institute (Francis Mdlongwa)
- Harare Polytechnic (Peter Banga)
- Higher School of Journalism (Feliciano Micavo)
- University of Dar es Salaam (Dr Bernadetta Killian)
- University of Limpopo (Professor Sheila Mmusi)
- Univeryst of Venda (Beverlyn Dube)
- University of Witwatersrand (Sarah Chiumbu)
- University of Swaziland (Adidi Uyo)
- University of Zambia (Sr Rose Nyondo)
- Midlands University (Peter Mandava)
- Malawi Polytechnic (Francis Chikunkhuzeni)

Members in media organisations

- Inter Press Service (Paula Fray)
- Media Institute of Southern Africa (Zoe Titus)
- International Federation of Journalists (Pamela Morinière)
- World Association for Christian Communication (WACC) - (Lavinia Mohr)

Independent representatives

- Sweden, Maria Edstrom (University of Gothenburg)
- India, Ammu Joseph
- United Kingdom, Margaret Gallagher
- Zimbabwe, Pat Made
- South Africa, Lizette Rabe
- Botswana, Pinkie Mekgwe

The objectives of the GMDC are to:
- Promote more analytical, responsive and contextual journalism.
- Develop and share a body of knowledge on gender and media diversity.
- Publicise the work of media scholars, students and practitioners.
- Provide resources that make the links between media theory and practice.
- Create a space for participatory discussion and debate on gender and media diversity.
- Develop global and local partnerships with strategic organisations.
- Become a centre of excellence on new approaches and fresh thinking.

To contact the GMDC:
9 Derrick Avenue, Cyrildene, 2198
Johannesburg, South Africa
http://www.gmdc.org.za
email: gmdcmanager@genderlinks.org.za
Twitter: @Genderlinks
Facebook: www.facebook.com/Genderlinks
Phone: +27 (0) 11 622 2877
Fax: +27 (0) 11 622 4732

Gender and Media Diversity Journal
Gender, Popular Culture and Media Freedom
Issue 10
© Copyright 2012
Gender Links
ISBN:978-1-920550-56-1
Editor: Saeanna Chingamuka and Danny Glenwright
Cover Photos: Saeanna Chingamuka, Women's Net, Financial Mail, Macdonald Phiri, Echoes, Gender Links Library, Dainess Nyirenda's facebook photo gallery
Design/Layout: Debi Lucas
Printer: D S Print

CONTENTS

CONTENTS

EDITORIAL

By Saeanna Chingamuka

"Right now there are more people on face book than there were on the planet 200 years ago. Humanity's greatest desire is to belong and connect, and now we see each other. We hear each other. We share what we love and it reminds us of what we have in common. And this connection is changing the way the world works. Governments are trying to keep up, and older generations are concerned.The game has new rules."

This is the introduction by the narrator of the viral video released by the *Invisible Children* on 5 March 2012 called *Stop Kony*. By the time of writing this editorial, the video had been viewed 89, 819, 046 times with 1,385,702 likes and 146,668 dislikes. *Invisible Children* uses film, creativity and social action to end the use of child soldiers in Joseph Kony's rebel way and restore Lord Resistance Army (LRA) affected communities in East and Central Africa to peace and prosperity.

The campaign to stop Joseph Kony, the leader of Uganda's Lord Resistance Army, drew controversy with some people questioning why an American charity should be leading campaigns in Africa and why it targeted US leaders instead of African leaders to stop Kony.

> *Love it or hate it, the online phenomenon that is KONY 2012 offers valuable lessons to development communicators.*
>
> -Riona McCormack, REPSSI Regional Communications Officer

However, there are many lessons to be learnt from the viral video about development communication by groups working on gender equality. The Internet provides a plethora of possibilities to campaign against gender inequalities in society. It is up to activist organisations to produce content that encourages citizens to act and be agents of change in society. Further, they are able to express themselves freely and demand equality.

The tenth edition of the Gender and Media Diversity Journal (GMDJ) focuses on freedom of expression. The theme is mainly informed by the 2011 Windhoek +20 celebrations of the Windhoek Declaration on Promoting Independent and Pluralistic Media, the recent debates on access to information and how freedom of expression is understood in today's society. The use of ICTs in order to enjoy freedom of expression is also tackled in this issue.

Freedom of expression comes and is enjoyed in many ways. In the first section, the journal explores how popular culture in the form of movies, hip-hop music, pornography and advertising perpetuate or condemn stereotypes. Dainty Smith writes about the 'bromance' culture and how the representation of gay people in popular culture has seen a breaking down of barriers between the heterosexual and homosexual communities. While the gay community has found soapies and movies as one way in which they can express themselves openly, another writer questions if the script writers of a popular soap in South Africa, *Generations*, understand gay issues so that they do not run into problems of perpetuating the same stereotypes that they condemn.

Freedom of expression or oppression? Three writers question the dilemmas that the women's movement is faced with as some women are objectified in pornography, hip-hop videos and advertising. The women may be enjoying their right to express themselves, but at the expense of their right to dignity.

At the Windhoek +20 celebrations, the media in Africa took stock of the state of media freedom and how the Declaration assisted many countries to mainstream media freedom in their constitutions. It is at these celebrations that a proposal to turn to access to information was deliberated.

The two freedom of expression issues, media freedom and access to information, are rooted in Article 19 of the Universal Declaration of Human Rights (UDHR). It guarantees to every citizen "the freedom to hold opinions without interference and to seek, receive and impart information and ideas through any media and regardless of frontiers." A very narrow understanding of the meaning of this right has led to different interpretations of the duties imposed on governments and much concentration on the negative obligations of governments in fulfilling this right. In addition, there is little understanding of the gender dimensions of media freedom of expression and access to information.

Saeanna Chingamuka, Daud Kayisi and Claudine Hingston argue that there are many ways in which citizens may be denied the right to be heard. As much as media freedom has been understood to be the absence of political censorship, women's voices may be excluded from the media. They recommend that for gender equality to be attained in society, there is need to take into consideration "gender based censorship" which ultimately disempowers, silences and makes invisible certain people in society.

The journal explores the gains and losses made in the recently adopted African Platform on Access to Information. GL CEO Colleen Lowe Morna and GMDC Manager Saeanna Chingamuka trace the campaign to make the Platform gender aware, and rate the gains at 49% of what gender activists had hoped for. Patience Zirima recommends that the Draft Model Law for AU Member States on Access to Information should mainstream gender so that when states draft national laws, they understand what a gender aware access to information policy looks like.

In order to ensure that gender is integrated in media content, Gender Links has launched a

Media Centres of Excellence project. Its aim is to contribute to the advancement of the SADC Protocol on Gender and Development target of gender equality in and through the media by 2015. Sikhonzile Ndlovu provides and update on the project and the monitoring and evaluation strategies that have been put in place to ensure sustainability of the long term goal to have gender mainstreamed in editorial practice, content and institutional practice.

At international level, UNESCO is facilitating the development of gender and media indicators that will enable media organisations and others - such as media workers' unions and gender activists - to evaluate the place and role of women in newsrooms (print, broadcasting and internet) as well as in news content. Building on the work done by several global, regional and national surveys that record the extent of the problem, Ammu Joseph points out that the indicators are meant to help assess the nature and degree of imbalance. Further, they point the way towards internal measures to address evident disparities.

The advent of ICTs comes with benefits and challenges for gender equality in society. ICTs can provide an alternative for women to be heard and access information as Fanisa Masia argues. Fungai Machirori reflects on her journey to expression through blogging. One of the main reasons why she started blogging is that the newspapers that she has contributed articles to censored so much of her language and what she aimed to articulate became shrouded in conservatism and political correctness. She concludes that the media should stop playing the safe game and dare to reflect the many faces of

society. That way, women and men in society may finally have their stories heard. However, ICTs have their own problems.

Glory Mushinge writes about cyber abuse and warns women on how they can protect themselves. On 18 April 2012, the *Daily Sun* in South Africa covered a story of how seven suspects were arrested for raping a mentally ill girl. The rape was recorded on a cellphone and the tabloid, together with the police used the video to identify the rapists and arrest them. Technology is thus as good as we use it.

Social media can also be used in a progressive way to advance women's rights. Its power cannot be underrated. Danny Glenwright presents a case study on how Gender Links has been using cyber dialogues to maximize the exchange of information among citizens online. In addition, social media has been used to fight despots, price increases and evil regimes among other things.

Social media can also be used to fight patriarchy and unequal power relations.

Can the Internet enhance access to information and provide an alternative platform for expression of voices generally excluded as a consequence of the dominant gender order, namely lesbian and transgender? Three writers consider the nature of regulatory policy in South Africa in relation to its potential impact on the freedom of sexual expression and the ways in which transgender and lesbian people use the internet to negotiate and perform their sexuality. Angela Shoko traces the gaps in the draft Zimbabwe ICT Bill in relation to gender equality.

We invite comments and feedback on this issue, as well as contributors for future issues. For information about upcoming themes and contributors guidelines, contact the GMDC Manager on: gmdcmanager@genderlinks.org.za

Happy reading!

Saeanna Chingamuka
Editor and GMDC Manager

The *Daily Sun*, a tabloid in South Africa, is the only paper that had a front page story of the rape of a mentally ill girl and narrated how video footage was used to arrest the suspects.

NEWS BRIEFS
NEWS BRIEFS

First woman president says the time is now!

Malawi's Joyce Banda has become the first female president in the region (Southern Africa) after the death of President Bingu wa Mutharika and the second in Africa after Ellen Johnson-Sirleaf of Liberia. Her appointment brings a wave of hope to Malawi and is one way in which the region is moving towards the attainment of 50/50 representation of women and men in politics and decision making by 2015. This is in line with the provisions of the 2008 SADC Protocol on Gender and Development.

Joyce Banda, Malawi's first female president.   *Photo: Macdonald Phiri*

President Banda has always emphasised the need for deliberate policies to challenge the patriarchal values still embedded in Malawi and in Southern Africa. In 2011, Forbes Magazine recognised her as the third most powerful female politician in Africa after Johnson-Sirleaf and Ngozi Okonjo-Iweal (currently vying for World Bank Presidency), Nigeria's Minister of Finance.

Banda has worked tirelessly to empower women economically in Malawi. She founded the National Association of Business Women (NABW) in 1990, a financial lending institution that aims to economically empower rural women. In addition, she has steered numerous women's rights initiatives in Malawi. As Minister of Gender, Child Welfare and Community Services, Banda fought for the Domestic Violence Bill to be passed into law. Parliament enacted the law, after it had previously failed to for seven years.

Her first major assignment will be in July 2012, when African Union (AU) delegates will gather in Malawi for the AU summit and election of the new chair following the last polls that ended in a deadlock. Nkosazana Dlamini-Zuma, South Africa's Home Affairs Minister will stand again for AU commission chair after stopping Jean Ping to a second term of office in the previous elections. Banda will therefore have to assert her power and ensure that African leaders support the appointment of Dlamini-Zuma.

The work being done by women leaders proves that putting women in leadership positions is not only democratically correct but it is the right thing to do. Women have shown that they are capable of delivering positive results in difficult circumstances, a thing that point to the fact that they can do much better if given full support. Banda has to now prove to the region that the time for female leaders in Africa is now.

Mainstreaming or malestreaming?
Gender@work in organisations

Gender is a cross cutting issue that concerns all development organisations and CSO's. Various approaches to attain gender equality have been adopted in CSO's. These include the Women in Development (WID); Women And Development (WAD); Gender and Development (GAD); Basic needs and the MDGs; Women's rights; and the Men and boys. The approaches work in different ways. What is the best approach, what are the shortcomings of each, what can be learnt? Have you ever thought about what your orgnaisations' theory of change is?

The Gender and Media Diversity Centre (GMDC), a GL partnership project that hosts regular dialogues on topical issues, is facilitating the discussion on how organisations are mainstreaming gender in their work. The GMDC will host two cyber dialogues and a seminar to discuss gender at work in organisations.

Some key questions arising include:
- **Approaches:** What is your theory of change with regard to gender and what approaches are you taking - women's rights; women and girls; gender mainstreaming; boys and men etc. If you are using a combination of approaches, why, when, where, and what has worked?
- **Tools and methods used:** Can we share tools and methods that we have used and found to be useful?
- **Case studies of what has worked:** Sharing examples of successes and failures. What have you learned in the process? How are you applying this?

The outcomes of the discussions include sharing of best practices around gender mainstreaming, tools that work and that do not work and demonstrating how civil society is contributing to gender equality. The discussions will be collated into a learning paper that will be shared on the GMDC website.

The first discussion centred on how media and journalism training are integrating gender into course content. Media and journalism trainers agree that it is important to mainstream gender in higher education. They agreed that a GAD approach will work in their contexts because men should understand the importance of gender mainstreaming processes and support them. Currently, there are more men than women in media and journalism training institutions.

SADC endorses Dlamini Zuma for next AU Commission Chairperson

As the July African Union (AU) Summit draws near, the election of the next AU Commission Chairperson remains a "hot issue" on the AU agenda, with a division occuring along traditional English-French fault lines.

Nkosazana Dlamini Zuma for AU's top job.   *Photo: GCIS*

After three rounds of voting at the first election in Addis Ababa, Ethiopia, in January 2012, neither South Africa's Nkosazana Dlamini Zuma nor

Gabon's Jean Ping was able to clinch the two-thirds majority needed to win the post at the election held.

Soon after, SADC's Extra-Ordinary Inter-State Politics and Diplomacy Committee (ISPDC) met and agreed to once again field Dlamini Zuma at the next election in July. In a statement issued from the Cape Town International Convention Centre in March, the committee said: "SADC remains committed and united to its candidate for the Chairperson of the AU Commission."

Dlamini Zuma, a seasoned diplomat and politician, is currently South Africa's home affairs minister. She has made significant contributions to South Africa's democracy and development.

Kenya's Erastus Mwencha will be the caretaker of the position until the next round of voting takes place July in Malawi.
Source: http://www.defenceweb.co.za

Women's freedom of dress threatened in Malawi and South Africa

Women in both Malawi and South Africa were sexually harassed and stripped in public because they were wearing trousers and mini-skirts, according to media reports out of these countries in early 2012.

In Malawi, where women were abused by street vendors, gender activists joined politicians to demonstrate on behalf of women's rights.

Women and freedom of dressing.
Photo: Trevor Davies

Women in Malawi also boycotted vendors involved in the abuse. The country's vendor association later apologised, distancing itself from the offensive acts.

In South Africa, the African National Congress (ANC) Women's League spearheaded demonstrations to protest the harassment of women at taxi ranks in the country. South Africa's Minister of Women, Children and People with Disabilities Lulu Xingwana, said: "The scourge of women abuse threatens to erode many of the hard-earned gains of the liberation struggle. It denies women their birth rights. It condemns them to a life of fear and prevents them from being productive members of society."

Traditional Courts Bill strips women of rights: activists

The South African (SA) National Council of Provinces has re-tabled a 2008 Traditional Courts Bill which would allow traditional leaders in rural communities to impose taxes and have legal clout within their jurisdiction. If the bill is adopted in its current form, traditional leaders will be presiding officers of the courts.

Gender activists are concerned this development opens the door for abuse on the part of tribal leaders and sets back women's rights in rural areas.

While the bill appears to guarantee women's participation, several clauses contradict this. For instance, one notes that the "Bill provides that women, when they come before the court as litigants, can be presented by their husbands or other family members in accordance with customary law."

The bill also contradicts several targets of the Southern Africa Development Community (SADC) Protocol on Gender and Development, to which South Africa is a signatory.

Grassroot Soccer selected for "Women Deliver 50"

Girls on Khayelitsha field. *Photo: Grassroot*

Grassroot Soccer (GRS), a Southern African organisation that uses sport to help stop the spread of HIV and AIDS, was honoured by global advocacy organisation Women Deliver a day prior to the 2012 International Women's Day.

GRS was awarded as part of "Women Deliver 50," an initiative to draw attention to the 50 most inspiring ideas and solutions currently being employed to help empower girls and women across the globe.

It was honoured especially for its Skillz Street programme, an after school soccer league for young women. Skillz Street challenges gender norms by creating a safe space where young women can be themselves and learn new skills, all while playing the male-dominated sport of football. Girls learn how to avoid risky behaviours and protect themselves from HIV and AIDS.

"We started the Skillz Street soccer initiative to educate girls in Southern Africa about sexual and reproductive health and to empower them with the skills they need to protect themselves from HIV," said Tommy Clark, GRS founder. "Our inclusion in this list, among so many inspiring organisations, gives us renewed energy as we inspire generations of strong-minded, confident young women, working towards our goal of educating one million youth by 2014."
Source: http://www.grassrootsoccer.org

Journalists have their say at COP17

A team of Gender Links and African Woman and Child Feature Service (AWCFS) journalists painted Durban green from 28 November to 9 December 2011 at two major international environmental meetings there.

The group took part in the 17th Conference of Parties (COP17) to the United Nations Framework Convention on Climate Change (UNFCCC) and the 7th Session of the COP serving as the Meeting of the Parties (CMP7) to the Kyoto Protocol. The meetings were also attended by activists, ministers, researchers, youth, heads of state and faith-based organisations.

GL and AWCFS joined the rest of the world at COP17 in Durban, South Africa. *Photo: Saeanna Chingamuka*

Two main issues dominated the agenda: the Kyoto Protocol and the creation of a fund to help developing countries tackle climate change.

Participants discussed the upcoming expiration of the current Kyoto Protocol in December 2012, noting the possibility of a second commitment that could start in January 2013.

Talks also revolved around creating a Green Climate Fund (GCF) to support capacity building and other projects aimed at tackling climate change in the developing world.

Through the Gender and Media Diversity Centre (GMDC), GL and AWCFS produced a daily e-newsletter that highlighted a range of issues around gender and climate change. This included findings from COP 17, opinion and commentary pieces from the 16 Days of Activism, as well as "I" Stories from GL's project on "healing through the power of the pen." The group produced ten e-newsletters, attended various meetings and joined in protests against climate change. Visit *http://www.genderlinks.org.za/page/publications-conference-newspapers* to read these Daily Links articles.

The power of campaigns: Right2Know in South Africa

While there are positive signs that many African governments are embracing the principles of free access to information, some South African activists are concerned their country seems to be regressing on this front. South Africa's controversial Protection of Information Bill, which was passed by the National Assembly in November 2011, is the main reason for concern.

Experts fear that if the bill, also referred to as the Secrecy Bill, is eventually signed into law it will not only muzzle media, but also impinge on the state of democracy in the country. Anton Harber, a journalism professor at Wits University, has argued against the bill, stating: "It is not just a battle for journalists and the media to do their job; it is a battle for citizens to be empowered by information and be able to assert their rights and aspirations. It is not just a battle for freedom of speech, but a fight to ensure our democracy is an open, participative and collaborative one, rather than a top-down authoritarian one."

Activists have called on opponents of the bill to support the Right2Know Campaign, a civil society coalition fighting to stop it. Right2Know members have already successfully lobbied the ruling ANC to rewrite several of the bill's more controversial clauses. Critics maintain that it is still unconstitutional because it fails to include a public interest defence clause.

From 31 January to 1 March 2012, the National Council of Provinces ad hoc committee on the Bill held public hearings in all nine provinces so citizens could speak out about the bill.

WACC encourages participation in Women Make the News

The World Association for Christian Communication (WACC) is trying to drum up excitement ahead of the 2012 UNESCO Women Make the News campaign aimed at creating gender equality in media. It launched its own campaign on 8 March to encourage both its members and partners from media and civil society to engage with the initiative.

The 2012 Women Make the News theme is "Rural women's access to media and information." It began on 8 March, International Women's Day, and will run until 30 April 2012.

Giving women a voice: BBC journalists interviews a female source during Tanzania's Business Unusual. *Photo: Trevor Davies*

The 2010 Global Media Monitoring Project found that internationally, just 12% of those interviewed in news stories about rural community concerns are female, yet women make up more than 50% of the rural population. This demonstrates a significant underrepresentation of rural women in media and a relative lack of visibility and voice in news stories on issues that are important to them.

WACC encouraged media editors and owners to entrust women journalists with editorial responsibilities in the newsroom for the period of the campaign and beyond.

Those with a stake in media are encouraged to share their thoughts on the theme at UNESCO's online platform. For more information visit: *http://www.unesco.org/new/en/communication-and-information/crosscutting-priorities/gender/women-make-the-news/*

Sun on Sunday replaces defunct *News of the World*

Rupert Murdoch's newest paper hit British newsstands for the first time in late February. The *Sun on Sunday* is the new Sunday edition of his News Corporation's most popular tabloid.

It replaces the *News of the World*, which the press magnate closed after senior figures at the paper were accused of hacking the phones of politicians, celebrities and the parents of a young girl murdered in 2002.

In its first editorial, *Sun on Sunday* pledged to meet high ethical standards. "Our journalists must abide by the Press Complaints Commission's editors code, the industry standard for ethical behaviour, and the News Corporation standards of business conduct," it stated.

The new paper is seen by many as Murdoch's way of reassuring US News Corp. Shareholders that the firm is trying to move on from the scandal.

It is reported that the paper has stuck largely to the Sun's daily format. However, it is being sold for 50 pence, a reduced price that has sparked a price war among its rivals.

Rupert Murdoch holds his newly launched newspaper. *Source: allvoices.com*

UPCOMING EVENTS

UPCOMING EVENTS

Third annual Gender Justice and Local Government Summit
23-25 April 2012
Johannesburg, South Africa

Gender Links will hold its third annual Gender Justice and Local Government Summit and Awards under the banner "365 Days of local action to end violence and empower women." Southern African local councils will be recognised for their work completing the six-stage process to become Centres of Excellence (COE) in mainstreaming gender at the local level. GL will award those councils that have shown exceptional commitment through leadership and implementation.The South Africa event follows in-country summits in six of the participating countries. The most exceptional councils following in-country summits will participate in the main regional summit. For more info:
http://www.genderlinks.org.za/page/gender-justice-and-local-government-summit-2012

World Press Freedom Day 2012
New Voices: Media Freedom Helping to Transform Societies
3-5 May 2012 Tunis, Tunisia

This year, we all have been encouraged by the unprecedented global socio-political democratic developments in which various media played an important part, even if not to the extent where some have spoken about the "social media revolution". Indeed, many factors came into play with the events taking place, particularly in the Arab states, including underlying economic woes and political suppression, which elicited mass organisation especially by young people. However, we cannot deny the fact that the freedom to harness the power of information and communication technologies (ICTs) and especially those of new media played a significant role, even while often being in conjunction with satellite television. This has reaffirmed what the World Press Freedom Day had been championing for the past twenty years - media freedom is part of the package of fundamental rights for which people will strive.

The confluence of press freedom and freedom of expression, through various traditional as well as new media, has given rise to an unprecedented level of media freedom. It is helping to enable civil society, young people and communities to bring about massive social and political transformations. Media freedom entails the right of any person to freedom of opinion and expression on a public basis, which includes freedom to hold opinions without interference and to seek, receive and impart information and ideas through any media and regardless of frontiers, as stated in Article 19 of the Universal Declaration of Human Rights.
Excerpt from the World Press Freedom Day 2012 UNESCO concept paper - www.unesco.org

Azerbaijani journalist wins 2012 UNESCO/Guillermo Cano World Press Freedom Prize

UNESCO has named an Azerbaijani journalist and human rights activists as winner of the 2012 UNESCO/Guillermo Cano World Press Freedom Prize.

Fatullayev: winner of 2012 UNESCO/Guillermo Cano World Press Freedom Prize.
Photo: UNESCO

Eynulla Fatullayev, 35, is the former editor-in-chief and founder of the popular independent Russian-language weekly *Realny Azerbaijan* (Real Azerbaijan) and the Azeri-language daily *Gundalik Azarbaycan* (Azerbaijan Daily) newspapers.

"Throughout his career, he has unfailingly and steadfastly spoken out for freedom of the press and freedom of expression," UNESCO stated in a news release. Imprisoned in 2007, he was released last year by presidential pardon on Azerbaijan's Republic Day, 26 May 2011- an event that was welcomed by the international community. In July 2011 Fatullayev founded the "Public Union for Human Rights", a non-governmental human rights organisation. UNESCO's Executive Board created the UNESCO Guillermo Cano World Press Freedom Prize in 1997. It is awarded annually during the celebration of World Press Freedom Day on 3 May, and honours the work of an individual or an organisation defending or promoting freedom of expression anywhere in the world, especially if this action puts the individual's life at risk. UNESCO Member States, and regional or international organizations that defend and promote freedom of expression propose candidates.

Guillermo Cano Isaza Prize is named in honour of the assassinated Colombian journalist. Isaza was killed on 17 December 1986. Candidates are proposed by UNESCO Member States, and regional or international organizations that defend and promote freedom of expression.

Previous recipients of the prize include Ahmad Zeidabadi (Iran, 2011), Mónica González Mujica (Chile, 2010), Lasantha Wickrematunge (Sri Lanka, 2009), Lydia Cacho (Mexico, 2008) and Anna Politkovskaya (Russia, 2007).

This year's World Press Freedom Day celebrations will take place in Tunisia under the theme New Voices: Media Freedom Helping to Transform Societies.
Source: http://www.unesco.org

Decriminalisation of freedom of expression in Africa
4-6 May 2012
Tunis, Tunisia

The Special Rapporteur on Freedom of Expression and Access to Information in Africa, Commissioner Pansy Tlakula, in partnership with the Centre for Human Rights (University of Pretoria, South Africa) and the United Nations Educational, Scientific and Cultural Organisation (UNESCO), will host a stakeholder consultative meeting in Tunis on 6 May. This meeting will follow UNESCO's World Press Freedom day conference in the same location from 4-5 May 2012. It will bring together organisations that have worked on the decriminalisation of laws limiting freedom of expression within Africa in the past, those that are well positioned to do so in the future, as well as representatives of media groupings whose activities are most jeopardised by the existence of these laws. It is intended as a kick-off organisational and planning event for extended work on repealing or "deactivating" these laws.

Open forum on money, sex and power
22-24 May 2012
Cape Town, South Africa

Put 22-24 May 2012 in your diaries - because that's when the four Africa Foundations of the Open Society Initiative of Southern Africa will host an unprecedented OpenForum on the theme of *Money, Power and Sex: The paradox of unequal growth.* Taking place at the International Convention Centre in Cape Town, the OpenForum will represent the first event of its kind and will provide a space for activists, academics, business people and policy-makers to talk about the economic, social and political implications for Africa of the emerging world order.

Within the broad overall theme, the OpenForum will focus particularly on the roles of India, Brazil and China as drivers of growth on the continent, but increasingly as important actors in the political and social affairs of African countries. Layered on top of this, will be an interest in how inequality - across money, power and sex - affects young people. In the shadow of the North African and Arab Spring revolutions, the Africa Foundations will be looking at who is being left behind as the race for resources plays itself out in Africa, and who - equally importantly - is being pushed aside.
Source: http://www.osisa.org

Rio+20: the future we want
June 2012
Rio de Janeiro, Brazil

Rio+20, the short name for the United Nations Conference on Sustainable Development to take place in Rio de Janeiro, Brazil, in June 2012, is a historic opportunity to define pathways to a safer, more equitable, cleaner, greener and more prosperous world for all. Twenty years after the 1992 Earth Summit in Rio, where countries adopted Agenda 21 - a blueprint to rethink economic growth, advance social equity and ensure environmental protection - the UN is again bringing together governments, international institutions and major groups to agree on a range of smart measures that can reduce poverty while promoting decent jobs, clean energy and a more sustainable and fair use of resources. Rio+20 provides an opportunity to move away from business-as-usual and to act to end poverty, address environmental destruction and build a bridge to the future.
Source and for more info visit:
http://www.uncsd2012.org/rio20/index.html

GENDER AND
POPULAR CULTURE

The "bromance" problem
By Dainty Smith

Abstract

A recent increase in the numbers of gay people represented in popular culture has seen a breaking down of barriers between the heterosexual and homosexual communities. It has also seen a shift in gender roles in relationships between straight men, and between straight men and gay men. This article looks at how this shift has affected popular vernacular with the creation of words such as bromance and hobromance. It also looks at those who have been left behind.

Key words
bromance, gender roles, hobromance, homosexual, heterosexual

In the last ten years those observing pop culture will have noticed a dramatic shift in its representation of friendships between heterosexual men. The increase in the visibility of friendships between straight men was accompanied by a term created to sum up the underlying intimacy straight men have with one another - what is now called a "bromance."

Dave Carnie, editor of the popular skateboard magazine *Big Brother*, coined the word in the mid 1990's. It has since caught on and become a part of the mainstream lexicon.

But what exactly is a 'bromance?" A tongue in cheek play on the words brother and romance, it is used to refer to a close friendship between two heterosexual who share similar interests, emotional closeness and physical affection.

This change in the cultural landscape and move away from alpha-male competitive straight relationships of the past, has been reflected in the English language and also in film and television. Films depicting bromances have proven popular. These include *I Love You Man*, *The Hangover* and *Sherlock Holmes*.

Kendrick Kang-Joh Jeong plays the part of a gay Chinese man called Mr Chow in *The Hangover* movie.   *Screenshot from YouTube*

The sudden rise in such films, not to mention television shows like *Scrubs* and *How I met your Mother*, reflect a changing attitude - a societal sea change where it is now permissible for straight men to have close friendships and not be perceived as gay.

Over the last decade, gay representation in the mainstream has also been on the rise. Gay men and women have become a major presence in pop culture and the public reception of this, while complex, has for the most part been positive. Television shows such as *Queer Eye for the Straight Guy, Queer as Folk, Will and Grace* and *Modern Family* showcase gay people in relationships, with children, and out of the closet and accepted by their families. There has been an ongoing "normalisation" of gay people in mainstream pop culture.

This has had a crossover effect into heterosexual culture. It has also led to increasing numbers of close friendships between gay men and straight men - what has been referred to as a "hobromance."

The idea of gay and straight men as friends has been taboo for such a long time that this development should only be perceived as a welcome step towards breaking down hatred, ignorance and discrimination. It brings with it a social relief: that there are more and more gay-straight alliances bridging the gap between gay and heterosexual communities. But the sudden inclusion and acceptance also brings with it conflicts and complications around masculinity and gender performance. There is still much hesitancy when it comes to heterosexual men entering friendships with homosexual men who are less "straight-acting," less "manly," and more effeminate.

Effeminate (and I feel it should be stated that the very word effeminate is an insult) gay men achieve acceptance in the straight world only as a heterosexual woman's shopping buddy or hairdresser. In societal norms, gay men who appear to behave like women are seen as too gay. This is a ridiculous concept: how can there be such a thing as too gay? Is there such a thing as too straight? This is hugely problematic because these gay men are rarely invited into straight male spaces.

Botswana television journalist covering a discussion on the role of men in Gaborone.   *Photo by Vincent Galatlhwe*

Heterosexual men typically also do not feel threatened if their wives or girlfriends spend an inordinate amount of time with their gay male friends because they are doing "girly" activities such as shopping, decorating, drinking cocktails and gossiping.

But many heterosexual men have far more difficultly engaging in friendships, and interacting, with effeminate gay men. They feel threatened by their lack of manliness and worry about being approached in a sexual way.

It would be easy and certainly less worrying to celebrate the grey areas between gay and heterosexual cultures, and how well we're all getting along, than to concern ourselves with what it takes to be included or accepted. But we need to worry about effeminate gay men being included and accepted. We need to worry far more than we currently do. Gay men who are read as too feminine are at risk of being attacked and they live in constant fear of being assaulted.

Although gender role expert Jean Lipman-Blumen first used the term "Homosociality" in 1976[1], it was scholar Eve Sedgewick who popularised the term while discussing male homosocial desire[2]. Homosociality describes same-sex relationships that are not sexual or romantic in their interactions.

There are no sexual interactions in bromances between heterosexual men and hobromances between heterosexual and homosexual men. But there are limitations around what is allowed and these limitations are dangerous. Gay men who blur gender roles are considered too gay and too feminine. This line of thinking isn't unique to heterosexual men: there are some gay men who take issue with this as well.

These rigid and enforced social constructs should be challenged. They should be destroyed. Gender is fluid; it is a state of mind. Men and women carry both feminine and masculine energy and, given our context and situation, we can and do perform both roles interchangeably.

This social shaming of effeminate men is damaging to both gay and straight men. If Johnny Depp can receive praise because he is daring enough to wear nail polish, then those nameless and faceless men who flirt with gender roles should also be lauded. It takes courage to be different and proud of it, to rebel against what is considered normal. It is revolutionary.

There is no right or wrong way to be a man. Masculinity isn't dependent on male swagger or posturing. The demands of constantly adhering

to the perceived qualities of "maleness" in this particular way result in men who become fathers raising emotionally stunted sons who then repeat the cycle.

How I met your mother: a screenshot from the comedy series.
Buzzsugar.com

Maleness and femaleness are not as simple and clear-cut as pop culture and society make them out to be. Masculinity is more layered and intricate than the stereotype offers. The problem is not that straight men can now wear pink and have close friendships with each other and not be "gay" about it. The problem is that some gay men who push the borders of masculinity are punished for doing so. Straight mainstream culture seems to pull from gay culture what is fashionable and easily likeable while dismissing and diminishing what is not. We do a disservice to gay men who challenge this "norm" by not protesting this behaviour.

Writer's Bio
Smith is a Jamaican-Canadian freelance writer, actress and performer.

Notes

[1] Lipman-Blumen, J. 1976. *Toward a homosocial theory of sex roles.* Signs. 1:3, pp. 15-31.
[2] Sedgwick, E., 1985. *Between men: Literature and male homosocial desire.*

Soap operas don't have to reinforce negative stereotypes
By Ntombi Mbadlanyana

It is estimated that around 4.9 million South Africans watch the famous soapie *Generations* every day. This is a huge number; more than the populations of Botswana and Namibia combined.

So what responsibility, if any, comes with attracting an audience of this size and should soap opera producers be obliged to present a responsible, fair, non-discriminatory version of society?

I think they should, which is why I recently complained to the Broadcasting Complaints Commission of South Africa (BCCSA) after I was offended by the portrayal of a gay character on *Generations.*

All soap operas have similar themes, characters and story lines: there is always a villain, a town gossip, a rich family, a poor family, never-ending love triangles, murder, sex and scandal. But what has also always been familiar about soap operas is their perpetuation of negative stereotypes in a very unrealistic television world.

Yet in recent years soaps have begun to incorporate marginalised groups and more realistic storylines, possibly in an effort to boost decreasing ratings. This has included people with disabilities, gays and lesbians and characters living with HIV.

When *Generations* first introduced a gay character viewers made their opinions known and a controversial kiss between two gay male characters caused an outcry among traditionalists and community leaders.

Generations performers pose for a picture during the soapie's 15th birthday celebrations.
Photo: TV SA

Admirably, at that time the show did not back down. Gays and lesbians are a part of the wonderful diversity of South African society and they are also viewers of shows like *Generations*.

However, soap operas also reinforce stereotypes of gay people just as they reinforce negative gender stereotypes about heterosexual women and men. Homosexual men are too often portrayed as effeminate, soft, gentle, and not masculine: subservient in relation to other men.

I was recently outraged watching *Generations* when one of the lead characters referred to a gay male character as "my girl." At first I thought I had heard incorrectly. Initially I laughed because I was processing what I had heard, but the laughter soon turned to anger. This was reinforcing a very negative stereotype about gay men - it was far from a progressive soapie's attempt to raise awareness.

Soap operas are powerful and their messages are taken seriously by many of their viewers (and this could be millions, knowing the numbers). When we know that gays and lesbians are daily targets of violence, bullying and rape in South Africa, this type of portrayal is incredibly dangerous and irresponsible.

Some friends thought I was overreacting but I compared it to the earlier black American battle to halt negative television stereotypes of African Americans. Through the National Association for the Achievement of Coloured People (NAACP)[1], black Americans once fought big production companies such as Warner and Metro Goldwyn Mayer (MGM) over the perpetuation of similar damaging stereotypes. Eventually the NAACP achieved success in ending pervasive and dangerous negative portrayals of black people.

Because South Africa is a diverse country with many cultures, ethnicities, languages, religions and ways of living it is inevitable that some stereotypes will be created and reinforced. This is why we have the Broadcasting Complaints Commission of South Africa (BCCSA), which is meant to arbitrate when there are cases of public commentary that may be deemed unfair or when language or vocabulary can amount to hate speech.

Thami Mngqolo (Senzo) and Zolisa Xalusa (Jason) portray as gay characters in *Generations* - a South African TV soapie.   *Photo: TV SA*

I complained to the BCCSA following the above mentioned episode and was told that although there was no contravention of BCCSA's code, SABC remains "committed to upholding and re-enforcing good values."

A code may not have been broken and broadcast decision-makers may well feel they are promoting good values, but this viewer is forever insulted. We need to change such harmful portrayal of gay characters in sitcoms, soap operas and all main-stream media if we want South Africa to stop making international headlines because of horrific, violent homophobic attacks. So long as our country stands out as a global hotspot for homophobia and hate crime, such issues should not be so quickly dismissed.

I challenge the writers and producers of *Generations* and other television shows to create characters and storylines that can help our country overcome violence, hate and discord. I challenge other progressive viewers to take up a pen and complain when, like me, you are offended by what you see on your screen or hear on your radio. It is only when we confront harmful stereotypes that our leaders actually stop perpetuating them.

Writer's Bio
Mbadlanyana is GL's South Africa Country Manager: Gender Justice and Local Government.

Notes

1 http://www.naacp.org/

Hip-hop perpetuates stereotypes
By Tichakunda Tsedu

Abstract
Hip-hop is one of the most popular music genres but also one of the most sexist. Hip-hop and rap lyrics are well known for being degrading to women and perpetuating gender stereotypes. This article analyses hip-hop videos and lyrics to underscore the extent of the problem in mainstream and less commercially successful hip-hop. It also illustrates how the problem is perpetuated by female artists both in local African and American hip-hop.

Key words
hip-hop, rap, gender stereotypes, Jezebel, song lyrics

Introduction

Originating in the homes and streets of New York in the 1970s, hip-hop has truly travelled across and beyond the Atlantic, similar to the slave ancestors of many pioneers of this legendary urban culture. On its journey it has embodied a spirit and authenticity that continues to make its social and economic impact all the more significant. Its commercial success is undeniable and countless rappers have made millions selling their music and lifestyles to the world.

Along with its growth and increased socio-cultural influence, hip-hop has retained its most funda-mental traits: a lyrical and factual engagement distinctly dominated by males. And what about the females in hip-hop? Well, we have commonly seen over the years that "misogynistic" and "demeaning" have become the clichés relied upon to describe the lyrics of many chart-topping singles produced by the genre. Indeed, gender equality is clearly not a hot topic in rap when you begin to dissect the lyrics and unearth the messages being delivered.

The woman represented in hip-hop is first and foremost empowered by her body - simply note the high numbers of underdressed females flaunting their bodies in bikinis and underwear in many hip-hop videos. The sheer proportion of women to men in some music videos effectively indicates strong gender and power relations favouring men. The fate of women is thus one which has left them voiceless and without real substance in music videos - and in the studio. What becomes clear is that the idea of "the Jezebel" still holds a firm place within the media, particularly in hip-hop/rap lyrics and music videos which continue to objectify women and reinforce stereotypical notions that a female's value is in ensuring men's sexual gratification. This paper aims to explore women in hip hop by considering how they are portrayed in rap lyrics and videos and looking at perspectives of male and female rappers.

Media effects

The media has a widespread influence and impact on individual perceptions of reality and beliefs about others. For instance, the lack of African Americans in early advertising and media in that country displayed white America's perceptions of blacks, as non-citizens in society. Moreover, the perpetual lack of diversity in the representation of women (i.e. media represents women as always thin with perfect skin) has indeed contributed to how young girls and women in general feel about their own bodies.

Numerous studies have indeed found some correlation between media consumption and body dissatisfaction, weight concerns and sexual attitudes, amongst others. This has significantly occurred especially amongst young girls and women. According to Ward and Harrison[1], exposure to sexual content (as opposed to nonsexual content) in music videos, television programs and magazines "is associated with stronger endorsement of stereotypical attitudes about sex. Women exposed to images depicting men as sex-driven, women as objects, or sex as recreation offered stronger support of these stereotypes than did women in control groups."

Jezebels in music videos

In modern popular culture, the Jezebel myth can be understood to be the prevailing stereotype that identifies black women as loose, sexually aggressive and promiscuous. This stereotype can be traced to pre-colonial times when European travelers encountered native women. Descriptions of these women mainly focused on their apparently insatiable lust for sex, and they were often depicted with large, sagging breasts. The international slave trade and slavery only entrenched these narrow, sexist, racist notions of women of colour.

From the 1940's onward, American television witnessed the downfall of the wise and respectable mammy as she was replaced by wilder depictions of sexually active black women. Fast forward to the 21st century and there has been little done by the media in terms of diversity in its mainstream representations of black women. One look at contemporary hip-hop music videos and it becomes all too clear that women of colour remain objects of sexual desire in the media.

Take Nelly's *Tip Drill*[2], certainly one of the most controversial and sexually explicit music videos to be released by a hip hop artist. The scene in the video is a party atmosphere with half-naked women dancing and stripping while men defile them by pouring champagne on them and even swipe a credit card between a woman's buttocks. At one point, a woman gyrates with such vigour and enthusiasm to the point that her bikini comes off.

Hip hop star: Nelly.   *Screenshot taken from Tip Drill video*

Another example of a video in which women are portrayed in sexually degrading ways is *Bucket Naked* by Papoose[3]. In the video the rapper walks around an office using a mobile phone that allows him to be able to see through women's clothing. Thus the entire video features Papoose exposing various women in their underwear as they try to go about their work. Certainly not all rap videos degrade women to such an extent but it is common to see men with cash, cars, alcohol and as many women as possible with as little clothing on as possible. Jay-Z's *Big Pimpin*[4] is an example of a video in which women outnumber the men. In this video, there are only a handful of men and dozens of bikini clad women. Representations such as this further strengthen the notion that male success and pleasure comes from having multiple female partners.

Case study: song lyrics

Screenshot taken from *MVP* video.

While videos visually display the way many are perceived in the world of hip-hop, song lyrics are the starting point. A critical analysis of hip-hop lyrics reveals an equally degrading representation of women. This section will look at two songs: one from South Africa (L-Tido's *It ain't my fault*) and one from America (Alchemist's *Keep the heels on*) to provide a sample of women's representation in hip-hop lyrics. The local song was selected because of its popularity on radio and television, while the American song is not as popular on mainstream radio. The purpose is to show that misogyny is common in both mainstream and less commercial hip-hop.

Alchemist featuring Prodigy: "Keep the heels on"[5]

Girl I wanna make you cry, I wanna make you scream/
I wanna make you sweat, make you wet when you dream/
Pick you up at lunch so we can do the back seat/
You can't concentrate at work, thinking about me/
Killing it, tip drilling it, I'm spilling it all over the place, yeah I got her feeling it/
Your man never made your body shake like that/
Bet he don't know his girl makes her face like that/
Off a long dick, hog spit in her ass crack while I long dick did it, yeah from the back huh/
Honey's sophisticated mommy raised her like a lady/
But every woman's got a freaky side I'm going crazy/
Ready to pop it off, you hit them with the proper talk/
They put their guard down and give a nigga what he wants/
Roll the blunt, pour a drink, nigga get the buzz going/
Keep em talking, don't let em think for a moment/
Turn the music up, lights down, we gon fuck right now/

Start sucking their tits and push their head right down/
Sloppy faced diva catch a breather coz her jaw hurt/
Then you lay em back, with their legs on your shoulder/
Dig her nails in my back, talking bout trying to kill her/
Grab the sheets like she's being raped, but she wants it nigga/

L-Tido: "It ain't my fault"[6]

It aint my fault, she smiling at me, eyeing my p, and likes what she sees
It aint my fault, that's why you're alone, calling her phone I might take her home
It aint my fault, pardon me please why cant you see that I'm just a G
It aint my fault, oh, said it aint my fault that your chick chose me

Damn, I see you doing it big homie/
In the club with some fine ass chicks homie/
Yeah, you popping bottles of Cris homie/
Man these girls got you spending all your chips homie/
You make it rain and make the shorties live/
When you scoop em up in your 7-45/
Now you getting big attention for real/
When they see you in your car and your mansion in the hills/
You blowing money fast, yeah you spend a couple g's/
But damn homie, you should get your girl on a leash/
Lil mama loose, she loves to be free/
Tido keep it G, you love women, cuff em/
Me I pass them on to the homies after I crush em/

In the first song, it is difficult to ascertain what message is being conveyed, besides explicit descriptions of engaging in sexual acts with a woman. This conforms with hip-hop norms of degrading women and limiting their role in society to one of sexual activity. Reading the lyrics one could say the rapper is providing guidelines for having sex with a woman. He encourages the listener to set the mood by smoking marijuana and drinking alcohol, that is when a woman will "put their guard down and give a nigga what he wants."

The woman's fidelity is questioned in the song as Prodigy claims he is intimate with her in a way his partner is not. This indicates that she is already in a relationship but has sex with other men, thus presenting the woman as unfaithful - a common representation of women in rap lyrics. Although he acknowledges proper and decent attributes to the subject, "sophisticated, mommy raised her like a lady," the rapper sees these characteristics as secondary to the woman's identity because according to him "every woman's got a freaky side." The imagery created by the last line about the woman grabbing the bed sheets "like she's being raped, but she wants it" is very shocking. Overall the song's portrayal of women is highly limited and inappropriate, promoting blatant stereotypes.

In the second song, the gender stereotyping is not as blatant because the woman is not the main subject of the song. In this song, the rapper is primarily addressing a big-spending man who uses money and status to attract women. However, despite the cash, cars and jewels, this man's girlfriend would rather leave him for the rapper, although the reasons for this are not so apparent. Initially, women are depicted as materialistic and interested in money, in the line "man these girls got you spending all your chips homie... now you getting big attention for real when they see you in your car and your mansion in the hills." What becomes clear is that the song is promoting the belief that women are loose, easily unsatisfied in their relationships, and ready to jump to the next best opportunity that comes their way.

The rapper should be minimally commended for his rather creative approach to demeaning women, as he does not take the obvious route identified in the first song. An analysis of the lyrics reveals intentional attempts to portray women as immoral, wild beings. L-Tido states that "you should get your girl on a leash, lil mama loose, she loves to be free," alluding to notions of female promiscuity. The idea of putting a woman on a leash is dehumanising and objectifying.

This song is popular on social networks, radio and television music shows, indicating the huge appeal of songs which put women down. As such, the American trend toward misogynistic music has crossed the Atlantic and continues to influence South African hip-hop music and reflect negative perceptions of women in society.

Momma's boys

Hip-hop, with all its misogyny and promotion of violence and materialistic lifestyles, is not exclusively negative toward women. Sometimes rappers try to deliver positive messages. Tupac Shakur famously said in *Dear Mama*[7]: "And even though you was a crack fiend mama, You were always a black queen mama."

Similarly, Kanye West sings about his love for his mother on *Hey Mama*,[8] telling a story of the sacrifices she made for him and his appreciation for all she did for him.

These two songs are indeed touching and worrying: Touching, because we see that some rappers have a soft side and can cherish and value the women who brought them into the world, but worrying because although there is recognition of the important role of mothers, all other women are typically depicted in negative ways.

Hip hop artist: 2 Pac and his mother.   *Source: The Maguire*

Female rappers

In a 2011 Forbes magazine article about hip-hop's top earners or "Cash Kings"[9], Nicki Minaj is the only female featured in the top 20. Besides the blatant gender blindness in the title, it is indeed clear that financially, female rappers are not doing as well as their male counterparts. But why is that? When we look at content, women certainly do their bit to lyrically present themselves in the typical rap style: gangster living, guns, money and of course typical degrading representations of women. It is interesting to note that many of the successful female rappers have entered the game on the back of popular male figures in the industry. Missy Elliot had Timbaland, Lil' Kim had Notorious BIG, Foxy Brown had Jay-Z and most recently Nicki Minaj had Lil Wayne.

Very seldom have female rappers been able to succeed on their own. Besides, the fact remains that women in rap continue to allow themselves to be used as sexual objects for the pleasure of audiences. For example, upon initially watching Nicki Minaj's first music video,[10] I was more interested in admiring her physical attributes than listening to what she was saying. I must mention, however, that I have now come to appreciate her lyrical skills as well. But the fact remains that she used sex, or rather her sex appeal, to get noticed, which will not help change stereotypes of women in hip-hop.

A more explicit example of females using sex to sell their music is Lil' Kim's "How many licks."[11] Although Lil' Kim started off her career embracing and portraying the gangster image and lifestyle commonly associated with hip-hop music, she soon began making music centered around anything and everything related to sexual intercourse. In the first verse, she describes by ethnicity, and in detail, the various types of men she has encountered (sexually). Although this is an extreme case, content such as this is common. Rapper Diamond (a female singer) released a song titled *Hit Dat Hoe*,[12] a reference to physically assaulting a woman. Why a female rapper decides to produce music with such content is a question of real concern.

Moving and grooving to house music

House music has over recent years become a major force in the industry, spawning a multitude of djs ready to rock Southern African crowds from Limpopo to Durban. Along with its ever increasing commercial success, house music has adopted, whether intentionally or not, the same tendency as hip-hop to depict women in a typical stereotypical and sexualised manner. Many house music videos feature women parading around wearing next to nothing, occasionally enjoying a cold quart of beer. Some of the most popular songs[13/14] refer to women as loose, unfaithful and promiscuous - reminiscent of what has been discussed in reference to women in hip-hop music.

Conclusion and way forward

Civil society and women's organisations must become more vocal about the stereotypes found within the hip-hop world. The industry clearly remains hostile territory for women and women's representation. This includes women in videos and those who rap, particularly in mainstream hip-hop. To affect real change, more women need to be in key decision-making positions at record labels and in other entertainment media sectors.

An example is www.femalerappers.net, a website seen to be a trusted and reliable source of information and news regarding the state of women in rap music. It is interesting to note, though, that a headline on one of its articles reads "Nicki Minaj sitting that ass down on Drake![15] It is essential that artists and producers make a better and conscious effort to bring a gender balance to music and videos.

Nicki Minaj and Lil Wayne.   *Source: hiphopjunkies.com*

There is a need for more research into gender representation in music, including comparisons between genres. This will give a broader, more comprehensive picture of the state of women in music videos, allowing for a more insightful analysis of women throughout the entire music industry.

In conclusion, lyrics remain the formative point of departure when seeking to understand perceptions of women in hip-hop. Many lyrics are highly offensive to women, yet the same songs top radio and video charts. As for female rappers, they remain largely underrepresented in the industry and have lagged behind male rappers in this respect. Finally, the content of some songs performed by females continues to degrade women and perpetuate stereotypical perceptions of women in society.

Writer's Bio

Tsedu recently completed a bachelor of social sciences at the University of Cape Town. He is an intern at Gender Links.

Notes

1 Ward, L. M., & Harrison, K. (2005). The impact of media use on girls' beliefs about gender roles, their bodies, and sexual relationships: A research synthesis. In E. Cole & J. H. Daniels (Eds.), Featuring Females: Feminist Analyses of Media. Washington, DC: American Psychological Association.
2 (http://www.youtube.com/watch?v=PK0QMrCA0hA)
3 (http://www.youtube.com/watch?v=CwcFl9LyO6o&feature=related)
4 (http://www.youtube.com/watch?v=Cgoqrgc_0cM&ob=av2n)
5 http://www.youtube.com/watch?v=hnNdJXv-FwM
6 http://www.youtube.com/watch?v=wLwZpFn_YCg
7 http://www.youtube.com/watch?v=JNcloTmvTeA
8 http://www.youtube.com/watch?v=RtpKqMpqGU0
9 http://www.forbes.com/special-report/2011/cash-king-11.html
10 http://www.youtube.com/watch?v=2ZCUtnuAXg8
11 http://www.youtube.com/watch?v=yhCD9qxlczo
12 http://www.youtube.com/watch?v=v6eykALaK1s
13 Professor -"Jezebel" - http://www.youtube.com/watch?v=eDMBB3IAMPE
14 Character ft. Professor - "Ex" - http://www.youtube.com/watch?v=jqJL9s0V6iQ
15 Attempts to get information regarding the gender composition of employees at the website were unsuccessful.

Sexualisation of women in the media: Freedom of expression or oppression?
By Doreen Gaura

Abstract
While many activists denounce the role played by the media in perpetuating stereotypes, the gender movement in Southern Africa seems to be missing the point of what freedom of expression really means. This article is a personal opinion about freedom of expression, what the author thinks it means and how it should be understood. It analyses three examples: imagery and lyrical content in hip-hop music; sexualised images of women in advertising; and pornography.

Key words
feminism, media, hip-hop, pornography, advertising

I have felt for a while that the largely growing movement against the sexual portrayal of women by and in the media is somewhat narrow, often making biased analyses informed largely by the personal. Of course the issue, in and of itself, is extremely personal as well as political in the broader sense. It is personal in that it is informed by gender activists' opinions, which are often validated by data. According to these activists, many women, including those whom they purport to represent, should support their opinions.

It is true that in the quest for gender equality it is pivotal that the media become more gender sensitive and not only practice but also encourage gender parity in its operations, publications and programming. However, as gender activists, we need not lose sight of what we mean by gender equality. Although the media in many instances presents a diminutive picture of women, the war waged against its portrayal of women ultimately makes collateral damage of those women who practice their right to freedom of expression and choice.

The absolute empowerment of women means giving them a choice in all aspects of their life. That is what freedom of expression is about. Most feminists tend to be very prescriptive and by doing so tend to have an approach that appears to reinforce the same patriarchal views that we fight against, only in a different way.

The gender movement in Africa seems mainly made up of the middle class academic elite, or the cultural or traditional moralists, who feel they know better about what it is that "less empowered" women should want. A case in point is the issue of sex, sexuality and sensuality and the expression thereof. Patriarchy, as a way of duct-taping female expression, has entrenched in society the archetypal "lady" - basically a woman who is modest, demure, and sexually "pure," who never aspires to sexual gratification or pleasure. This woman should view sex as a way of fulfilling her maternal and reproductive roles. Anything more, we are led to believe, would make her a whore.

The only thing worth wearing this summer...

POLICE

Sexiest advert: What has a half-naked woman got to do with police sunglasses? *Photo: Trevor Davies*

Media in the region should be monitored and taken to task for its contribution to negative and harmful reinforcements, especially because it has a responsibility bestowed on it by article 30 of the SADC Protocol on Gender and Development. However, we should be careful not to wage a war on women who would rather subscribe to these

stereotypes - the same women we claim to be representing, and yet we often have very little knowledge, understanding or acceptance of them.

The hip-hop scene, pornography and advertising have been identified as the biggest culprits of perpetuating stereotypes. I attempt to look objectively at these three areas, taking into consideration both sides of the argument before drawing my conclusions.

Imagery and lyrics in hip-hop

Over the past two decades hip-hop has grown from its roots in black culture to a multimillion dollar industry that now champions materialism, violence, sex, drugs and misogyny. The videos for most hip-hop songs feature women wearing less and less with each new release. They portray women as sexual objects and commodities. This visual imagery is accompanied by denigrating lyrics that reduce these women to "bitches" and "hos." This trend has understandably been the source of much dismay and anger for both feminists and moralists alike. However, we need a more analytical approach to understand women in these videos.

In his online blog *Hip Hop News*, Khalil Amani tackles the denigration and abuse of these women at the hands of both the public and the media. At one point he writes:

These are grown... women who choose (some out of necessity and some because they love it!) to expose their bodies for our consumption! It is art! We certainly don't view male strippers as exploited! (Having been a male stripper myself, it was the most liberating feeling to shake my tallywacker in the faces of adoring women!... and get paid!)[1]

Amani notes that women who expose their bodies in music videos still deserve respect. In the same article, he berates a fellow blogger, Juan, for his disparaging remarks against Buffie the Body, a well-known video vixen (as these women prefer to be called). Juan accuses her of being "ghetto trash" and having an "offensive face" and a "skewed perception of her worth in this world."

Amani points out that Juan's opinion of Buffie the Body, and other brown-skinned women, is a racist one he would not apply to Caucasian women with the same physique and in the same profession. He encourages people to look at these women as a symbol of black sexual womanhood instead of as sluts or victims.

He also makes reference to the "ho" paradigm, which he says "is an old one used to keep women as second class citizens in a patriarchal society." The same can be said of the feminist movement's attempt to deter women from expressing their sexuality and claiming ownership of their bodies. The lines are blurry when it comes to determining whether or not these video vixens, who have been belittled by society, are disempowered and ultimately denied the right to freedom of expression through sexuality. Again, there are no set parameters that divide what is, and what is not, sexual expression. Sexuality is a very individual concept.

Sabrina Ford (2004), writing on the *Golden Gate X Press* website, acknowledges that for all its misogynistic content, hip-hop has awarded women of colour and women with fuller figures the chance to have a more positive view of their bodies in a world laden with a history of determining the beauty of women by a European standard. This is important given the history of treatment of brown-skinned women, including the example of

Saartjie Baartman, who was exploited and treated as a freak because of her physique. The hip-hop scene takes back the reverence of that stature and build, with women across all races now aspiring for a big "booty."

Ford states that hip-hop has in some ways reinforced a sense of sexual empowerment in women. She cites female rappers such as Trina, Foxy Brown and Lil Kim, who have never shied away from sexual themes. These women have defended their images and their lyrics are believed to have led women to realise sex is one tool that renders men helpless and makes women powerful.

Further, she says many women reference sex in their music, and they are as cavalier and una-shamed as their male counterparts. Ford is of the view that this is an attempt on the part of these female artists to position themselves as equals - the hip-hop version of a feminist movement.

The Hip Hop Summit South Africa 2011[2] website sets out pointers for aspiring video vixens that may shock some feminist groupings. The how-to guide opens like this:

> The coolest thing about hip-hop modelling is that rap video vixens come in all shapes and sizes. In the vast majority of the modelling world, they're really only looking for a very specific type of girl, they all want someone who's impossibly tall and stick thin. Hip-hop honeys, on the other hand, can have a shapely figure, they can be tall or short, thick or thin and everything in between.[3]

The British documentary *Music, Money and Hip Hop Honeys* looks into the lives of some of these hip-hop women. It finds that most "hip-hop honeys" not only purposely chose their career path, but also dedicated a lot time, and invested a lot of money, so they could become a video vixen. Many achieved this goal with as much tenacity and perseverance as a law student or aspiring biologist achieves theirs.

However, there is always a dark side. For all the aid in shifting society's idea of what constitutes women's beauty, this movement has also dictated how women should look. This has resulted in many going under the knife to get "butt" implants. Something that began as a celebration (if you choose to view it as such) of the natural physical build of some women has now created its own model of what an attractive woman should look like. Some women now feel pressure to subscribe to this model, which has negative financial, emotional and physical implications.

Inasmuch as these video vixens have made these choices and taken up their own agency by taking part in these videos, this does not change the fact that the videos they appear in (and the song lyrics) are misogynistic. Most of the songs refer to women as hos, sluts and bitches. They imply that women are not worthy of respect, and they objectify women and treat them as commodities. Although some hip-hop artists and their fans argue that this is simply entertainment, and fine because of freedom of expression, many hip-hop lyrics are tantamount to hate speech. This has a negative impact on societies, particularly those with high incidences of gender-based violence like South Africa.

The lyrics provide inconsiderate and harmful entertainment and also send a message to hip-hop fans. Young men and boys may begin to believe that women are nothing more than sexual possessions and young women and girls may feel that their entire worth is determined by how sexy

they look and how sexy men consider them to be. This can result in self loathing and low self esteem, which is documented in filmmaker Tamika Guishard's *Hip Hop Gurlz*: "Girls do what they see in videos," a black, pre-teen girl says in the film. "If I can get skinny, dress, and dance like that, I can be in videos too."

Just like in advertising, women are also objectified in hip hop music lyrics and videos.   *Photo: Trevor Davies*

Participants watched this eight minute film at a US conference called "Feminism and Hip Hop," which was hosted by the Center for the Study of Race, Politics, and Culture (CSRPC) in Chicago.

Facilitators then asked participants where objecti-fication and anger towards women comes from. Their answers ranged from "the capitalist influence of the corporate enterprise on the music industry, sexuality, drugs, crime, misogyny, consumerism and nihilism" to the complexities of American black masculinities as suggested by Byron Hurt, a former marine and current antisexism activist *(Brown, 2009)*.

Whatever the reasons, it goes without saying that there needs to be a paradigm shift in the hip-hop industry. Calling for the end of the sexualisation of women is not the ideal way to actually end the sexualisation of women. More spaces need to be created where women can address their issues;

reclaim their dignity as defined by themselves; empower other women, including those who choose different lifestyles, for example video vixens; as well as challenge the way they are presented by hip-hop artists who undeniably have a lot of influence.

Sexualised images of women in advertising

Much like the world of hip-hop, advertising is under attack. In Southern Africa, media and feminist networks have long played a watchdog role. They have succeeded in getting some advertisements stripped from billboards or removed from the airwaves on the grounds of objectification and sexualisation of women.

In 2009, a South African billboard advertising the Sexpo adult exhibition came under scrutiny because it depicted a woman taking off her underwear. The picture showed only the lower half of the woman's body, which promted the Advertising Standards Authority to pull it down and ban the advertisement.

Those objecting were angry because the advert did not show the woman's upper body or face, therefore marring all identity. Nevertheless, it was not surprising that a sexualised image was used

The media should be held accountable for sexist adverts.
Photo: Colleen Lowe Morna

to publicise an event dedicated to sex. Activists, however, should have questioned why the Sexpo ad campaign only featured women and not men. This is not to say that there are no sexualised images of men in the media, just fewer than those depicting women. Media watchdogs remain mum on this issue, which makes one wonder if, consciously or not, gender activists also consider women the weaker sex.

There is generally little consideration of the women who appear in these ads, nor acknowledgement that they have the aptitude to decide for themselves what career path they want to follow or what advertising campaign they want to take part in. Instead of belittling, judging and vilifying these women, activists should help empower them so they can avoid expoitation.

While this argument might appear to reinforce the idea that women are only valued for their physical appearance, it can also be argued that it is acceptable to value a woman for this quality among others. This might be compared to the academic or professional woman who prefers acknowledgement for her intellect and is not interested in being judged on how she looks. In order to support and represent the former woman, it is important to help empower her to realise her worth so she does not sell herself short. To let her know her power lies in her hands and not in the hands of men who would exploit her.

There is a great need to inform women of their options and show them how to protect themselves. I concede that many women feel the only option they have involves exploiting themselves. This is thanks to socialisation and messaging in our society, which typically endorses misogynistic views.

In addition, we need a commitment from the

media that it will stop propagating and normalising harmful practices and beliefs in its messaging (and this is not to say that this should be done by splitting hairs and pushing individual ideas and agendas). The media plays an integral role in how information is disseminated and its messages are far reaching and taken as the gospel truth by most. The media can achieve this by maintaining a balance between the sensuality and the intellect and strength of women. There is a need, in its messaging, to deconstruct the belief that women's bodies are products to be acquired, or something men are entitled to.

Pornography: friend or foe?

The concepts highlighted above also apply to this industry. This topic has been the cause of many a divisive debate amongst feminists since the 1980s. It can be seen in the outbreak of what is known today as the "feminist sex wars" which resulted in the feminist movement being split into the categories of Anti-Pornography Feminism and Pro-Sex Feminism, or Sex Positive Feminism.

Those who see pornography as a form of sexual liberation and freedom for women say that attacks on the sex industry trivialise the agency of women in this industry. The argument that pornography is synonymous with violence against women reinforces the neo-Victorian idea that men want sex and women merely endure it, or, in the cultural context in Africa, women should not want it because sex is not for women to enjoy. This ignores the fact that women also like to watch other people have sex. While the opposite is the norm, there are many pornographic films in which women play the dominant role.

The 1990s saw the emergence of the sexually-empowered woman in the form of pop culture figures like Madonna and Sharon Stone. Although these women have come under much scrutiny and been accused by the more scholarly feminists of bringing about the death of feminism, these women are anything but disempowered. They are sexually liberated.

The same can be said for self-described sex-positive feminist porn stars like Nina Hartley, Ovidie, Madison Young and Sasha Grey who do not see themselves as victims of sexism. In fact, they defend their decision to star in pornography and maintain that much of what they do on camera is an expression of their sexuality. They also maintain that in most cases women get paid more compared to their male colleagues.

On the other hand, the anti-pornography feminist faction claims women are coerced into pornography, either by a male figure or because of unfortunate circumstances. They feel the industry should be regarded as violence against women. These feminists would hold up the book Ordeal, about the life of former porn star Linda Boreman, as one example of this. The book is Boreman's story of being pimped out by her husband, who also forced her into pornography and raped and physically abused her.

Of course there is a risk of abuse and exploitation in any profession. The risk of encountering unscrupulous and violent people is present in all spaces, public or private, and our focus should be to ensure safety in all spaces, rather than trying to remove spaces altogether.

Feminist scholars like Catherine Mackinnon believe that pornography enforces a male-dominated social hierarchy in which rape is socially acceptable. Others believe that the sometimes violent nature in some of these films desensitises viewers to violence against women. I cannot dispute the validity of these concerns, as I share many of them, but only as far as the narrative is concerned, not regarding the industry as a whole.

The debate about whether pornography consumption increases the likelihood a man will rape women is ongoing. In a paper on the subject, Todd Kendall (2007) cites a study which notes that pornography and rape are economically complementary: one is used to arouse the consumer, who will then channel that arousal into a demand for sex. However, Kendall cites another study which claims the opposite: that consumers are already aroused when they seek out pornography, which then acts as a function to relieve their arousal, thereby making pornography a complement of masturbation and consensual sex, and a deterrent of rape.

I believe the more productive endeavour, which serves both the women who choose to work in this industry and all other women, is the approach taken by filmmakers like Erika Lust, Petra Joy and Anna Span. These women make porn for women, which can be enjoyed by women.

They acknowledge that women use pornography as an avenue of sexual expression and therefore they should be able to consume it without feeling violated. In an interview with the *Guardian*[4], Lust says she realised pornography has historically been made by men for men and she identified a gap that needed to be filled. This, in my opinion, is more productive than calling for a ban of pornography. We should instead demand that pornography producers use a more gender-sensitive approach.

I appreciate that in most societies, particularly in the South African context, gender-based violence is an epidemic and some believe the sex industry perpetuates this. But in fighting GBV by demonising sexuality, are we not, much like patriarchy, stereotyping women as victims and depriving them of their sexual rights and the freedom to express these rights?

What now?

Sexuality and sensuality and the expression thereof are still mostly unattainable and taboo for women, even in the eyes of many women's rights activists. Some gender activists maintain that those who choose to embrace their femininity, sexuality and sensuality, as prescribed by patriarchy, do so as a result of patriarchal social conditioning, which renders these women disempowered. To some degree this is true but it ignores the possibility that these women may have also considered this and made a conscious decision that it is what they want. We need to ask ourselves: when does socialisation stop and when does preference begin?

Does pornography fuel incidences of rape in society?

Photo: Sikhonzile Ndlovu

In my view, instead of shaming these women or relegating them to victim status, desperately in need of rescuing, we should applaud and encourage their agency. We should appreciate that the beauty and sensuality of a woman and her body, whatever shape or size, is neither a curse nor something to be ashamed of.

Indeed, we must encourage women to realise that their potential is not limited to their sensuality and sexuality. We must make men see that a woman is much more than her body; that her strengths lie in so many other places too. If a woman chooses a career as a video vixen she should not be judged as a result of that choice.

Rather than calling for the removal of advertisements showing women who have decided to celebrate their physical attributes, we must focus our efforts on ensuring that the media delivers a message of non-violence and respect for all women.

Writer's Bio
Gaura is a gender activist and writer based in Cape Town.

References
Amani, K. (2009) Hip Hop News, http://hiphopnews.yuku.com/topic/992#.Tqqaa5tXRW8 (last checked September 2009).

Brown, R.N. (2009) Black Girlhood Celebration: Toward a hip-hop feminist pedagogy. New York, Peter Lang.

Bynoe, Y. (2008) Hip Hop News, http://hiphopnews.yuku.com/topic/992#.Tqqaa5tXRW8 (last checked September 2009).

Ford, S. (2004) Golden Gate X Press, http://xpress.sfsu.edu/archives/editorials/001990.html

Kendall, T. (2007) Pornography, Rape and the Internet, paper for the The John E. Walker Department of Economics, Clemson University.

Lippi, T. (2011), Comment on Gender Links facebook page.

Weissheiss (2011) Hip Hop Summit South Africa, http://www.hiphopsummitsouthafrica.com/?p=884

Notes

[1] http://hoodgrownonline.com/buffie-the-body-hip-hop%E2%80%99s-mary-magdalene-hottentot-venus.html
[2] http://www.hiphopsummitsouthafrica.com/
[3] http://www.articlesbase.com/cosmetics-articles/learn-to-be-a-hip-hop-honey-4279093.html
[4] http://www.guardian.co.uk/lifeandstyle/2011/mar/22/porn-women?INTCMP=SRCH

What messages are adverts imparting?
By Thato Phakela

Abstract
Advertising is one mode of communication used to pass messages to audiences. While both women and men appear in media advertisements trying to sell products, women are more often seen than heard. This article seeks to find out why this is the case. It analyses representation of women and men in adverts, and the types of information each sex shares and discusses. This article will also look at the different products women and men advertise and the impact of this on the public.

Key words
advertising, sexualisation, access to information

Media should always be held accountable for the information it imparts to society and the way it represents men and women. One of the roles of the media should be to promote and empower women in all aspects of life. However, it often does the opposite when it comes to advertising. Women continue to be used as objects and victimised in and through media adverts.

Advertisers claim they are committed to truth, objectivity and accuracy. This article seeks to analyse the extent media and advertisers are actually committed to these tenets. It uses a gender lens to look at information imparted through advertisements in order to uncover their potential harm to women's rights. This article will look at several advertisements which frequently appear in print and broadcast media.

Case study one: analysis

In 2011, Britain's Advertising Standards Authority banned a L'Oreal make-up ad starring Julia Roberts after an MP complained it had been excessively airbrushed[1]. The advert is just one of many ads featuring airbrushed women regularly seen in the media. In the ad the 44-year-old actress is seen with flawless skin and no wrinkles. The photo is clearly too good to be true and does not look real, but rather resembles a painting.

This extreme manipulation of images is misleading to many women, especially young women who are more particular about their looks. This advert gives women the wrong impression about what defines beauty. It is also deceiving. Consumers will surely not get the same result they see on

Roberts' face. This may lead to lack of self confidence or worse. Advertisers are profit-orientated first, presenting their products in a way that ensures the most sales.

The writer concurs with the banning of this advert.
Source: National News and Pictures

While this ad was banned, there are many like it still appearing on TV and in print that should also be banned. Those authorities that police and monitor advertising must step up the pressure on advertisers. There is a long way to go before informative and gender-aware advertising is the norm and not the exception.

Women's representation in advertising

Airbrushed adverts are popular and can be seen in all types of media: on billboards, television and in magazines. Airbrushing is mostly used on women, especially women advertising make-up and facial products. These are common in women's magazines. Advertisers use airbrushing in order to promote their product and show how effective it is. However, this does not help most women who buy a product hoping to improve their skin. The purchase is often in vain.

The fact remains that the media's idea of female beauty is unattainable for all but a very small number of women. Advertisers use computers to create perfect models to sell their products. Most of the products advertised do not perform the same "miracle" women see on TV or in magazines.

A great number of women and girls even face health consequences trying to look like the women they see on TV.

Women are brainwashed by this type of advertising, made to feel beautiful and confident because they use a certain product. Some women even get addicted to products and feel they cannot face the world without them.

While women's magazines should be a tool for empowering women and helping them gain confidence, the information within them often does the opposite. Adverts found in women's magazines are degrading to women, undercutting their self confidence, self esteem and dignity. Many adverts make women believe they are not beautiful with their natural skin or body and instead need artificial help such as make-up to be acceptable to the world. This is wrong and harmful to women. Women, like men, should have the confidence to believe in their natural beauty, but most advertising aimed at women has over the years led many women to believe otherwise.

In monitoring several local women's magazines it was surprising to find at least three advertisements for weight loss products in each. What message is this passing to women? Many women struggle to lose weight, trying different products every day. This is because advertisers have made women believe that to be beautiful one has to be slim. This is deceiving and costs women a lot of money. With the money spent on weight loss and beauty products, many women could develop a small business and achieve financial independence.

Research has shown that advertisers use young, slim and good-looking girls to sell their products to older women[2]. Many women are suffering because of these deceiving messages advertisers transmit through the media. This kind of advertising should be banned from media.

This type of advertising also raises several questions: are women's magazines actually for women and do they serve the purpose of empowering women and helping them develop. Does the information in these adverts serve women's best interest?

The information in beauty and make-up adverts seems far from empowering. These ads portray women as beauty without brains - more concerned about their looks than anything else.

These magazines are filled with adverts for the best artificial hair, artificial nails, make-up, and weight loss advice. Advertisers pass the message: "You will never be more beautiful and feel better about yourself than if you use this product."

The message sent to women is that they are not good enough as they are. Most women reading these magazines do not have perfect skin, hair and nails. They are easy targets because the magazines also show them the standards of "beauty" they should attempt to achieve. Looking at this type of magazine reveals that women are still oppressed and there is a long way to go in order to obtain women's empowerment and gender equality.

These types of magazines are also full of adverts that urge women to use certain products for cooking and cleaning - in order to ensure women perform as the best wives and housekeepers. These adverts perpetuate the gender stereotype that a woman's job is in the home and her place is in the private and not public sphere.

A look at men's representation in such magazines presents a stark contrast. Men are seen advertising business products, or in adverts about ideas, education, finance and politics. Men are portrayed as leaders - people who are always in control. Yet women share the same size brain as men, they should be given a similar platform. While there are many women who are dominating in the public sphere, media and advertising have little time for such women.

Media has the right to inform but it should be held accountable for the kind of information it passes to society. Information imparted to the public should not harm or mislead.

Case study two

Description
The magazine, Top Women in Business and Government, promotes top women in business. It shows women who have made it in the top management positions in different organisations. It is about women who are challenging stereotypes and dominating in the public sphere. However, the very first advert in the magazine perpetuates a gender stereotype. It shows a beautiful naked woman covered in jewellery. This advert has been given prominence - it is at the front of the magazine and covers two full pages. This says a lot about how advertisers view women and how they continue to market and perpetuate stereo-types.

JENNA CLIFFORD

What has a woman's sexuality got to do with selling of jewels?
Source: Top Women in Business and Government

Analysis: visual image

This advert is a blatant stereotype that shows the woman as a sex object. This is an example of a woman being seen and not heard - her beauty is used to sell a product. This woman is not depicted as a professional, which contradicts the content in the rest of the magazine. Her sexuality is given prominence over all else.

The photo also seems to infer that once a woman becomes successful all she cares about is how she looks, including jewellery and accessories. The woman in the photo appears as someone not interested in business or development. While women are known to enjoy jewellery, which is perfectly acceptable, this advert is stereotypical and presents the woman as an object.

I think this company could have used a different approach by showing a photo of a well-dressed professional woman wearing jewelry. Such a photo would have had greater relevance in this magazine.

Women are seen but not heard

Compared to men, women's voices are rarely heard on radio and television. According to *Gender and Advertising Southern Africa* research by Gender Links (2007), women comprise 41% of all subjects in advertising and constitute only 29% of voiceover on radio and television. This huge gap illustrates that men have more power when it comes to imparting information to society.

This gap also leads women and men to believe that women are subordinate and men dominate. Meanwhile, men's voices in advertising sell "important" products such as cars, education and financial products.

If women advertise the same products, for example a car, they are likely to be seen posing naked with it or lying on top of it. Again, women are seen as sex objects and not voices of authority or knowledge. A gender-aware car advert would depict a fully-clothed woman using the car to get to a business meeting.

Instead, women's voices are mostly heard advertising food products or cleaning products. This perpetuates the stereotype that women belong in the domestic sphere and men in the public sphere.

Conclusion

Women should be given more and better opportunities to air their voices and views on radio and television, including about women's issues and women's rights. Denying them this opportunity is counter to the African Platform on Access to Information[3]. It states that public and private bodies should be obliged to proactively release information about their functions, powers, structures, officials, decisions, expenditure and other information relating to the activities of bodies of public interest.

There are many women's organisations fighting for better women's representation in the media. These organisations strive to ensure that women are no longer targeted by advertisers who have historically misrepresented products for women, as well as misrepresented women.

Women should be given more and better chances to give informative and empowering information to other women and society at large. Advertising authorities should stop allowing degrading adverts of women to appear in media.

Writer's Bio
Phakela is a gender activist from Lesotho. She is currently based in South Africa.

Notes

1 http://www.guardian.co.uk/media/2011/jul/27/loreal-julia-roberts-ad-banned
2 http://www.valt.helsinki.fi/comm/fi/english/WP2.pdf
3 http://windhoekplus20.org/african-platform-on-access-to-information/

GENDER AND MEDIA FREEDOM 20 YEARS AFTER THE WINDHOEK DECLARATION

Defending their democracy: South Africa's Right2Know protesters demanding media freedom and access to information without government's interference.   *Photo Saeanna Chingamuka*

Putting SADC gender and media freedom into perspective
By Saeanna Chingamuka and Daud Kayisi

Abstract
This article looks at media freedom in Southern Africa 20 years after the historic endorsement of the Windhoek Declaration. The authors analyse some current setbacks in the region which are leading to concern about backtracking on commitments made under the Declaration. In addition, the article discusses gender equality as it relates to media freedom and freedom of expression.

Key words
Windhoek Declaration, African Charter on Broadcasting, Protection of Information Bill, Right2Know, Media Institute of Southern Africa, Declaration of Principles of Freedom of Expression

In 2011, Africa marked 20 years of the Windhoek Declaration on Promoting Independent and Pluralistic Media, which UNESCO and the United Nations General Assembly endorsed in 1991. This endorsement ultimately led to the creation of 3 May as World Press Freedom Day.

In 1991, heavy state control characterised much of the African media landscape. Following the Windhoek Declaration, things began to change. Acknowledging that media freedom is a necessary condition for democratisation, many African countries mainstreamed this into their constitutions in the first decade following the Declaration. At the Windhoek +10 conference in 2001, the right to press freedom was extended to include broadcasting freedom, which was brought about through the adoption of the African Charter on Broadcasting. The Charter in turn fed into the influential Declaration of Principles of Freedom of Expression, as adopted by the African Commission on Human and Peoples' Rights of the African Union.

While positive signals elsewhere in the continent show that governments are embracing principles of free access to information, the Southern African Development Community (SADC) seems to be retrogressing. Namibia and South Africa, once beacons of media freedom in the region, are no longer conducive environments for the press, according to Freedom House, an independent watchdog organisation. Egocentric political interests in the region are the main cause of this relapse.

State of media freedom in SADC

The controversial Protection of Information Bill in South Africa, dubbed the "Secrecy Bill" by critics, is the most recent attack on, and cause of worry for, the media industry in the country. Critics argue that the bill, which has been in the public domain since 2010, is not only a threat to the media but also civil society organisations, academia and members of the public, just to mention a few.

Responding to the development, Witwatersrand University journalism professor Anton Harber said: "It is not just a battle for journalists and the media to do their job; it is a battle for citizens to be empowered by information and be able to assert their rights and aspirations. It is not just a battle for freedom of speech, but a fight to ensure our democracy is an open, participative and collaborative one, rather than a top-down authoritarian one."

The bill, which is currently under review after Right2Know (a civil society coalition created to oppose its passing) and opposition parties lambasted the ruling African National Congress (ANC) when it tried to use "clause 18" of the draft bill to force journalists to reveal their sources. Surprisingly, the ANC is preparing to pass this draconian bill after backing down from its threat to establish a Media Appeals Tribunal.

Similarly, Malawi's ruling Democratic Progressive Party recently amended section 46 of its penal code, bringing in a law that also undemocratically targets freedom of the press and freedom of information. The law empowers the information minister to close any newspaper that publishes information that s/he deems "contrary to the public interest." Despite numerous petitions from within the country, the region and the world, Malawi's former president, the late Bingu Wa Mutharika, signed and implemented the law in 2011. Critics believe it is meant to silence the newspaper industry, which has been very critical about governance issues in the country.

Ironically, Malawi's politicians have been sitting on the Access to Information Bill since it was drafted in 2003. A draft law currently gathering dust on government shelves aims to empower information seekers to access and obtain information with ease, as opposed to the current situation.

Farah Shaik: Capturing news with a gender perspective during gender and media training in Kwazulu Natal, South Africa.
Photo: Trevor Davies

Further, other media houses have been slapped with advertising bans in politically motivated decisions. According to the Media Institute of Southern Africa (MISA), advertising bans are the most common political strategy used to punish media houses that are critical of the conduct of the ruling elite around issues of governance, policy, human rights and rule of law, to mention a few. This chokes operations of the affected media houses because governments are among the biggest advertising clients in the region. Surprisingly, governments in the region ignore the fact that state revenues are public funds; therefore they should not use these revenues to punish independent media.

In countries such as Namibia, this has even become policy. *The Namibian* newspaper has been under such a ban since 2002. Malawi's Nation Publications Limited, one of the leading private media houses in the country, is under a similar advertising ban implemented by the Mutharika administration last year. Over the years, this practice has also been used in South Africa, Zimbabwe, Botswana, Lesotho and Swaziland.

Colonial and draconian laws of defamation, libel and treason continue to muzzle the media. According to MISA, "in Lesotho and Swaziland, journalist and civic activists can be arrested under treason laws that guise political repression."

However, one wonders why the ruling elite continue to come up with policies that contradict core principles of most hard-won democracies in the region. Freedom of the press, which extends to broadcasting, is the most famous clause in most republic constitutions in SADC, yet the reality on the ground contradicts what this clause stipulates.

The Secrecy Bill, for instance, if passed into law, will not only deny South African citizens their right to access and disseminate information, but to development as well. Imagine NGOs, researchers, academics, the corporate world and members of the general public unable to conduct campaigns, research, business and any other activities because they cannot use or access "classified information" because of a Protection of Information law?

Politicians in the region should bear in mind that laws such as newspapers bans and the proposed Secrecy Bill "[do] not stay in the statute books only for one administration or one term of government," says Ayesha Kajee, former executive director of the Freedom of Expression Institute. "It stays well into the future... history has shown that repressive laws are not usually misused by the administration that passes them but rather by administrations into the future." This makes it incumbent on politicians to come up with laws

that are democratic and contribute to the greater common good.

However, there is hope.

Efforts by South Africa's Right2Know (R2K) coalition have shown that persistent spot checks on politicians can yield positive results. The grouping has been advocating for further review of the Secrecy Bill since the ANC tabled in 2009. R2K is also amongst the forces that helped stop the ruling party from establishing the Media Tribunal, which critics believed was another threat to the media.

Elston Seppie of Freedom of Expression Institute stresses a need for media freedom and access to information at Gender Links' seminar in Johannesburg.   *Photo: Thato Phakela*

Numerous R2K campaigns, demonstrations and petitions with support from members of the public, politicians, academia and the media have seen the ANC change its mind around some of clauses of the bill. Delay in the process forces those who support suppression laws to rethink their motives. Other countries in the region ought to learn that establishing civil coalition groups like R2K can yield positive results if similar situations arise. Seeking legal redress of draconian laws is another option that media, civil society and concerned citizens should consider. The prevailing conditions in the region are reason enough why media practitioners should execute their duties ethically and responsibly so that the ruling elite do not take advantage of avoidable mistakes.

Elsewhere, and contrary to developments in SADC, Nigeria adopted a progressive freedom of information law in 2010 and Uganda passed an Access to Information Act in 2005. In 2010, Uganda debated the Whistle Blowers Protection Bill, which is aimed to create an enabling environment for citizens to freely disclose information on corrupt or improper conduct in public and private sectors.

What has gender got to do with media freedom?

The media landscape envisaged in the Declaration of 1991 is still far from being realised. This is due to various new laws and bills that ultimately threaten freedom of the media, for instance the 2011 Newspaper Ban Law in Malawi. These type of laws and others continue to infringe on the freedom of the media and undermine democracy.

The Declaration also addresses other pertinent issues such as freedom of information and expression, free flow of ideas by word and image, independent and pluralistic press, repression of media professionals, and establishment of associations that safeguard the fundamental freedoms in the Declaration and training of journalists. The Declaration puts women and men in the same bracket of media freedom.

Whereas media freedom has been understood to mean the absence of political censorship, there are many other ways in which citizens may be denied the right to be heard. As noted by the 2006 *Gender Review of Media Development Organisations*, women's voices may be excluded from the media. It is thus important to look at

media freedom in a way that takes into consideration "gender-based censorship" which ultimately disempowers, silences and makes invisible certain people in society.

Women are grossly underrepresented in the media.
Photo: Ncane Maziya

Whilst the Windhoek Declaration has in many ways been successful at changing the overall African media landscape, the focus in the next decade should be on how citizens, both women and men, can be empowered by its provisions. This can only be realised if the Declaration clearly articulates the different ways media freedom impacts women and men.

Interestingly, the 20th anniversary of the Windhoek Declaration took place at a time when the 2008 SADC Protocol on Gender and Development is closer than ever to coming into force. The Protocol brings together and enhances international and African commitments to gender equality by setting 28 targets to be achieved by 2015. Specific provisions for media include achieving parity in decision-making (rapid strides have already been made in the political realm); giving equal voice to women and men; challenging gender stereotypes; sensitive coverage of HIV and AIDS and gender violence. The Protocol also calls on the media to mainstream gender in all laws, training and policy.

Gender equality is entirely consistent with freedom of expression. Nothing is more central to this ideal than giving voice to all segments of the population. When women comprise about 52% of the population, but only constitute 24% of news sources (according to the 2010 Global Media Monitoring Project), censorship of a very real kind exists. The 2010 Gender Links *Gender and Media Progress Study* (GMPS) found that there has been a marginal increase in the proportion of women sources in Southern African media: from 17% in the 2003 *Gender and Media Baseline Study*, to 19% in the GMPS.

Mozambican beer advert: women are mostly objectified in the media, particularly in advertising.   *Photo: Mercedes Sayagues*

These findings beg the question: what do we really understand by freedom of expression, democracy and citizen participation? While more blatant forms of censorship may be subsiding, our media daily silences large segments of the population, notably women. Gender disparities in the news occur because of a lack of diversity in media ownership and because of "armchair" journalism, which results in the media seeking out a few voices of authority, usually men.

Further, the media often applies double standards to men and women. Women are objectified and their physical attributes highlighted in ways that do not apply to men. The explosion of tabloid media has further perpetuated these stereotypes.

Gender equality is implicit in the notions of a pluralistic press; reflecting the widest possible range of opinion within the community; the fulfilment of human aspirations; freedom of the press; and freedom of association as espoused in the Windhoek Declaration. But the failure to state this explicitly has led to gross gender disparities in the media.

The Declaration encourages the establishment of professional associations that safeguard various freedoms. These associations should include women's media associations. Media development organisations have the opportunity, through the work they do, to lead by example in showing that gender is intrinsic to free speech, citizen participation, and progressive media practice and content.

Thus after 20 years of the Windhoek Declaration it is time to acknowledge these silent forms of censorship that daily occur in the media. The debates on mainstreaming gender in the declaration should be taken forward so that the next decade can see a region that truly exemplifies the freedoms espoused in the original document.

Writer's Bio
Chingamuka is the Gender Links GMDC Manager and Kayisi is the GMDC Programme Officer.

The gender, media freedom and access to information nexus

By Claudine Hingston

Abstract

The Windhoek Declaration (1991) calls for the promotion of independent, pluralistic and free press. Twenty years down the line, it is important to review how successful this has been especially in relation to gender, media and access to information. The following questions need to be asked and analysed within a gender framework. How free is the media? Is information accessible to all? For until men and women have equal involvement and participation in the media and equal access to information, media freedom and access to information by all will not be fully achieved. This article will critically examine the concepts of gender, media freedom and access to information and tease out the interplay between the three. This article is based on the hypothesis that media freedom and access to information by all will only be fully realised when grounded within a gender framework.

Key words
gender, media freedom, access to information, Windhoek Declaration

This article sets out to examine the concept of media freedom, gender and access to information and look at the inter-relationship of the three issues. It is based on the hypothesis that media freedom and access to information by all will only be totally realised when grounded within a gender framework. It is examined against the 1991 Windhoek Declaration and the 1948 Declaration of Human Rights. The focus is on the African media, women's inclusion, position and representation in it and women's accessibility to information.

Media freedom can best be described as media that has the ability to publish news and ideas without government control. This concept gained significance in 1991, when African journalists came together in Windhoek, Namibia, to discuss the way African newspaper journalists had their work censored, some were also intimidated and imprisoned. Journalists wanted to look at ways to address these problems. Gadzekpo (2009) states that prior to the liberalisation of the press in Africa in the 1990's, editors and journalists that did not tow the government's line were often jailed or

hounded into exile. A caged media reported mostly government news and pronouncements.

The Windhoek Declaration (1991) calls for the promotion of independent, pluralistic and free press. The meeting focused on the print media, although recommendations were made to address problems in broadcast media at a later conference. A new document was adopted at the tenth anniversary that addressed issues specific to broadcast media. The UN General Assembly chose 3 May, the date the Windhoek Declaration was adopted, as World Press Freedom Day.

Gender refers to the social attributes and oppor-tunities associated with being male and female, and the relationship between men and women, girls and boys, as well the relations between women, and those between men. These attributes, opportunities and relationships are socially constructed and learned through socialisation processes. They are context/time-specific and changeable (UN, 2000). Gender has a transforming quality. It can be seen as a constraint upon the ways in which people do things, a barrier to free participation, and a palimpsest for creative expressions on which cultural and social practices are worked out, contested, resisted and often redefined *(Essed et al., 2009)*.

Give us access to speak through the media. *Photo: Colleen Lowe Morna*

Access to information simply means the rights of individuals to use and obtain information gene-rated by other people. The right to information is a core principle of good governance. The African Union Draft Model Law on Access to Infor-mation was released for public comments in 2011. It has very good recommendations on improving accessibility of information to all, although its gendered nature is questionable.

The 1948 Universal Declaration of Human Rights best brings out the interrelationship between gender, media freedom and access to information. It asserts the inherent dignity and the equal and inalienable rights of all members of the human family as the foundation of freedom, justice and peace in the world. It also proclaims the advent of a world in which human beings shall enjoy freedom from fear as the highest aspiration of the common people. Article 19 specifically calls for the right to freedom of opinion and expression by all and this is applicable to institutions made up of people, such as the media. The human family consists of men and women (gender), freedom from fear and want (access to informa-tion), the rights to freedom and of opinion and expression (media freedom). It is the denial of these rights to the media that culminated in the Windhoek Declaration.

Twenty years after, we may tend to ask the question whether the media is really free, but let us first examine the concept of freedom. Freedom is described as the power or right to act, speak or think freely. Has the media really achieved this? Freedom comes along with equality. It is not just about gaining freedom from government interference, but freedom should also be inherent within the media. Are men and women equally represented in the media? Do men and women have equal opportunities to managerial or senior positions within the media? Do they have equal say in decision making? Are they allocated the same tasks? Are they portrayed as equals by the media? Do they have equal access to the media? So many questions, but until all are answered in the affirmative, can the media be said to have achieved true media freedom. Unfortunately, this is not the case. Before looking at the gender situation in the African media, it is worth looking briefly at the gender situation in society in general.

Most societies are patriarchal in nature and discrimination against women is sadly still found throughout the world. The 2010 *Human Development Report* states that gender inequality remains a major barrier to human development, and although girls and women have made major strides since 1990, they have not yet gained gender equity. There are tremendous variations in gender inequality, with the Netherlands topping the list as the closest to attaining gender equality, while the bottom ten are Cameroon, Cote d'Ivoire, Liberia, Central African Republic, Papua New Guinea, Afghanistan, Mali, Niger, the Democratic Republic of Congo and Yemen. Other countries high in gender inequality are Benin, Malawi, Saudi Arabia and Sierra Leone (UNDP, 2010). It is of note that out of the 14 countries above, ten are African countries.

Gender inequality is reflected in the private and public sector and the media is no exception. According to Ndlela (2003), most countries in Africa inherited and sustained sexist and undemoc-

The SADC Barometer 2011 monitors the implementation of the SADC Gender Protocol.   *Photo: Loga Virahsawmy*

ratic broadcasting structures and hardware that were set up under colonial governments. Female journalists still complain of being asked to report the soft news, such as beauty and health, whilst men cover hard news, such as politics and the economy. In contrast to news, women are most likely to feature in advertisements where they are stereotypically presented (Lowe Morna and Ndlovu, 2009). Media portrays women in stereotypical roles including as sex symbols, beauty objects, caregivers, home-makers and housewives. According to Gallagher (2002), the tendency to ignore women, or at best, talk about them, rather than to them, is deeply embedded in the normative cultural practices that filter into newsroom cultures and routines. Articles 29-31 of the Protocol on Gender and Development signed by SADC heads of states in August 2008 specifically calls for changes in the media content and the challenging of gender stereotypes.

Zimbabwean gender and media activist Thabani Mpofu works with Zimpapers journalists to mainstream gender in editorial content.
Photo: Trevor Davies

Though the African media has made strides towards bridging the gender gap, it needs to do much more. Until then, media freedom is just a catchword. In a 2008 report by East African journalists, it was noted that only 3% of the total numbers of women in nine East African countries are employed in the decision-making organs of their institutions. In a 2007 report by the South African National editors, it was noted that the majority of decision-makers overseeing production routines in South African media houses are men with women occupying less influential positions.

According to Gadzekpo (2007), there are very few female media owners in the world, but the situation is even worse in Africa. It is therefore not surprising that the emerging class of African media and communications technology entrepreneurs are almost all men. The importance of including women in the media, as well as positive representation and portrayal of women, cannot be overemphasized. Lowe Morna (2002) best sums this up, stating: "If our reporting is guided by human rights ethos, if we agree that the media has a role to play in challenging racism, surely we must also agree that it has a role to play in challenging sexism."

The importance of gender in the media is not a new discourse and various conferences have been held to promote this, including the Women Empowering conference held in Bangkok, Thailand (1994); the UNESCO International Symposium on Women and the Media: Access to Expression and decision making held in Toronto, Canada (1995); and the International Women and Media Seminar convened in Kalmar, Sweden (1995). Section J, paragraph 234-245 of the Beijing Platform of Action outlines action to be taken by governments, national and international media and other institutions. The first is to increase women's participation and access to expression and decision-making in and through the media and new technologies of communication. Secondly to promote a balanced and non-stereotypical portrayal of women and girls in the media and encourage gender-sensitive training for media professionals and take effective measures against pornography. In fact, these forward-looking strategies suggest that access to the media is one way women can be empowered.

It will strengthen their ability to combat negative portrayals of women internationally and allow them to challenge instances of abuse of power in an increasingly important industry. As noted by Pratt (2004), gender (men and women), plus access to the media, minus socio-cultural barriers and discriminatory practices, equals gender equality.

Women at a Tanzania Media Women Association meeting.
Photo: Gender Links library

Access to information is vital for all, and it is true that women have less access to information than men because of socio-cultural barriers. The majority of African women have little or no access to the mass media. In some homes, computers, television, magazines, newspaper and the radio are the man's property. The situation is further complicated by the low literacy rates amongst African women. Girls are denied education, which limits their access to information. The many tasks of the African woman also limit her access to information. Many women are ignorant of the existence of laws that recognise their rights and can be evoked for their protection.

According to Zirman (2011), women have had limited participation in the processes that led to the formulation, enactment and implementation of laws or policies that enable citizens to enjoy freedom of information, especially information held by public bodies. She adds that factors such as geographical location, education and literacy, levels of economic empowerment and access to various media, put women as a group at a disadvantage. These factors mean women remain in a vicious cycle, although it could easily be mitigated by conscious efforts to ensure that women access information that can help them make informed choices. It is therefore worrying that the Draft Model Law on Access to Information which is supposed to promote access to information for all has no specific measures around how information can be made available to women who have little or no access to it. FEMNET research has found that the advancement of African women has been affected by lack of access to vital information that relates to their rights. Therefore there is a crucial need for legislation that guarantees free access to relevant and timely information.

On a positive note, many women's organisations are making use of the media to achieve their aim. The Forum for African Women (Sierra Leone Chapter), for instance, has been very instrumental in using the media to achieve its aim of encouraging parents to send their girl children to school. Advances in information technology and telecommunications have continued to broaden access to information and open new possibilities for women's participation in the development process. Many women's organisations are now making use of information technology to network and communicate with each other.

The African Women's Media Centre is one such organisation. It links women throughout the continent and offers training and other facilities to them. In addition, many African countries not only have a national media association, but they also have women's media groups, such as the

Tanzanian Women's Group, Association of Media Women in Kenya and Women in the Media, Sierra Leone. These groups are instrumental in advocating for gender equality in the media and working to find ways for more women to be able to access information.

Many NGOs are also making a concerted effort to mainstream gender into African media, including Fesmedia Africa, which supports programmes and projects that promote balance in and through the media. On the southern front, there are organisations like Gender Links.

However, the fact remains that many African women still have little or no access to information. Until men and women have equal involvement and participation in the media and equal access to information, media freedom and access to information for all will not be fully achieved.

References

AU Draft model law on access to information:Available at: http://www.achpr.org/english/other/MODEL%20LAW%20 FINAL.pdf. Accessed 14/08/11

Beijing Platform of Action. Available at : http://www.un.org/womenwatch/daw/beijing/platform/ Accessed:10/08/11

East African Journalist Forum (EAJA), (2008), Enhancing Gender Equality in the media in Eastern Africa. Available: http://africa,ifj.org/assets/docs/175/137/cb64af-8ab2089,pdf Accessed: 15/08/11

Essed, P. Goldberg. D. and Kobayashi, A.2009. A Companion to Gender Studies (Wiley Blackwell).

Hambuba, C. and Kajoiya, R. 2009.Freedom of Information (FOI) and Women's right in Africa. FEMNET

Gadzekpo, A. (2009), Missing Links: African media studies and feminist concerns, Journal of African media Studies Vol. 1(1), p 69-80

Gallagher, M. (2002) Women, Media and Democratic Society: In pursuits of rights and freedom.

Lowe Morna, C. (ed) (2007) The Glass Ceiling and beyond-the status of women and diversity in the South Africa news media, South Africa National Editors Forum (Sanef) and Gender Links.

Lowe Morna, C. (2002) 'Promoting Gender Equality in and through the media. A Southern African Case Study. Available: www.un.org/womenwatch/daw/egm/media2002/reports/EP5Morna. Accessed: 07/08/11

Protocol of Gender and Development, 2008: Available at http://www.sadc.int/index/browse/page/465

Ndlela, N. (2003), Critical analysis of the media law in Zimbabwe. Konran Adenauer Foundation: Harare United Nations, 2000 Available at http://www.itu.int/gender/about/gender.html. Accessed: 09/08/11

United Nations Human Development Report. Available at http://hdr.undp.org/en/reports/global/hdr2010/chapters/en Accessed: 10/08/11

United Nation Declaration of Human Rights: Available at http://www.un.org/en/documents/udhr Accessed: 12/08/11

Windhoek Declaration 1991, Available at http://www.cpu.org.uk/userfiles/WINDHOEK%20DECLARATION.PDF Accessed: 15/08/11

Zirman, P. (2011) Ensuring women's right to access to information. Available at http:/www.genderlinks.org.za/article/ensuring-women-rights-to-access-to-information-ati-2011-07-09. Accessed 15/08/2011

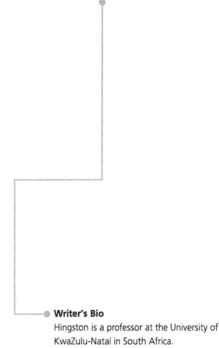

Writer's Bio

Hingston is a professor at the University of KwaZulu-Natal in South Africa.

Half full or half empty: Gender gains and losses in APAI

By Saeanna Chingamuka and Colleen Lowe Morna

Abstract

This article concerns the process that saw the gender lobby provide input about the African Platform on Access to Information (APAI) declaration. Adopted in 2011, the declaration encourages governments to implement Access to Information (ATI) laws. To date, only nine African countries have such laws. The Gender and Media Diversity Centre (GMDC), a Gender Links project, hosted seminars in three SADC countries in order to solicit input about gender and the ATI. Seminar deliberations were collated and shared with the task team that drafted the Declaration. Some of the proposed amendments were implemented while others were not. Subsequently, the gender lobby has scored the task team 49% for integrating gender in its final declaration. The article thus details the gender gains and losses made, as well as what the GMDC has learnt from this process.

Key words

access to information, gender equality, media, ICTs

Background and context

While celebrating the Windhoek +20 anniversary on 3 May 2011, media experts praised the declaration, noting that to a great extent it had assisted many African countries in enacting media freedom laws. The state of media freedom in Africa 20 years ago was very different than it is today. The situation in many countries around freedom of the press has been enhanced because of the Windhoek Declaration. It was also at the World Press Freedom Day, 3 May 2011, in Windhoek where media experts tabled a desire to implement a declaration to improve access to information (ATI) in Africa.

In many African countries, access to information has not been on the top of the agenda. Only nine, including South Africa, Uganda, Angola, Ethiopia, Liberia, Zimbabwe, Guinea and Nigeria, have access to information laws. In Mozambique for instance, parliament has yet to table a draft bill presented by a group of civil society organisations in November 2005. The same is true in Kenya, Sierra Leone, and Tanzania, while policymakers in Rwanda, Sudan, Zambia and Ghana have struggled to push tabled draft bills through parliaments.

Paige Ekandjo, a final-year journalism student at the PoN, poses a question to the panel. *Photo: Echoes*

Society has a right to be informed and therefore access to information is crucial for democracy and good governance in any given country. For this reason media experts drafted a declaration that encourages African states to create and implement ATI laws. The declaration underwent several changes and a process was initiated for the public to comment on the document.

Adoption of the declaration

On 19 September 2011, the Africa Information and Media Summit (AIMS), a meeting that brought together the Pan African Conference on Access to Information (PACAI) as well as the Highway Africa Conference, adopted the African Platform on Access to Information (APAI) in Cape Town. Advocate Pansy Faith Tlakula, the African Union Special Rapporteur for Freedom of Expression and Access to Information signed the declaration, which will be presented to the African Union in 2012.

The objectives of the PACAI were:
- To concentrate the insight and power of stakeholders in information rights and access, particularly in Africa, to exchange knowledge and experience;
- To advance the momentum for transparency, public domain information and ICT-accessibility, particularly in Africa;
- To initiate a process for the adoption of an instrument (the APAI) which elaborates the right of access to information, sets standards and provides guidance to countries in the enactment and implementation of access to information laws, and which may be put to the African Union Commission for its November session (consultations with the African Union will take place mid-June 2012); and
- To contribute to the international community a call for the United Nations to give formal recognition of an International Day of Access to Information. (To date, the following have agreed to assist in drafting the declaration: UNESCO, UN Special Rapporteur for Freedom of Expression, Article 19).

The APAI was crafted around a similar process as the one which informed the adoption of the 1991 Windhoek Declaration. It is envisaged that the

APAI will assist African states to commit to developing ATI laws.

At the AIMS Summit, Frank la Rue, UN special rapporteur on the promotion and protection of the right to free-  dom of expression, said it is relevant that a document which will set global standards on access to information comes from Africa. He added that rapporteurs should not only criticise but also praise good practices such as the APAI. Tlakula said the importance of access to information cannot be overemphasised. "Secrecy builds suspicion and information opens doors of neutral trust between the state and citizen," she said.

More than 200 delegates signed the African Platform on Access to Information, which states that "access to information is a fundamental human right" and "the right of access to infor- mation shall be established by law in each African country." Among other things, the conference has called on UNESCO to endorse the African Platform on Access to Information. It also identified 28 September as a date that should be declared International Right to Information Day.

In another development, a model law for AU member states on Access to Information has been drafted by the Special Rapporteur on Freedom of Expression of the African Commission for Human and Peoples' Rights. Consultations on the draft model law are being carried out in different regions in Africa.

Gender awareness in access to information

One may wonder why access to information laws should be gender-aware. However, any development process requires that attention be given to gender perspectives. This involves making gender perspectives - what women and men do and the resources and decision-making processes they have access to - more central to all policy development, advocacy, development, implemen- tation and monitoring of norms and standards. It is imperative that gender is a component of development processes because it informs what needs to be done, where the gaps are, how and to whom interventions should be targeted at.

A gender-aware policy is one that uses gender- neutral language; it is fair in its approach to how an issue affects women and men differently, challenges stereotypes and recognises the importance of sex-disaggregated data. The objective of gender neutral language is to steer clear of implicit or explicit mention of gender or sex. Language should be inclusive and avoid assumptions about professions and roles and their attachment to one sex or another. General rules include avoiding gender specific words like fireman; use phrases such as his or her rather than he/him to refer to both sexes; avoid language that excludes one sex, such as mankind; and avoid gender stereotypes.

Taking stock: a media trainer during women in politics workshop in Madagascar. *Photo: Loga Virahsawmy*

The *Gender and Media Progress Study* (2011) found out that women constitute only 19% of those speaking in SADC media. Gender equality is not given top priority in regional media constituting only 1% of all topics covered. The research further found that women are still more often found in images than as news sources. They are more likely to be seen than heard, constituting 27% of all images in newspapers in the region compared to 18% of news sources in the print media and 19% overall.

The paucity of women in the media requires a deliberate approach that makes integration of issues that affect women mandatory. For as long as gender mainstreaming is not at the core of all development issues, women will continue to be further marginalised. It is against this background that the GMDC initiated a process to mainstream gender in the draft declaration on access to information.

Women are more likely to be seen than heard in the media.
Photo: Frank Windeck

The GMDC informs regional processes

The GMDC, a partnership unit of Gender Links which convenes monthly seminars to discuss pertinent gender, media and diversity issues, contributed to the process that developed the final APAI declaration. In August 2011, it convened three seminars in Namibia, Tanzania and South Africa. The seminar discussions were based around the question: "What has gender got to do with access to information?"

What has gender got to do with access to information?		
Country	**Date**	**Who**
Namibia	8 August 2011	Clement Daniels (Media Ombudsman); Eberhard Hofmann (Chair, Editors' Forum); Graham Hopwood (Director, Institute for Public Policy Research); David Lush (Media Consultant & Trainer); Marbeline Mwashekele, (Director, MISA Namibia); Ronelle Rademeyer, (Senior Journalist); Sandra Williams (General Manager, 99 FM) and citizens.
Tanzania	9 August 2011	Editors from GL's Media COEs in Tanzania, DFID partners, citizens.
South Africa	16 August 2011	Guy Berger, Karen Mohan, Joe Thloloe (Press Ombudsperson), Elston Seppie (Executive Director, Freedom of Expression Institute), GL Media COEs facilitators, citizens.

The proposed gender entry points were submitted to the think tank tasked with drafting the bill. Some proposals were fully adopted, some were diluted and some were rejected outright. In the table we look at the final declaration, noting what did and did not make it in. Each category item has been scored out of five marks. There were a total of 17 categories that the GMDC contributed to, which means the final total is out of 85. The total number out of 85, similar to a rating, was then calculated as a percentage.

The full declaration can be accessed from:
http://www.pacaia.org/index.php?option=com_content&view=article&id=57&Itemid=120

Item	Original document (22 July 2011 draft)	Proposed amendments	Final	Gain or loss	Score out of 5
Preamble	Stating that access to information (ATI) is the right of all natural and legal persons to seek, access and obtain information from public bodies and private bodies acting in a public nature.	Stating that access to information (ATI) is the right of all natural and legal persons, **women and men**, which implies the right to seek, access and obtain information from public bodies and private bodies acting in a public domain.	Stating that access to information (ATI) is the right of all natural and legal persons, which consists of the right to seek, access and receive information from public bodies and private bodies performing a public function and the duty of the state to prove such information.	Loss: From the outset, access to information should be problematised and the differential impact between women and men underscored.	0
	Emphasising that access to information is a fundamental human right essential for the recognition and achievement of every person's human rights and socio-economic rights, and as a mechanism to promote democratic accountability, good governance, access to health care, a clean environment, sustainable development and fight corruption.	Emphasising that access to information is an integral part of the fundamental human right of freedom of expression, essential for the recognition and achievement of every person's civil, political and socio-economic rights, and as a mechanism to promote democratic accountability, good governance and equality.	Emphasising that access to information is an integral part of the fundamental human right of freedom of expression, essential for the recognition and achievement of every person's civil, political and socio-economic rights, and as a mechanism to promote democratic accountability, good governance.	Loss: The declaration does not emphasise that access to information is integral to attaining equality.	0
	No mention of the SADC Protocol on Gender and Development.	Acknowledging the SADC Protocol on Gender and Development that cites gender equality in and through the media and ICT's as central to development.	No mention of the SADC Protocol on Gender and Development.	Loss: The regional instrument is quite progressive on attaining gender equality in and through the media. This remarkable regional instrument should be acknowledged.	0
	Cognisant that questions around "whose information" and "who has access to information" highlight	Cognisant that questions around "whose information" and "who has access to information" highlight	Cognisant of the African Union Convention on Preventing and Combating Corruption, the African Charter on Values and	Loss: The phrasing is imprecise. The inequalities in society need to be addressed by levelling the	0

Item	Original document (22 July 2011 draft)	Proposed amendments	Final	Gain or loss	Score out of 5
	(problems in society that need to be addressed in terms of equality of access.	(problems in society that need to be addressed in terms of equality of access).	Principles of Public Service and Administration, the African Charter on Democracy, Elections and Governance, the African Youth Charter and the African Statistics Charter, all of which promote transparency in public life.	playing field on many fronts, the most cross-cutting of which is gender equality.	
Key principles					
Fundamental right	Access to information is a fundamental human right, in accordance with Article 9 of the African Charter on Human and Peoples' Rights. It is open to everyone, and no one should be privileged or preju-diced in the exercise of this right on account of belonging to a class or group howsoever defined. It should expressly not be required that anyone has to demonstrate a specific legal or personal interest in the information requested or sought or otherwise required to provide justification for seeking access to the information.	Fundamental Right Accessible to (Everyone) all women and men: Access to information is a fundamental human right, in accordance with Article 9 of the African Charter on Human and Peoples' Rights.	Fundamental Right Accessible to Everyone. Access to information is a fundamental human right, in accordance with Article 9 of the African Charter on Human and Peoples' Rights. It is open to everyone, and no one should be privileged or prejudiced in the exercise of this right on account of belonging to a class or group howsoever defined, and whether in terms of gender, class, race, political association, occupation, sexual orientation, age, nationality, HIV status, and other bases as cited in many African constitutions. It is not required that anyone must demonstrate a specific legal or personal interest in the information requested or sought or otherwise required to provide justification for seeking access to the information.	Loss: "Everyone" casts a shadow on who currently has access and who does not. Placing women and men in the same bracket implies that the current gaps affect them equally. Gain: It mentions that "no one should be prejudiced in the exercise of this right on account of belonging to a class, group, howsoever defined."	5

Item	Original document (22 July 2011 draft)	Proposed amendments	Final	Gain or loss	Score out of 5
Language and Accessibility	To the greatest extent possible, information should be available in the language of the person seeking it, and in a format that is as accessible as possible.	To the greatest extent possible, information should be available in the language of the person seeking it, and in a format that is as accessible as possible, especially radio, which remains the most accessible format in Africa.	To the greatest extent possible, information should be available in the language of the person seeking it, in an accessible location, in a format that is as accessible as possible, and, in particular, ensures that it is accessible to those who may be particularly affected by the subject matter of the information.	Loss: Gender is implicitly referred to.	3
Right to personal data	All persons have a right to access and correct their personal data held by third parties.	All persons have a right to access and correct their personal data held by third parties. Women shall have a right to be identified according the surname of their choice and not necessarily their surname by marriage.	All persons have a right to access and correct their personal data held by third parties.	Loss: This provision is subject to interpretation by parties involved. It can be problematic to those who are supposed to be served by it.	2
Duty to collect and manage information	Public and private bodies have a duty to collect and manage information on their operations and activities on behalf of their citizens. This includes procedures for ensuring that the information is easily accessible.	Public and relevant private bodies have a duty to collect and manage information on their operations and activities on behalf of their citizens.	Public and relevant private bodies have a duty to collect information on their operations and activities on behalf of their citizens. They also have a duty to respect minimum standards in relation to the management of this information to ensure that it may easily be made accessible to citizens.	Loss: Sex disaggregated data is often missing in Africa. The fact that this is not clearly defined means that development interventions will be gender blind.	2
Duty to fully implement	Public and private bodies have an obligation to ensure the law is fully implemented. This includes internal procedures and processes and the designation of responsible	Public and relevant private bodies have an obligation to ensure the law is fully implemented. This includes internal procedures and processes and the designation	Public and relevant private bodies have an obligation to ensure the law is fully implemented. This includes internal procedures and processes and the designation	Loss: It does not point to some of the indicators for implementation.	0

Item	Original document (22 July 2011 draft)	Proposed amendments	Final	Gain or loss	Score out of 5
	officials. An independent body such as an ombudsman or commissioner should be established to monitor and ensure implementation.	of responsible officials. An independent body such as an ombuds (man - person) or commissioner should be established to monitor and ensure implementation.	of responsible officials.		
		Application of principles These principles are essential to development, democracy, equality and the provision of public service, and are applicable to, amongst others, the following:	Removed completely	Loss: The proposed principle included equality.	0
Disadvantaged communities	Governments have a further obligation to ensure that information is provided to disadvantaged communities including minority groups and minority language speakers, women, rural people, the poor and disabled. They have an obligation to ensure equitable and affordable access to ICTs for the disabled and for other disadvantaged persons.	Governments have a (further-particular?) obligation to (provide- patronising? Maybe facilitate access to) information to disadvantaged minority groups and minority language speakers, as well as marginalised people (groups?) - order, this should come first such as women, children, rural people, the poor and persons with disabilities. This especially applies to information that contributes to the long-term empowerment of people (???) Governments also have an obligation to ensure equitable and affordable access to ICTs for (those with special needs and for other disadvantaged persons)	Governments have a particular obligation to facilitate access to information by disadvantaged minority groups and minority language speakers, as well as marginalised groups including women, children, rural people, the poor and persons with disabilities. This especially applies to information that contributes to the long-term empowerment of the groups. Governments also have an obligation to ensure equitable and affordable access to ICTs for those with special needs and for other disadvantaged persons and groups.	Gain: The application of this principle recognises women as one of the disadvantaged groups. It further acknowledges the goal for long-term empowerment and the need to ensure equitable and affordable access to ICTs.	5

Item	Original document (22 July 2011 draft)	Proposed amendments	Final	Gain or loss	Score out of 5
Women	Governments, civil society and media should facilitate women's access to information, thereby contributing to promoting and defending their rights in public life. Civil society organisations should make use of access to information mechanisms to monitor governments' fulfilment of commitments to further gender equality, to demand the enhanced delivery of services targeted at women and to ensure that the public funds they are entitled to are received. The collection, management and release of information should reflect gender distinctions where possible.	Governments, civil society and the media (should- have an obligation to) facilitate women's equal access to information, (thereby contributing to promoting and defending - so that they can defend) their rights and participate in public life. Civil society organisations should make (the best?) use of access to information mechanisms to monitor governments' fulfilment of commitments to further gender equality, to demand the enhanced delivery of services targeted at women and to ensure that the public funds they are entitled to are received. The collection, management and release of information should (reflect gender distinctions where relevant- be gender disaggregated. NB there are hardly any instances in which this is not relevant).	Governments, civil society and the media have an obligation to facilitate women's equal access to information, so that they can defend) their rights and participate in public life. Civil society organisations should be encouraged to make the best use of access to information mechanisms to monitor governments' fulfilment of commitments to further gender equality, to demand the enhanced delivery of services targeted at women and to ensure that the public funds they are entitled to actually reach them. The collection, management and release of information should be gender disaggregated.	Gains: This principle is detailed and acknowledges that the collection and management of information should be gender disaggregated. This is progressive and can inform gender aware interventions.	5
Media and information literacy	Governments, civil society and the media have an obligation to promote media and information literacy, to assist individuals and communities to ensure that all members of society can understand and take advantage of new	Governments, civil society and the media have an obligation to promote media and information literacy, including gender and media literacy, to ensure that all members of society can understand and take advantage of new	Governments, civil society, education institutions, and the media have an obligation to promote media and information literacy, to assist individuals and communities to ensure that all members of society can understand and	Loss: The principle does not mention gender and media literacy, which has become an empowering tool for citizens to better understand the media and its operations. Women are often not quoted as	3

Item	Original document (22 July 2011 draft)	Proposed amendments	Final	Gain or loss	Score out of 5
	technologies, and to be able to participate intelligently and actively in public matters and enforce their right of access to information.	technologies, and to be able to participate intelligently and actively in public matters, and enforce their right of access to information. Citizens should be empowered to consume information critically and express their views on such information, as well as seek corrections where applicable.	take advantage of new technologies, and to be able to participate intelligently and actively in public matters, and enforce their right of access to information. Citizens should be empowered to be able to consume information critically and express their views on such information, as well as be enabled to seek corrections where applicable.	sources, presented as sex objects in news and adverts. Gender and media literacy enables citizens, both women and men, to create their own media.	
National governments of AU member states	Adopt comprehensive laws on access to information in line with the principles and the AU Model Law and fully implement them; Harmonise legal frameworks to ensure access to information including repealing or reforming anti-quoted laws which restrict access; Engage with civil society and other stakeholders in implementation; Join multi-stakeholder efforts on transparency; Promote availability of public domain information through ICTs and public access to ICTs; Support AU efforts to adopt instrument on access to information; Officially recognise 28 September as International and African "Access to Information Day."	Adopt comprehensive gender-aware laws on access to information in line with the principles in this Declaration and the proposed AU Model Law, and fully implement them; Engage with civil society and other stakeholders to ensure widespread information demand and effective implementation of laws and policies to advance access to information by all citizens, especially marginalised groups.	Engage with civil society and other stakeholders to ensure widespread information demand and effective implementation of laws and policies to advance access to information by all citizens, especially marginalised groups.	Loss: This responsibility does not call on governments to adopt gender-aware laws. They can come up with laws that are gender blind which will not serve those who currently do not have access to information.	2

Item	Original document (22 July 2011 draft)	Proposed amendments	Final	Gain or loss	Score out of 5
Civil society	Civil society to: Engage with governments in developing, enhancing and implementing ATI laws; Monitor progress on implementation of ATI laws; Create awareness on ATI and provide assistance to the public on access; Ensure that their activities are transparent; Promote 28 September as African and International Access to Information Day and, in particular, carry out activities on 28 September of every year aimed at advancing the recognition, awareness and enjoyment of the right of access to information by all sectors of the society.	Create awareness on ATI and provide assistance to facilitate information access by the general public as well as by specific audiences (including minority groups and minority language speakers: This should include groups that have larger numbers - women, children, rural communities, individuals with disabilities or those living in poverty).	Create awareness on ATI and provide assistance to facilitate information access by the general public as well as by specific audiences (including women, minority groups and minority language speakers, children, rural communities, individuals with disabilities or living in poverty).	Gain: Women are listed as one of the groups that need to be given assistance in accessing information.	5
Media	Respect equality, and provide equitable representation within their information output.	Promote gender equality within the media and in media content.	Respect and promote equality, and provide equitable representation within their information output.	Gain: Equality is explicitly mentioned in the media as well as in the manner in which it represents women and men.	5
	Recognise gender differences in regard to audience and market research.	Recognise and be responsive to gender differences in regard to audience and market research.	Recognise and be responsive to gender differences in regard to audience and market research.	Gain: The declaration calls on the media not just to recognise but to respond to gender differences especially in audience research.	5
Total					42/85 = 49%

GENDER AND MEDIA FREEDOM

The APAI declaration does more than simply set out principles on ATI, it also gives direction on how these principles should be applied, taking into account the various issues that affect different sectors of society. The declaration makes special provision for children, women, disadvantaged communities, health care, and education, among others.

Women traders can benefit from ATI laws.   *Photo: Daud Kayisi*

The document was given a final rating of 49% following the proposal of many amendments and the incorporation of some. While this is less than a passing score of 50%, the qualitative process cannot be discounted. Gender is not often understood in freedom of expression issues. Some of the gains made include:
• Women being recognised as a disadvantaged group in ATI.
• Equality is explicitly mentioned in some of the principles around ATI.
• There is special mention that women need to be given assistance in accessing information.
• Calls on the media to respond to gender differences especially in audience research.
• Underscoring the importance of collecting and managing sex disaggregated data.

The losses include:
• ATI is not problematised in the preamble and therefore the differential impact of ATI between women and men is not acknowledged.
• The SADC Protocol on Gender and Development is not mentioned as one of the progressive regional instruments.
• It does not point to the indicators that should be put in place to monitor implementation
• Gender and media literacy is not mentioned.
• Governments are not encouraged to adopt gender-aware laws.

Lessons learned

The quest for gender equality in and through the media is far from over. There remains a lack of understanding of gender equality in freedom of expression discourse.

• The GMDC seminars on access to information and the input made into the APAI declaration changed the discourse on access to information in Africa. If Gender Links had not convened seminars through the GMDC, most of these gains around gender equality would not have been made. There was constant engagement with the think tank that crafted the declaration.

• The think tank argued that some of gender provisions could not be easily integrated. The question often asked was: "How about transgender people?" Somehow, this became an excuse for not specifically mentioning how ATI affects women and men differently. This is not a problem in this instance. Transgender issues are diluting the gender equality discourse. Policymakers need to be very careful in how they apply transgender recognition.

- The processes around media freedom and access to information in Africa are dominated by men. There should be a critical mass of women who understand these issues and the gender dimensions to them so that any decisions made are ultimately gender-sensitive.
- However, men should also be targeted in promoting gender equality in and through the media. They need to be sensitised to appreciate that women and men have different needs and unless these needs are explicitly underlined, the laws that are put in place will further marginalise women.
- Constant engagement and persuasion for the inclusion of gender in media laws can yield results. Gender Links actively participated in the discussions of the draft APAI document. Though not all contributions were accepted in the final document, we anticipate that what we managed to integrate will go a long way in enhancing access to information for women and men on the continent. In addition, this is one impact the organisation can claim credit for.

Way forward

The APAI document will inform the drafting of access to information laws in Africa. The draft

Gloria Masanza, a Malawian Journalist, engaging with Capital FM's gender policy.   *Photo: Danny Glenwright*

Model Law for AU Member States on Access to Information should also be scrutinised from a gender point of view so that gender is explicitly mentioned. The draft law will be used by member states to draft ATI laws. It is therefore important for gender to be explicit so that it is not lost in the discourse.

Countries should be monitored to ensure that the ATI laws they put in place make a difference for both women and men. This will enable women and men to make informed decisions on development and participate more fully.

Writer's Bio
Chingamuka is the Gender Links GMDC Manager and Lowe Morna is the CEO of Gender Links.

Gender censorship: None but ourselves can free our minds!
By Colleen Lowe Morna

When Agnes Callamard, Executive Director of Article 19, coined the phrase "gender censorship" at the launch of the third Global Media Monitoring Project in 2005, the Fleet Street audience she stood before in London stopped short of pummelling her with tomatoes.

Time has marched on but not much has changed. Since the first global study in 1995, to the latest in 2010, the proportion of women sources in the media has risen from 17 to 25% globally, and from 16 to 19% in Africa. Yet censorship is still viewed through the narrow lens of politically barred content, rather than the broader societal lens of exclusion.

Three studies over the last two years initiated by Gender Links with various partners have provided stark data of the gender gaps in the media. The *Gender in Media Education Audit* shows that there are more women than men in media studies, but many more male than female lecturers. *Glass Ceilings* in Southern African media shows that women constitute 41% of media employees (32% if South Africa is excluded) but less than a quarter of managers and only a handful of board members and top executives.

The 2010 *Gender and Media Progress Study* (GMPS), a follow up to the baseline study in 2003,

confirms the global findings that on average women now constitute a mere 19% of news sources in the region. This study broke new ground by asking some pointed questions about basic media practise, finding, for example, that a startling 67% percent of news stories are based on single sources.

What are the chances, in our society, that if only one source is consulted, that source will be a man? And how free are societies in which half the population is effectively silenced without us even aware this is so? Do we think twice when a report on a South African TV station tells us about an award for African soccer players at which none of the players showed up, when in fact the top African woman soccer player did show up? Or an article in a Zambian newspaper about elections titled "Peoples views on the elections" in which only men are quoted, and the final caption reads "the best man for the job" (even though two women candidates stood in that particular election).

It is this gender blindness that in 2011 prompted activists to demand that the Windhoek Plus Twenty Declaration state explicitly that freedom of expression must be understood as equal voice for women and men - not just for "people." This plea is strengthened by the Southern African

Development Community (SADC) Protocol on Gender and Development that calls for equality in and through the media; gender mainstreaming in policies and training; as well as sensitive coverage of difficult issues like gender violence, HIV and AIDS.

Many a cynical editor argues that gender biases in the media are just "the way of the world," and that no band of NGO crusaders is going to change that! The fourth Gender and Media Summit held under the banner "*Gender, Media, Diversity and Change*" late last year made the case, through vivid examples, that *change is possible*.

For example, in 2003 women constituted 14% of sources at the Mauritius Broadcasting Corporation, the first media house to work with GL in developing a gender policy. The GMPS shows that this figure has since doubled. What's more,

the gender policy has prompted the public broadcaster to think more broadly and critically about what it means to serve the public, half of whom are women.

Armed with the SADC Gender Protocol and evidence from the ground, GL is working with media education partners in the Gender and Media Diversity Centre as well as 100 media houses across the region on creating Gender and Media Centres of Excellence. The collective target is to ensure that women constitute *at least* 30% news sources by 2015: a target good for business, good for democracy, and good for media freedom.

As Bob Marley might have said: who feels it knows it (so let them speak!) and none but ourselves (caught in this silent censorship) can free our minds. So let's do a little reasoning. Ya mon!

Writer's Bio
Lowe Morna is the Chief Executive Officer at Gender Links.

Freedom of information and women's rights instruments
By Carlyn Hambuba

Abstract

Women in Africa continue to experience various forms of discrimination despite the adoption of several regional and international instruments that protect and promote women's rights. These include the Convention on Elimination of all Forms of Discrimination against Women (CEDAW), the African Union (AU) protocol on women's rights, and others. Many women are not aware of these groundbreaking legal instruments, and others which their governments have signed or ratified, which could help them claim their basic human rights. Most of the discrimination faced by women has been perpetuated by the fact that millions of women on the continent lack critical information that would stand between life and death. This is mainly due to the inability of governments to provide adequate information. Additionally, many women are not aware of the power of freedom of information (FOI) and how it can transform their lives. Even in countries where FOI laws exist, civil society has not utilised these bills to demand implementation of instruments that promote women's rights. In many African countries, it is difficult to access even the most basic information. For example, young girls should be able to access information about family planning and birth control. This would help save the lives of young girls who are reportedly abusing the emergency birth control pill which is readily available in pharmacies, but comes with no information warning of its dangers. This paper will look at the key provisions in international and regional instruments to promote women's rights that have not been fully utilised due to lack of information.

Key words
freedom of information, legislations, women's rights, access to information

Introduction

Despite several attempts by the United Nations and the African Union to implement measures that promote gender equality and women's empowerment, women in African continue to be disadvantaged. This is mainly attributed to highly patriarchal societies. The disparity between men and women is evident in many aspects of life. For example, women still constitute the majority of illiterate citizens[1], and there are still few women in decision-making positions. Currently, Africa has just two female heads of state: Liberian president Ellen Johnson Sirleaf and Malawian president

Joyce Banda. At parliamentary level, almost all countries, except Rwanda, have more male legislators.[2] It is widely acknowledged in Africa that poverty has a female face, affecting almost all aspects of women's lives and their basic human rights. Poverty reduction continues to represent an urgent and persistent challenge.[3] In most developing countries, women make up a substantial portion of the lowest income groups and play a central role in the wellbeing of their family and community. For this reason, information is incredibly valuable for women, affecting all aspects of their lives. It is important that women's access to information is increased,

Protesters demanding their fundamental human rights.

Photo: Colleen Lowe Morna

especially in the context of the various roles women play in society. These include productive (small and medium enterprises, food production and trading); reproductive (child care, subsistence agriculture, health care and education); and community (community infrastructure, water and sanitation, and natural resource management) responsibilities.

This paper seeks to highlight the importance of freedom of information in promoting women's rights in Africa. The first section introduces the topic while the second looks at some of the regional and international freedom of information initiatives that promote women's rights. The third section highlights reasons why FOI remains a missing link in women's rights advocacy. Finally, the last section looks at the importance of FOI in promoting women's rights. A conclusion in the form of recommendations has also been provided.

Freedom of Information (FOI) law

FOI is a fundamental human right enshrined in Article 19 of the 1948 Universal Declaration of Human Rights.[4] However, despite the fact it is recognised as an essential requirement for democracy, good governance, and development and poverty reduction, many African countries have not incorporated FOI laws into their constitutions.[5] FOI is important in any democratic state because it is fundamentally related to citizen empowerment, good governance and development. Its benefits include:

- ***Promotion of transparency:*** FOI enables citizens to see and understand how government and public office work;
- ***Promotion of accountability:*** Once citizens know what their government is doing they are in a position to hold those in office accountable for their decisions and actions. The same applies for designated oversight bodies such as parliamentary committees: they need information to be able to fulfill their mandate;
- ***Reduction of corruption:*** Secrecy and lack of information create a breeding ground for corruption and abuses of power. By promoting transparency and accountability, FOI curbs such abuses;

- **_Improvement of service delivery and government functioning:_** By making those in office accountable for their actions and giving citizens a voice, FOI helps ensure the former work for the benefit of the latter. It thus promotes better planning and service delivery, i.e. improved education and health care.

FOI also empowers citizens to demand their rights and entitlements and ensures that policy-making and implementation are geared toward bringing about equitable development. Good governance, an essential component of any thriving democratic state, is premised on a system of openness, trust and government accountability. This can only be achieved if the public is involved in the process of governance. If the general public is aware of the functions, policies and decisions made by government, they can question government on the basis of this information, and, most importantly, ask about the reasons for their government's actions. It is thus necessary that governments develops clear policy on FOI to ensure that subsequent legislation is implemented effectively and based on accepted international principles and best practices. FOI is a cornerstone for other human rights and is critical in enhancing women's development. Women's current lack of access to information should be a major concern for African governments.

The FOI and mechanisms for promoting women's rights

Global instruments promoting women's rights

There are currently several global instruments that promote women's rights, but lack of proper implementation and domestication prevent women from enjoying their benefits. For example, Article 2[7] of the CEDAW states: "State Parties condemn discrimination against women in all its forms,

agree to pursue by all appropriate means and without delay a policy of eliminating discrimination against women." However, not many African women are aware of this instrument.[8] The Accra Agenda for Action (AAA) acknowledges the importance of gender equality in accelerating development. It is aimed at accelerating and deepening implementation of the Paris Declaration on Aid Effectiveness (2 March 2005). However, to date there are still limited funds available to support women's rights advocacy.

The year 2010 marked several major milestones for improvements around women's human rights, both globally and regionally. It provided several opportunities for the advancement of women's rights because of commemorations of various significant events. These included the 15th anniversary of the Beijing Declaration and Platform for Action (BPFA); the tenth anniversary of the United Nations Security Council Resolution (UNSCR) 1325 on Women, Peace and Security; the fifth anniversary of the African Union's Solemn Declaration on Gender Equality in Africa (SDGEA); and the tenth anniversary of the Millennium Development Goals (MDGs). In July 2010, the UN General Assembly created UN Women, the UN Entity for Gender Equality and the Empowerment of Women. This development was part of the UN's reform agenda, dedicated to bringing together resources and mandates for greater impact. The formation of UN women merges and builds on the important work of four previously distinct parts of the UN system which focused exclusively on gender equality and women's empowerment.

The Beijing (BPfA +15) Synthesis Report[9] calls for African economic and social policies and programmes to include a gender perspective, specifically in respect to their impact on women. However, there is still not enough government information to enable women to track processes like the BPfA.[10] A survey carried out in 37 countries by African civil society organisations in 2009 as part of the Fifteen-Year Review of the Implementation of the BPfA+15 indicates that more than 70% have formulated and/or implemented national development strategies and Poverty Reduction Strategy Papers (PRSP). The main strategy adopted in most appeared to be dispensing microcredit and formulation and implementation of social protection programmes to address poverty among women. For example, Burkina Faso has set up several funds to support income-generating activities for women.

In 2008, Chad reviewed its national strategy document on growth, poverty reduction and microfinance in order to mainstream gender. Ghana has also allocated funds to national gender mainstreaming from its highly indebted poor countries funds. Zambia has created the Citizen's Economic Empowerment Fund, 40% of which is reserved for designated groups, including women and people with disabilities. In Uganda, organisations seeking funding through the Local Government Development Programme, which is the main funding modality for its development budget, have to meet the basic criteria of gender main-streaming. Gabon has put in place a small credit facility for women. However, lack of access to information keeps women from benefiting from such initiatives. Bureaucracy around obtaining information also keeps such initiatives from achieving intended goals.

In February 2012, the African Charter on Democracy, Elections and Good Governance[11] came into force. One of the Charter's objectives is the promotion of establishment of the necessary conditions to foster citizen participation, transparency, access to information, freedom of the press and accountability in the management of public affairs.

Regional instruments promoting women's rights

Article 2 of the Protocol to the African Charter on Human and People's Rights on the Rights of Women in Africa (commonly referred to as AU Protocol on the Rights of Women in Africa)[12] emphasises that States Parties shall combat all forms of discrimination against women through appropriate legislative, institutional and other measures. Additionally, the Constitutive Act of

Alliance members standing firm in advocating gender equality in SADC.
Photo: Gender Links Library

the African Union mandates the organisation to focus on the promotion and protection of human rights, including the rights of women, and promoting civil society participation in regional, sub-regional and national policy processes. Article 4(1) of the Constitutive Act provides that the AU shall function in accordance with the principle of the promotion of gender equality.

African Women's Decade: Women at COP17 march in Durban, South Africa.
Photo: Saeanna Chingamuka

In the Solemn Declaration on Gender Equality in Africa (SDGEA), AU member states commit themselves to ensure the full and effective participation and represen-tation of women in peace processes, including the prevention, resolution, management of conflicts and post-conflict reconstruction in Africa as stipulated in UN Resolutions 1325 (2000) and 1820 (2008). However, despite this provision, women's rights activists, such as the Solidarity for Women Rights (SOAWR) coalition, still encounter difficulties in accessing information, especially during AU summits. CSOs are only observers at these events and only permitted access during opening and closing ceremonies. Because of this, representatives miss actual discussions.

Additionally, during the African monitoring of the SDGEA, conducted by the Gender is My Agenda Campaign (GIMAC), African countries frequently submit late reports that do not comply with the reporting format. This means plenty of information that could have been useful in tracking the implementation of these important instruments is missing.

Sub-regional instruments promoting women's rights

The Southern African Development Community (SADC) Protocol on Gender and Development commits member countries to ensure 50/50 representation of women in all decision-making positions, including the political arena, by 2015.[13]
According to the 2011 *SADC Gender Barometer*, conducted by Gender Links, representation of women in SADC parliaments has increased from an average of 21% in 2005 to 25% in 2011.

The above international and regional instruments provide a solid foundation for lobbying for women's rights in the region. However, lack of information about these provisions negates their proper implementation. Without access to information it is difficult for African women to follow-up and pin down their governments. The fact that not all African governments have ratified the AU Protocol on Women's Rights in Africa is another challenge, hence the need for continuous lobbying and awareness raising.

As a result of the continued disparity between men and women in African, women's rights activists and other actors have intensified their lobbying efforts. Every year new lobbying strategies emerge. For example, in October 2010, the AU launched the African Women's Decade (2010-2020), as declared by the heads of state and governments in Africa in January 2009. The decade is aimed at pushing governments to implement various international and regional commitments they have made around the promotion of gender equality and women's empowerment. Now that this has been launched, African women have the mammoth task of ensuring that its objectives are achieved.

Access to information will be critical in this process. The inititave stipulates that governments are required to support women's organisations to generate and use sex-disaggregated data, qualitative information, conduct gender analyses and put in place gender-sensitive monitoring and evaluation systems to measure the extent to which gender equality objectives are met, and changes in gender relations achieved. The onset of the Decade also challenges all AU member states to ratify and begin implementation of the Protocol to the African Charter on Human and People's Rights on the Rights of Women in Africa.

FOI: Missing link in women's rights advocacy

The vital need for access to information has often been ignored as women's rights activists lobby for gender equality, including the implementation of regional and international commitments. Many women's rights activists in Africa do not clearly understand why having an FOI bill would add value to their work. Such

a bill is critical in the process of lobbying and advocating for women rights. Out of the 54 African countries, only nine have right to information laws. Many others, including Ghana, Sierra Leone, Cameroon, Rwanda, Kenya, Tanzania and Zambia, have tried without success to implement such legislation for more than a decade. Even South Africa, a model of implementation, faces challenges on transparency and accountability. Such a bill can empower women to demand information from governments and other stakeholders. It would also allow them to enquire whether their governments have met financial pledges to under-funded bodies such as UN women.

Access to information would enable gender activists to hold their governments accountable. *Photo: Botswana Women's Affairs Department*

African women can therefore use FOI bills as they monitor and review important global, regional and national commitments on women's rights. Women also need information to analyse how their governments are using aid. With an FOI bill in place, women can easily demand information which could help them identify achievements, gaps and challenges in implementing instruments and policies signed by their governments.

The advancement of African women's rights continues to be hindered by lack of access to vital information, including at the micro level. In most rural parts of Africa, women shun antenatal and post-natal care in hospitals because they lack basic information on the importance of such care. Information about access to family planning and birth control should also be more accessible in order to save the lives of young girls who are reportedly abusing the emergency birth control pill that is readily available in pharmacies.[14] Lack of access to information means many African women are unable to contribute to development processes of the continent. Information can play a critical role in building on the successes of African women, allowing them to take part in the development of their country.

Lack of access to vital information also denies women access to medical care.
Photo: Trevor Davies

Rising to the challenge and promoting women's rights

African women's organisations need to incorporate FOI into their advocacy discourse. The importance of free access to information must not be underestimated. Having a FOI law makes the government more sensitive and responsive to the needs and demands of ordinary people.

There is a need for women's rights advocates to form alliances with FOI advocates and collectively lobby African governments to adopt and implement FOI laws. African women can use FOI bills as they monitor and review global, regional and national commitments that favour women, such as the Beijing Platform for Action, Millennium Development Goals, the Maputo Plan of Action on Reproductive Health and Rights and the Accra Agenda for Action on Aid effectiveness.

Keeping women from accessing information is an infringement of their basic human rights. In many cases, women are already exposed to poverty, conflict, HIV and AIDS, sexual exploitation and gender-based violence. Women are not aware of their rights or the laws in place to protect their rights. In other cases, women do not know where to seek help and they fear victimisation. FOI is therefore a vital tool to ensure the enrichment of women's lives.

Conclusion

In this paper I have argued that despite the abundance of regional and international instruments that call for equality between men and women, women's rights in Africa and the world over will remain elusive if women's rights advocates do not have freedom of information. Women must be able to participate in processes aimed at lobbying for adoption and implementation of FOI laws in Africa. A good starting point for women's rights advocates is to partner with FOI advocates such as the Africa Freedom of Information Centre; Media Foundation for West Africa; Open Democracy Advice Centre of South Africa; Media Rights Agenda; Media Institute of Southern Africa;

International Federation of Journalists; Article 19 and other organisations already working towards pushing African governments to adopt and implement FOI laws.

FOI is an essential element in lobbying for women's rights in Africa because it hinges on making governments more accountable and increases public participation in national affairs. Additionally, an FOI law would contribute to making private companies more accountable and help in fighting corruption. It is therefore necessary that

FOI lobbyists enhance the collective participation of African women in lobbying for the enactment and implementation of FOI laws in their respective countries, and also demonstrate the relevance of FOI laws for advocacy. With an FOI bill in place, women can easily demand information which could help them to identify achievements, gaps and challenges in implementing instruments signed by governments. This highlights the urgent need for African women to join campaigns for FOI laws in Africa.

Writer's Bio
Hambuba is a development dommunication specialist and head of communications at the African Women's Development and Communication (FEMNET) in Nairobi, Kenya.

References
African Women's Regional Shadow Report on Beijing +15 November, 2009

All Africa.com: http://allafrica.com/stories/200809250776.html?page=2

Article 19, Universal Declaration of Human Rights

Beijing +15 Synthesis Report 1995 - 2009

http://www.un.org/womenwatch/daw/cedaw/

http://www.africa-union.org

http://www.un.org/democracyfund/Docs/AfricanCharterDemocracy.pdf

Freedom of Information and Women Rights in Africa -FEMNET 2009

The AU's African Charter on Democracy, Elections and Governance - adopted at the AU Assembly of the AU on 30 January 2007

http://www.un.org/womenwatch/daw/cedaw/

http://www.africa-union.org

New Media 'The Press Freedom Dimension, UNESCO Report 15-16th February, 2007

Operationalising the African Women's Decade (2010-2020) FEMNET, January 2011

Toby Mendel, Freedom of Information A Comparative Legal Survey, UNESCO 2008.
UNESCO publication: Freedom of Expression, Access to Information and Empowerment of People(2008) page 13-15

Notes

1 http://www.rockefellerfoundation.org/what-we-do/where-we-work/africa/grants-grantees/forum-african-women-educationalists/
2 Beijing +15 Synthesis Report 1995 - 2009
3 Gender and ICTs: Reducing the gender digital divide in Africa ICT4D Issue Paper ISTD/ECA, 2008 http://awro.uneca.org/downloads/ICTs%20&%20Gender%20Issue%20Paper.pdf
4 Freedom of information, Protection & Promotion of Human Rights, Priscilla Nyokabi, FEMNET News May-August 2009
5 All Africa.com: http://allafrica.com/stories/200809250776.html?page=2
6 The AU's African Charter on Democracy, Elections and Governance - adopted at the AU Assembly of the AU on 30 January 2007.
7 http://www.un.org/womenwatch/daw/cedaw/
8 The Accra Agenda for Action was the outcome document at the 3rd High Level Forum on Aid Effectiveness which was held in Accra Ghana in 2008.
9 http://www.femnet.or.ke/viewdocument.asp?ID=128
10 Beijing +15 Synthesis Report 1995 - 2009.
11 http://www.un.org/democracyfund/Docs/AfricanCharterDemocracy.pdf
12 http://www.africa-union.org
13 Genderlinks website: http://www.genderlinks.org.za/article/red-lights-flash-in-sadc-gender-protocol-2011-2011-08-11
14 African Journal of Reproductive Health / La Revue Africaine de la Santé Reproductive © 2000 Women's Health and Action Research Centre (WHARC) http://www.jstor.org/pss/3583245

The media's gender blackout
By Rosemary Okello-Orlale

On 3 May 2011 journalists the world over commemorated World Press Freedom Day with gusto and pomp. They used the opportunity to reflect on the past, present and future events that have shaped the profession.

But as the world commemorated, there were concerns in a Declaration issued by a Namibian conference about the lack of gender equality in the media. Indeed, the findings of the Africa regional report of the 2010 Global Media Monitoring Project (GMMP) shows that women are underrepresented in news content and in media structures. Women account for only 19% of news sources in African media, unchanged since 2005.

In his analysis of African media 20 years after the Windhoek Declaration, Rhodes University Professor Guy Berger argues that in 1991 the Declaration focused mostly on print media. During the Windhoek +10 review, it was expanded to deal with broadcasting.

Berger posed the question: "Can we do the same as with Windhoek?" in reference to the Cape Town Conference, dubbed Windhoek+20, held in September 2011.

There appears to be a very real need to expand the Windhoek Declaration, this time to include gender.

Guy Berger proposes that the Windhoek declaration should include broadcasting. What about gender?   *Photo: Daud Kayisi*

Many media and gender experts are arguing that in this era of enormous change, the media can only play a critical role in the lives of Africans - a majority of whom are women - if the following questions are tackled: Information for what and for whom? Why are we collecting this information and what difference is it making in the lives of women? What do we do with the information once it is collected?

Media development scholars generally agree that information can empower women and enable them to forge links for gender equality. The Nairobi Forward Looking Strategies and the Beijing Platform for Action recognise media as one of the fundamental tools for achieving gender equality and the economic empowerment of women. Yet women continue to be underrepresented and portrayed in a narrow range of roles in the mainstream media: most often either as victims of violence or as sex objects.

During the conference in Namibia, concerns were raised about the fact that African media has failed to commit itself to ensuring that the gender question becomes a standard of measure for press freedom and access to information on the continent.

Meanwhile, many media practitioners have been content to argue that since society is male-dominated, it is this reality they convey. There has been little willingness to grapple with what is meant by freedom of expression when half the population is virtually mute - nor the more philosophical question of the role of the media in a democracy: to project only what is, or what could be?

Another important discussion revolves around media ethics and codes of conduct. For instance, why do women continue to be objectified and portrayed as sex objects and why are their voices and opinions ignored. If this approach is considered unethical, then which codes are African media houses using?

Therefore, as the Windhoek Declaration is expanded to embrace access to information, there is also a need to develop a gender addendum which takes cognisance of the context in which media is produced.

What this means is that an "engendered" Windhoek Declaration can help media managers to address these problems, making it a duty to increase representation of women, and give women space and visibility on issues of national importance.

The main areas of focus should be to increase women's access to, and use of, the media; improve the portrayal of women in the media; increase women's representation in decision-making structures in media houses and develop structures and frameworks for gender mainstreaming based on laws and policies.

If the Windhoek Declaration is to continue to be a guiding, constructive document in this era of intense media transformation, any expansion must include the issue of gender justice in the media.

Writer's Bio
Okello-Orlale is the Executive Director of the Africa Woman and Child Feature Service based in Nairobi.

Ensuring women's rights to access to information
By Patience Zirima

The release of the Draft Model Law for African Union (AU) Member States on Access to Information for public comments provided an opportunity for gender dimensions of Access to Information (ATI) to be explored before it was adopted in 2012.

While this is a positive development to ensure improved accessibility of information, as well as increased openness and accountability of public institutions, it remains worrisome that the model is silent on the gendered nature of ATI. Yet, it is expected to inform continent-wide ATI laws.

Evidence from Africa shows that there has been limited participation by women in the processes that have led to the formulation, enactment and implementation of laws or policies that enable citizens to enjoy freedom of information, especially information held by public bodies. A research conducted by the African Women's Development Network (FEMNET) titled *Freedom of Information and Women's Rights in Africa* noted that few women's organisations have actively campaigned for Freedom of Information (FOI) legislation.

This is despite the acknowledgement that: "The right to information is a core principle of good governance, and can provide decision and action leverages to women to effectively participate in important developmental issues like poverty alleviation strategy papers, the attainment of UN Millennium Development Goals, international instruments that protect women like CEDAW, Beijing Platform for Action and the AU's NEPAD initiative."

This disconnect between what women want and expect in terms of ATI, and their interaction with ATI laws, is worrisome. Very few women's organisations actively participate in the formulation of media laws, probably because they may not

Lack of and access to information denies women the much needed knowledge to make informal decisions.   *Photo: Trevor Davies*

see the added benefit of these laws to their constituency. Zambian organisations interviewed by FEMNET perceived the FOI law as an issue that affects only the media. They did not see how it affects them. In Ghana, women's organisations felt that this campaign would unnecessarily add to their workload. However, this is not true as ATI is one of the major reasons why women continue to suffer inequalities on the continent.

Unfortunately the AU draft model law risks coming up against the same disinterest from women if no conscious effort is made to ensure that the law relates to women and their rights, and addresses women's interests within its ambit. In order to ensure it is effective for women, the law will need to make a deliberate attempt to ensure ATI for women as a disadvantaged group. Women are deprived by factors including geographical location, education and literacy, levels of economic empowerment, access to various media, as well as other societal barriers that limit their access to knowledge. These factors mean women remain enmeshed in a vicious cycle which can only be mitigated by a conscious effort to ensure they are able to access information that can assist them to make informed choices.

In Zimbabwe for example, young girls have lower access to education than their male counterparts. The lower literacy levels in turn imply lower levels of knowledge, and therefore lower levels of access to information and resources. The model law needs to be more proactive in providing information in many languages. Section 20 of the model law says that "Where information exists in more than one language, the information shall be provided to the requester in such of those languages as the requester prefers." English is the official language in most African countries and the bulk of public information held by public bodies is in

Policies should be in a language that both women and men understand.
Photo: Ntolo Lekau

English. However, it is not the main language most citizens use. Accessing information may be difficult for women and men who do not speak or understand English.

It is worth noting that the majority of African women reside in rural areas where there are fewer public services and institutions where they can access information. Rural areas are also poorly serviced by public and private media, a key source of information. The model should thus stipulate proactive measures states must put in place to ensure women who have limited access to the media are still able to access the information they need.

Part VI of the draft model law makes provisions for the establishment of an oversight mechanism. It has, however, conveniently forgotten commitments made by the African Union, or regional bodies such as SADC, in the Protocol on Gender and Development (2008), to ensure equal representation of women in all decision-making bodies. The oversight mechanism as a decision-making body should ensure 50% representation of women who can influence access to information policy processes. In section 60 (2) of the model law, deliberate concessions to multi-partyism are stated, but it fails to take into consideration other factors such as gender in oversight mechanisms.

A questionable section in the model notes that ATI can be denied when the information officer deems the request for information "manifestly frivolous or vexatious." The information officer has the discretion of dismissing information requests on this basis but the question is: how is it determined if a request is frivolous or vexatious?

The draft model law on ATI will potentially change the dynamics of ATI on the continent. However, if it remains inaccessible to women it risks alienating half of those it purports to give rights to inform-ation. It has been proven numerous times that laws are not gender neutral and it is important to ensure proactive mechanisms are put in place to ensure access to legislation by women.

Writer's Bio
Zirima is the Media Alliance of Zimbabwe Coordinator.

Zimbabwe's government media reforms cosmetic
By Njabulo Ncube

Abstract
This article explores recent media reforms undertaken by Zimbabwe's coalition government, criticising them for their inability to address freedom of expression and gender equality in state and private media. Despite the creation of dozens of new media outlets, it is argued that Zimbabwe remains far from achieving its international and regional commitments around access to information and media freedom for all.

Key words
Global Political Agreement, media freedom, gender policies, broadcast media, Broadcasting Services Act, access to information, African Charter on Broadcasting

Recent media reforms in Zimbabwe are silent on gender mainstreaming and continue to stifle media freedom and access to information.

At least 20 media houses have been licenced to operate in Zimbabwe under the Global Political Agreement (GPA) signed between President Robert Mugabe, Prime Minister Morgan Tsvangirai and Deputy Prime Minister Arthur Mutambara. This has seen a plethora of newspapers and other publications hit the streets of Zimbabwe's major cities and towns, including *NewsDay, The Daily News, The Daily News On Sunday* and *The Patriot.*

The new publications, although enjoying mixed fortunes in terms of readership and circulation, joined a long list of other already established government and privately-owned titles such as the state-controlled *The Herald, The Chronicle, The Sunday Mail, The Sunday News, The Chronicle, The Sunday News, The Manica Post, The Zimbabwe Independent, The Standard* and the *Financial Gazette.* There are a host of other specialist publications covering lifestyle, sports, and other areas.

While media stakeholders, among them journalist trade unions and advocacy groups, have welcomed the media reforms with guarded optimism, it is, however, shocking that reforms fell short of ensuring gender balance, media freedom and access to information for citizens.

It is undisputed that scores of unemployed journalists and other support staff have been snapped up by the new publications and other media houses, including new foreign agencies and broadcasting networks that have set up shop in Harare. However, there is clear evidence of a lack of commitment on the part of most of these media houses to mainstream gender in reporting and recruitment. It is also an undisputed fact that the majority of these media houses do not have gender policies.

Many of those that do have gender policies lack living documents. This is a firm indicator that gender mainstreaming is not a priority, not just for owners, publishers and journalists, but even for media activists who lobby the country's parliamentarians and parliament, week in and week out, on media reform issues.

Apart from the absence of gender mainstreaming in an expanded media environment, especially in the print sector, the principals in the GPA have failed to facilitate the passage or enactment of media sector legislation that is gender sensitive. It is my submission that under the present transitional government, media reforms in Zimbabwe should include an audit of the present media laws to ensure they have provisions and clauses that mainstream gender.

It is also equally worrisome that the three political parties' signatories to the GPA - ZANU-PF and the two formations of the Movement for Democratic Change (MDC) - have maintained draconian laws that criminalise the practice of journalism as a profession. This keeps citizens of Zimbabwe from enjoying media freedom and access to information.

No attempts have been made to repeal the repressive Access to Information and Protection of Privacy Act (AIPPA), a piece of legislation that the previous administration of President Mugabe used in 2003 to close the popular *Daily News*. The coalition government still relies on the Public Order and Security Act (POSA), the Criminal Law Codification and Reform Act, the Official Secrets Act and the Interception of Communications Act, to stifle media freedom and access to information. Instead of AIPPA facilitating access to information, it has emerged as the major stumbling block for journalists.

Under AIPPA, journalists are still required to register with the new Zimbabwe Media Commission (ZMC), whose commissioners were cherry-picked by three political parties that are signatories to the GPA. The ZMC, which to all intents and purposes is a statutory body, is presently in the process of establishing a statutory Media Complaints Council intended to rival the Voluntary Media Council of Zimbabwe, a self-regulatory body set up by journalists that includes media activists and journalists drawn from the private media.

The coalition government has also failed to repeal or amend the Broadcasting Services Act (BSA), which perpetuates the monopoly of the Zimbabwe Broadcasting Corporation (ZBC) despite evidence that most of the population would prefer alternative broadcasters. There is a general consensus that the state broadcaster churns out ZANU-PF propaganda. Although the Broadcasting Authority of Zimbabwe (BAZ) advertised on 26 May 2011 a call for applications for licences to establish independent national broadcasting stations, there has been a deafening silence surrounding the processing of applications for the two commercial radio broadcasters.

Sandra Mujokoro and Kholiwe Nyoni at the Gender and Media Summit in Johannesburg.
Photo: Trevor Davies

Since the submission of applications by 15 aspiring broadcasters and the subsequent publication of the applicants' names in the media, there had been no update on the progress of the adjudication process. BAZ has not published a comprehensive list of the applicants, neither has it furnished the public with useful details of directorship and ownership of respective companies that applied, which would have assisted the public in making objections as required under the broadcasting law.

Although BAZ has no legal obligation to do this, the issue is of public interest, and it should appraise the nation to ensure transparency and build public confidence in the licensing process. It is my submission that even if the new broadcasters were to eventually be licensed, this may not necessarily translate to the provision of alternative information for the citizenry because of the stipulated content restrictions in BSA. By their very nature private broadcasters are profit-oriented and therefore need to structure their programming in a manner that attracts listenership, thereby drawing advertising revenue. Therefore, they need to operate within a framework that accords them considerable editorial autonomy for their sustainability.

However, the current operating framework as stipulated under the repressive BSA imposes content requirements that interfere with independence. Among these are the compulsory 75% quota for local content; the allocation of an hour of broadcasting space per week to government; and the stipulations on airing of political and electoral matters. For example, in terms of Part II of the fifth schedule of the BSA, a broadcaster is required to report to BAZ and keep records of any broadcast of a political matter. According to the interpretation clause, a political matter is "any political matter, including the policy launch of a political party." This definition is vague and can cover a broad spectrum of the broadcasters' content. Restrictions such as these are bound to compromise private broadcasters' role as independent sources of alternative information. It is for this reason that advocacy and lobby groups in Zimbabwe reiterate calls for the repeal of the BSA and its replacement with a democratic law that will ensure transparency in the licensing process, as well as promote the establishment of a three-tier broadcasting system. This will allow Zimbabweans to freely express themselves and access information of their choice.

Ten years after the crafting of the African Charter on Broadcasting (ACB), Zimbabwe is still far from fulfilling the three-tier broadcasting system it envisaged. The three-tier system comprises public broadcasting, private commercial broadcasting and establishment of community radio stations. Against this background, the coalition is receiving loud calls from media activists to free the airwaves now. While the bulk of the 15 member states of the Southern African Development Community (SADC) boast a plethora of privately-owned broadcasting stations and community radio stations, Zimbabwe remains stagnated as a monolithic pariah state whose airwaves continue to be monopolised by ZBC.

With this said, it has not been a stroll in the park for media activists to campaign for media freedom and access to information despite the fact media reforms top the agenda of the coalition government. Police have had no qualms in using draconian laws to disrupt advocacy activists. On 23 July 2011, police barred the Media Institute of Southern Africa (MISA)-Zimbabwe and Artists for Democracy Trust Zimbabwe from staging a joint Free the Airwaves concert at Warren Park Shopping Centre in Harare. This is despite the fact that the organisers of the event had notified police of the event and had been cleared to proceed with the concert.

Officers argued that the notification letter did not state that the activity was a public awareness activity. The police said they only became aware of the scope of the event following an article published in the *NewsDay* of 20 July 2011.

The preview article quoted MISA-Zimbabwe Advocacy Officer Tabani Moyo saying: "It is our right as people of Zimbabwe to have diverse views. Such views can only be promoted through a level playing field in the media. We need a diverse broadcasting sector as we are only limited to ZBC products. There should be public, private and community media." MISA-Zimbabwe employs free the airwaves concerts to build public support in lobbying the authorities about the need for wholesale broadcasting reforms that will completely liberate the airwaves in line with regional and international treaties on freedom of expression.

The Zimbabwean broadcasting sector continues to be dominated by the state-run ZBC 31 years after independence. The banning of this peaceful civil event was not only undemocratic but indicative of the extent to which the police arbitrarily abuse their authority to violate citizens' constitutionally guaranteed rights. The government should urgently address and curb such arbitrary actions to prevent the country's plunge into a police state.

Despite these setbacks, civil society organisations involved in media remain undeterred in their demands for a diverse broadcasting sector. I therefore call on the government of Zimbabwe to embrace the provisions of the African Charter on Broadcasting (2001), which enjoins member states to facilitate the development of a three tier broadcasting system through the establishment of public, commercial and community broad-casters. That way, there will be several platforms for gender equality issues to be projected.

Writer's Bio
Ncube is the current Chairperson of Misa-Zimbabwe and a practising journalist. He writes this article in his personal capacity.

GENDER IN THE MEDIA

Participants at Zimpapers Media Centres of Excellence inception workshop.   *Photo: Trevor Davies*

Making every voice count: the media Centres of Excellence project
By Sikhonzile Ndlovu

Abstract
This article discusses the Centres of Excellence (COE) for gender in the media concept, its rationale and progress to date. The COE project is a culmination of Gender Links' (GL) ten-year endeavour to transform gender relations in and through the media. Over the last ten years GL has worked on gender and media research, advocacy, policy and training in Southern Africa and beyond. This has included creating a powerful gender movement, which resulted in the signing of the 2008 SADC Protocol on Gender and Development. With its 28 targets, the Protocol has one time bound target for media, attaining gender equality in the media by 2015. It encourages the media and media related bodies to mainstream gender in their codes of conduct, policies and procedures and adopt and implement gender-aware ethical principles, codes of practice and policies in accordance with the Protocol on Culture, Information and Sport. The COE project is GL's final drive to ensure that media houses meet their mandate in the build-up to 2015. The evidence of key gender gaps in the media informs this drive for gender equality.

Key words
gender equality, gender mainstreaming, media, SADC Protocol on Gender and Development, Centres of Excellence

Background and rationale

The media COE project borrows from GL's local government COE project, which has seen GL work with 240 councils to mainstream gender in their operations. Whilst building on media research, advocacy and training, this project is mainly anchored by GL's experience in supporting media houses and newsrooms to develop and implement gender policies. However, the COE project goes beyond the six-stage gender policy development process (buy in; situation analysis; inception workshop; drafting; adoption; monitoring and evaluation) by ensuring training, ongoing backstopping and support. This has resulted in GL offering media houses a full gender-mainstreaming package that draws from all research and training conducted to date. GL is currently working with 100 newsrooms on this initiative.

Since 2003, GL and partner organisations have conducted ground-breaking media research in SADC, much of which came together in the 2010 Gender and Media Progress Study (GMPS). The GMPS looked at general media practice, gender in media content, gender in newsrooms as well as the gendered dimensions of gender-based violence and HIV and AIDS coverage.

The Gender and Media (GEM) summits, held every two years, have served as a useful platform to deliberate and discuss emerging gender and media issues in the region. Since 2004, participants from Southern Africa and beyond have gathered in Johannesburg to share best practices in this area of work. Participants have included academics, researchers, students, civil society, women's rights groups and gender activists. The summits are now a key component of the COE process, as GL will use them to recognise good practice through the awards. All participating COEs send a representative to present a best practice and share ideas on taking the work forward.

In the past, advocacy work has flowed into the various policy initiatives undertaken with media houses throughout the region. After in-country consultations with individual media houses, GL has assisted partners to put in place mechanisms that create conducive media environments for women and men. So far GL has worked with media houses to develop HIV and AIDS and gender policies. The policies were part of the Media Action Plan (MAP) on HIV and AIDS and Gender, which started in 2005. GL then followed the MAP process by working with newsrooms to develop gender policies.

The new COE approach, launched in 2011, is informed amongst others by the results of the 2009 Glass Ceilings in Southern African Media

and the 2010 Gender and Media Progress Study (GMPS), which showed a lack of improvement in gender in and through the media compared to earlier studies.

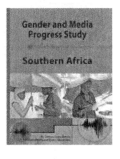

The GMPS found that the average proportion of women sources in the region increased by just two percentage points from 17% in the 2003 Gender and Media Baseline Study (GMBS) to 19% in the 2010 GMPS.

On the other hand, the Glass Ceilings study showed that whilst women are under-represented in media in general, they are also glaringly absent from decision-making positions. Women constituted 28% of boards of directors and senior management; and 23% of those in top management.

GL used the findings of these studies to reflect on its strategies and explore possibilities for a more holistic and sustained approach to addressing gender gaps in and through the media.

Aim of the project

The main objective of the COE project is to contribute to the advancement of the SADC Protocol on Gender and Development target of gender equality in and through the media by 2015. This project seeks to ensure that media houses mainstream gender into editorial practice and content as well as in institutional practice. This is part of broader efforts to address gender gaps in media and other sectors.

Media provisions in the SADC Protocol

Ensure gender is mainstreamed in all information, communication and media policies, programmes, laws and training in accordance with the Protocol on Culture, Information and Sport.

Encourage the media and media-related bodies to mainstream gender in their codes of conduct, policies and procedures, and adopt and imple-ment gender-aware ethical principles, codes of practice and policies in accordance with the
Protocol on Culture, Information and Sport.

Take measures to promote the equal representation of women in the ownership and decision-making structures of the media, in accordance with Article 12.1 that provides for equal representation of women in decision-making positions by 2015.

Take measures to discourage the media from:

• Promoting pornography and violence against all persons, especially women and children;
• Depicting women as helpless victims of violence and abuse;
• Degrading or exploiting women, especially in the area of entertainment and advertising, and undermining their role and position in society; and
• Reinforcing gender oppression and stereotypes.

Encourage the media to give equal voice to women and men in all areas of coverage, including increasing the number of programmes for, by and about women on gender-specific topics that challenge gender stereotypes.

Take appropriate measures to encourage the media to play a constructive role in the eradication of gender-based violence by adopting guidelines which ensure gender-sensitive coverage.

The SGDI

In 2011, GL developed the SADC Gender and Development Index (SGDI), which is an empirical measure that weighs how governments are performing against the targets of the Protocol. The SGDI on the status of women in SADC countries is based on 23 indicators which are further grouped under six categories: Governance (3 indicators) Education (3), Economy (5), Sexual and Reproductive Health (3), HIV and AIDS (3) and Media (6). Regarding the media, the score consists of:

• *Women employees as percentage of total:* The number of women employees working in media institutions expressed as a percentage of all employees in media institutions.
• *Women as percentage of board of directors:* The number of women directors of media institutions expressed as a percentage of all directors of media institutions.
• *Women as percentage of management:* The number of women managers in media institutions expressed as a percentage of all managers in media institutions.

- *Female percentage of staff in institutions of media learning:* The number of female staff in institutions of media learning expressed as a percentage of all staff in institutions of media training.
- *Female percentage of students in institutions of media learning:* The number of

female students in institutions of media learning expressed as a percentage of all students in institutions of media learning.

- *Percent women sources:* The number of women referenced as sources in the media expressed as a percentage of all people referenced as sources.

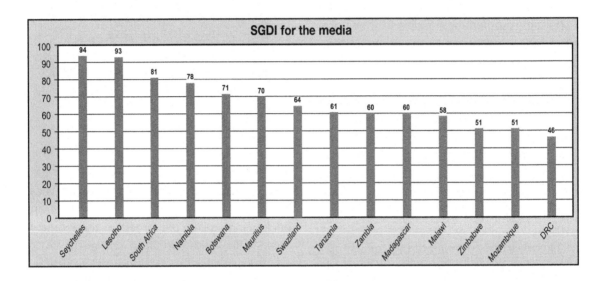

The SGDI gives SADC an overall score of 67%. Recent GL research on gender in media education, in newsrooms and in media content has provided rich empirical media data. Seychelles, Lesotho, South Africa and Namibia lead the way, with Malawi, Zimbabwe, Mozambique and DRC at the rear. These indicators combine institutional indicators as well as a measure of voice (percentage women sources). The latter is somewhat outweighed by the institutional indicators that may skew the results in some cases. For example South Africa and Namibia now have quite high proportions of women in the media (including, in Namibia, in decision-making positions) but they do not fare well in women sources (19% and 20% respectively). Lesotho does well on both. Mozambique and DRC perform poorly in both areas. In future, voice measures may be given

more weight, especially in the absence of many rights-based indicators within the SGDI.

Towards a more holistic approach to media transformation

Recent research findings have called for a multi-pronged approach to creating an enabling environment for gender equality in the media to flourish. This includes regulators, critical citizens, media and journalism institutions and activists and decision-makers. The media COE project fits within the larger framework of a holistic approach to attaining gender equality. Whilst media is a powerful tool as an agent of change, there is need to include other key industry players and stakeholders.

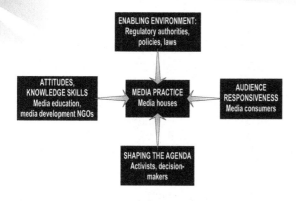

this broader framework of empowering media consumers to hold the media accountable. Media activists and decision-makers are key players in shaping the agenda whilst media educators and media development agencies shape the attitudes and knowledge on gender.

The media COE project should therefore not be seen as an end in itself, but an important component of the sector as it deals directly with media content and content producers.

An enabling environment is crucial for transformation to take place. GL has been working with media regulators in mainstreaming gender in their codes of practice and ethics. This framework will help ensure media compliance. Regulators are key partners in working towards the SADC Protocol targets. Audience responsiveness is also important. GL's media literacy efforts and advocacy around key gender and media issues fits within

Evidence from the GMPS found that while macro level results show slow change in transforming gender relations in and through the media, institutional level change is possible and it strengthens the COE approach. One such example is the Mauritian Broadcasting Corporation, one of the first media houses that worked with GL to develop a gender policy.

Case study: MBC champions gender mainstreaming in its operations

MBC Director General Dan Callikan with GL Francophone Director Loga Virahsawmy officially opening a GBV training workshop at MBC offices in Mauritius.   *Photo: Davinah Sholay*

The Mauritius Broadcasting Corporation (MBC), which signed a Memorandum of Understanding (MOU) with Gender Links in October 2011, was one of the first media

houses to work with GL to develop a gender policy.

In 2003, women comprised just 14% of news sources in MBC's reporting. GL worked with the MBC to draft its first gender policy in 2003 and it was approved in 2004. In 2006 GL held a three-day workshop with all MBC departments to advance the policy and develop a gender-aware HIV and AIDS policy. MBC approved both policies, which were printed and launched during the 16 Days Campaign in 2006.

The MBC has worked systematically to promote gender equality in its ranks. The broadcaster received the award for best practice on gender at the inaugural GL and Sol Plaatje Institute for Media Leadership -

Media Action Plan (SPI-MAP) Institutional Excellence Media Awards in September 2007. The award recognised progress made in its radio section, which is headed by a woman, as well as the considerable progress made in diversifying editorial content.

In the 2010 GMPS, the proportion of women sources at the MBC had doubled to 28%, making MBC a success story and gender-reporting leader in Mauritius and the region. For this it also received the institutional award at the 2010 Gender and Media (GEM) Summit. What is significant is that the MBC not only acknowledges the improvement with regard to gender responsive reporting, but it believes this has improved its overall reporting.

Speaking at the GEM Summit in 2010, Deputy Director General Soondree Devi Soborun said gender awareness had improved the responsiveness of the public broadcaster. GMPS research found that the MBC also displayed a high standard of reporting, with primary sources accounting for 94% of those sourced in its stories.

A key ingredient in this success is buy-in from the highest levels of management. Dan Callikan, MBC director-general, assured GL that MBC will implement the action plan that accompanies its gender policy. In a letter addressed to the Director of GL (Mauritius and Francophone office) dated 10 November 2010, the deputy director general, writing on behalf of the director general, stated:

"The MBC has always been a close collaboration of GL and takes pride in its firm commitment towards gender equality at the Corporation. We assure you that the Corporation will continue to give its support in making gender justice a reality in Mauritius and we thank you for your collaboration and assure you of our commitment to the SADC Protocol and our Gender Policy."

On the face of it, progress has been slow. In 2003, women constituted 30% of overall staff. The *Glass Ceilings* study (2009) showed that this has since only increased by three percentage points. However, the proportion of women in top and senior management has increased from 4 to 20%. Luximbye Samboo, principal officer in charge of the human resources division noted, "the corporation is doing its level best to ensure that there is gender equality in its operations."

The GMPS showed that 51% of stories monitored were by women reporters. In 2009, the MBC appointed a female acting director general for the first time.

Civil society gender and media watchdog, Mauritius Media Watch Organisation, has noted that the MBC consistently seeks the voices of women from different walks of life to comment on various issues. This includes the country's budget; HIV and AIDS; security and other topical issues. The MBC also has regular gender-specific programmes that aim to empower women.

As part of its commitment to the media COE process, the MBC played an active role during the 2011 16 days of activism campaign. MBC staff, with support from the GL Mauritius office, identified a series of story ideas not only to create awareness about GBV but also to find solutions. Callikan told GL: "We are showing the other face of Mauritius where people live in poverty, where gender-based violence is rife and where children cannot go to school because men just leave and refuse to bear the family responsibility. In some cases GBV is due to alcohol. We know how to get people to talk. A lot of women are given voices in our programmes and they are not afraid to break the silence and we are breaking new ground. Our programmes have fantastic impact and we go beyond. We make sure with the authorities and Ministries concerned that these people are given all the support, help, and infrastructure needed. Our broadcast is an eye opener."

The media COE process

The MBC case study demonstrates that micro level interventions can bring about change in media practice and content. As mentioned above, GL has now adopted a ten-stage process which is a step-by-step guide for media managers to mainstream gender in their operations.

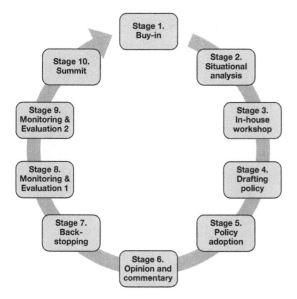

Stage one: Buy in - Identifying and working with 100 newsrooms to develop gender policies by 2014. GL conducts a high-level seminar on gender and the media for top managers. Participating media houses sign an MOU with GL to ensure commitment to the COE process.

Stage two: Obtaining baseline data that is media house specific. This stage seeks to update the data gathered during the Glass Ceiling study. This stage is very critical in establishing baselines against which progress is measured. The situation analysis mainly looks at institutional practice, such as staff composition and positioning, as well as the policy framework.

Stage three: In-house workshop for representatives from different departments: This ensures that media decision-makers are equipped with the knowledge and skills to mainstream gender in institutional practice.

Stage four: Drafting the policy by a cross disciplinary team appointed at the workshop.

Stage five: Adoption of the policy at a formal event.

Stage six: Opinion and Commentary Service: This stage involves media practitioners becoming familiar with the GL Opinion and Commentary Service for further dissemination with participating media houses. Journalists can also contribute to the service.

Stage seven: On-the-job training and capacity-building on key thematic areas. This is based on the SADC Gender Protocol provisions that offer possibilities on themes such as governance and political participation, economic justice, HIV and AIDS, gender-based violence and implementation.

Stage eight and nine: Monitoring and evaluation: Administration of media house scorecards, knowledge and attitudes surveys, situational analysis forms and other monitoring and evaluation tools that can be used to measure change in the immediate, medium and long term. GL has devised a self-monitoring tool to enable media houses to evaluate their performance against set targets. This ensures participation and ownership of the project.

M and E will take two forms:

Tracking change: After six months: This periodic monitoring takes place at six month intervals and is implemented by media houses. As part of capacity building, GL is training media houses to use a simple self-monitoring tool to track progress. This stage includes ongoing identification and documentation of best practice.

Measuring change in the lead up to the GEM summit: GL will carry out this evaluation on a larger scale. This will involve more in-depth quantitative and qualitative monitoring leading up to the fifth GEM summit. This monitoring will contribute significantly to the selection of case studies which media COEs will present at the regional media event.

Stage ten: Affirming good practice, know-ledge creation and distribution of gender-aware articles and training materials: Content and other examples of best practice produced as part of the various capacity building initiatives will be used as resource materials for the GL Virtual Resource Centre for trainers as well as to inspire other media houses. Similarly, GL will use the print media as outlets for the GL Opinion and Commentary Service. Throughout the period, GL will work towards gathering and disseminating best practices and case studies that media houses will present at the GEM summits.

On-the-job training and capacity building

Stage seven of the COE project involves on-the-job support and training. This stage seeks to equip media personnel with a theoretical understanding of key gender and media issues as well as provide them with practical on-the-job support to ensure full implementation of the gender policy. The SADC Gender Protocol serves as the guiding framework for this training.

GL has developed a training manual, *Making Every Voice Count: Reporting Southern Africa*, which helps media houses to understand the practical steps to take towards mainstreaming gender into newsroom management and  editorial content. The training manual facilitates Stage 7 of the COE process.

Individual country contexts determine the schedule of modules and activities. These include:
* Understanding the context: SADC Protocol on Gender and Development;
* Constitutional and legal rights;
* Governance;
* Education and training;
* Productive resources, employment and economic empowerment;
* Gender-based violence;

- Health and HIV and AIDS;
- Peace building;
- Media, information and communication;
- Implementation; and
- Management and editing.

Affirming good practice: The Gender and Media (GEM) summit

The GEM summits provide a platform for media COEs to share best practices and experiences in mainstreaming gender into institutional practice. This part of the COE, stage 10, will see all participating COEs send representatives to the summit. The GEM summits have become significant marketplaces of knowledge-sharing, strategies and successes in driving the gender and media agenda forward.

These summits also solidify GL's efforts at regional level, where COE media professionals get the space to engage with people from other like-minded organisations and institutions. There are different learning streams that will enhance people's understanding and knowledge around gender mainstreaming in the media.

The summit recognises best practices through the GEM awards. GL rewards media houses that have excelled at institutional and editorial transformation. Awards are presented in categories linked to all the SADC Protocol thematic areas, as well as institutional practice. The awards also recognise the efforts of media managers who are serving as gender champions in their media houses.

The COE project has thus provided GL with an opportunity to review its GEM award categories and reward institutions and individuals on COE-specific areas. This is a slight shift from the past where awards were classified by genre and

medium mostly, with one thematic category on Gender and Economic reporting.

A COE verification process precedes the GEM summits and awards. This is to verify whether media COEs are fully implementing the action plans developed during the policy drafting process.

Monitoring and evaluating (M and E) progress

Beata Kasale: Botswana Media COE country facilitator.   *Photo: Trevor Davies*

The COE's have prompted GL to review and customise M and E tools to institution-level work (for example gender scorecards that are used to track progress over time) as well as enhance automation of data gathering methods. COE's bring together GL's "way of working"- research, advocacy, policies and action plans, sharing best practice, monitoring and evaluating for impact - as well as its different programmes, focusing these in one geographical space where change can be measured.

GL has developed a self-monitoring tool that gives media houses the capacity to use an electronic database to measure progress on content and institutional indicators. The tool has a built-in analysis capacity that allows media houses to produce profiles as soon as the monitoring is complete. At the touch of a button, media houses may produce profiles and compare their performance to previous results.

For M and E to make sense, it is important to set baselines against which to measure progress. In

July 2011, GL conducted in-house monitoring for an additional 30 newsrooms that did not participate in the GMPS. The findings of this study corroborated GMPS findings. This attests to the urgency for strengthened advocacy efforts in the SADC region. Some of the key findings included:

Women constitute 19% of news sources in SADC. This is the same as the GMPS figure of 19%. This shows that regionally, men have continued to be given more say by the media. Women have remained on the sidelines of main dialogues and debate. To its credit, *Harare Metro*, a Zimpapers daily tabloid based in Zimbabwe, recorded the highest proportion of women news sources during this monitoring at 49%. This places it second regionally after Madagascar's FMA which has 52% women sources (recorded during GMPS monitoring). Country averages have changed in some instances, while some have remained the same. In Zimbabwe, for example, the proportion of women sources is up one percentage point to 17%. Botswana remained at 20%. Madagascar went up from 23 to 26%. Tanzania dropped from 21 to 20%. Zambia remained at 14%.

Women constitute 26% of those in images. As in the GMPS, men also still dominate in media images. The GMPS recorded 26% for women in images. This shows that women are mainly absent as both sources and in media images. News still has a male face and perspective.

There are fewer women reporters at 29%. Like in the GMPS, male reporters (81%) dominate newsrooms. The COE process aims to ensure equal numbers of women and men at all media levels by 2015. This figure illustrates that a lot of work needs to be done before parity is reached.

Progress

GL measures the targets of all 100 participating newsrooms against baselines. The target setting process is part of inception workshops. The new targets are built into institutional MOUs to ensure commitment and compliance. GL has shared individual newsroom profiles with participating COEs to give them a quantitative overview of their performance. The profiles combine newsroom and news content data.

Innocent Gore at the Zimpapers media COE inception workshop.
Photo: Thabani Mpofu

So far, GL has managed to sign MOUs with media houses in Botswana, DRC, Lesotho, Madagascar, Malawi, Mauritius, Tanzania, Zambia and Zimbabwe. Media houses in other SADC countries yet to sign on. The COE process is at different stages in different places. Tanzania, Mauritius and DRC are further along at Stage 6, while other countries are still at the very nascent stages of the process.

The GEM summits will serve as a progress checkpoint when COEs gather to share best practices and strategies in taking the work forward.

Conclusion

The COEs for gender in the media concept is a new innovation within GL. It is an example of uses and applying lessons learnt after a decade of media-centred initiatives in the SADC region. The findings of earlier studies corroborated by the in-house monitoring points to the need for a more vigorous and coordinated approach to achieve gender equality in the media. These findings have also proved that changing mindsets and attitudes requires much more effort and a more comprehensive strategy.

The COE project brings together media research, advocacy, policy and training components of the GL Media Programme. This has ensured that GL offers a full package that allows media houses to effectively participate in the drive for gender equality.

This new approach has ensured synergy between different GL programme areas. The other strength of the COE project is that GL has tailored media training around the SADC Gender Protocol thematic areas. This has ensured that the organisation works in a synergised manner bringing together media, governance, justice, and, to a certain extent, the Gender and Media Diversity Centre (GMDC). The COE project has a module on education and training, which is one of the key areas of focus for the GMDC.

The participatory type of monitoring and evaluation will go a long way toward ensuring that media COEs take ownership and accountability for their performance. GEM summits hosted by GL will serve as an important checkpoint for progress leading up to 2015. Finally, the self-monitoring tool, which is an adaptation of the GMPS methodology, can draw individual newsroom profiles at the click of a button.

Writer's Bio
Ndlovu is the Gender Links Media Programme Manager.

Gender sensitive indicators for the media
By Ammu Joseph

Abstract
This article discusses the creation of a set of gender-sensitive indicators that can be used internationally to enable media organisations and others - such as media workers' unions and gender activists - to evaluate the place and role of women in newsrooms (print, broadcasting and internet) as well as in news content. Building on the work done by several global, regional and national surveys that have recorded the extent of inequality in news coverage and within media houses, the indicators are meant to help assess the nature and degree of imbalance and point the way towards internal measures to address evident disparities.

Key words
gender-sensitive indicators, media, representation

Some facts:

- Women account for less than a quarter (24%) of those heard or read about in print, radio and television news across the globe.
- News media continue to portray a world in which men outnumber women in almost all occupational categories.
- As persons interviewed or heard in the news, women remain lodged in the "ordinary" people categories, whereas men predominate in the "expert" categories.
- Female news subjects are identified by their family status four times more often than male news subjects.
- Only 13% of all stories focus specifically on women.
- Only 6% of stories highlight issues of gender equality or inequality.
- Nearly half (46%) of stories reinforce gender stereotypes, almost eight times higher than stories challenging stereotypes.

(*Who Makes the News?* Global Media Monitoring Project 2010)

- Nearly three quarters (73%) of the top management jobs in media companies across the globe are occupied by men.
- Women hold 26% of jobs at the governance level and 27% of top management jobs.
- Among reporters, men hold nearly two-thirds of the jobs, while women hold 36% of them.

- Among senior professionals, however, women are nearing parity, working in 41% of news-gathering, editing and writing jobs.
- Only slightly more than half of the companies surveyed have an established company-wide policy on gender equity.

(*Global Report on the Status of Women in the News Media*, International Women's Media Foundation, 2011)

The World Association of Christian Communication's (WACC) 2010 global research report *Who makes the News*[1] found that 24% of the people interviewed, heard, seen or read about in mainstream broadcast and print news are female. On the other hand, the International Women's Media Foundation's (IWMF) *Global Report on the Status Women in the News Media*,[2] has revealed that almost three quarters of the top jobs in media houses are held by men.

Because of such imbalances, the International Federation of Journalists (IFJ) is in the process of finalising a set of indicators for media houses to help bring about gender equality in news content and in newsroom structures. The 2010 Global Media Monitoring Project[3] noted that "The cultural underpinnings of gender inequality and discrimination against women are reinforced through the media." The end result is that women are deprived of their right to freedom of expression.

These facts are not any different to most regions in the world. For example, the *Gender and Media Progress Study* (Gender Links, 2010) found that there had been only a marginal increase in the proportion of women sources in the media in Southern Africa, from 17% in the 2003 *Gender and Media Baseline Study* to 19% in the 2010 GMPS (slightly lower than the global average of 24% yielded by the GMMP the same year).

Likewise, the *Glass Ceilings: Women and Men in Southern African Media* research (Gender Links, 2009) revealed that the region's media industry is fairly male-dominated, with men constituting 59% of employees in media houses compared to 41% women. The governance structures of media houses are also firmly in the hands of men (72%), with women constituting only 28% of those on boards of directors. Women constitute less than a quarter (23%) of top management and only marginally more (28%) of senior management. Only 16% of the media houses surveyed stated that they have gender policies and even those often could not specify what such policies comprise.

Journalists at work: *Daily Times* newsroom in Malawi.
Photo: Danny Glenwright

The media's role in promoting gender equality through content and professional practice is now widely acknowledged, but the link between media freedom and gender equality within the media is not as commonly recognised. This is largely because discussions on the latter issues tend to proceed on parallel tracks that rarely meet.

There is also a misconception that the two are incompatible, that any focus on "sectoral" concerns such as gender would infringe on freedom. But freedom of the press (media) is part of the broader fundamental right to freedom of opinion and expression to which all human beings, including women, are entitled. Access to media and the right to both receive and convey information and ideas through media is a vital aspect of freedom of expression.

Accordingly, gender equality in access to media is entirely consistent with freedom of expression and, thereby, media freedom. In fact, there can be no real freedom of expression as long as some sections of society, including women, are denied equal access to, and representation, in the media. Something is clearly wrong with the state of media freedom if, when women comprise half or more of the population, they constitute less than a quarter of news sources and hold only about a quarter of the decision-making positions in media houses.

In recognition of the fact that inclusion and representation in the media is crucial to women's human rights and empowerment, the 1995 Beijing Platform for Action listed two strategic objectives to promote gender equality in the media:
1. Increase the participation and access of women to expression and decision-making in and through the media and new technologies of communication.
2. Promote a balanced and non-stereotyped portrayal of women in the media.

Since there seems to have been little progress on either of these objectives in the intervening 15 years, UNESCO and the International Federation of Journalists (IFJ) recently collaborated in a project designed to help media houses track the situation within their organisations.

Targeted: Emily Brown, Namibian gender and media activist.
Photo: Trevor Davies

The project set out to identify gender-sensitive indicators that would enable media organisations and others - such as media workers' unions and gender activists - to evaluate the place and role of women in newsrooms (print, broadcasting and internet) as well as in news content. Building on the work done by several global, regional and national surveys that record the extent of the problem, the indicators are meant to help assess the nature and degree of imbalance and point the way towards internal measures to address evident disparities.

In the first phase of the project the IFJ asked Rosa María Alfaro Moreno and Ammu Joseph to map existing initiatives to define gender-sensitive indicators, looking in particular for indicators that could be of special relevance to media.

They found that while there is an abundance of material across the globe on gender-sensitive indicators, very little of it relates directly to media. In fact, only a third of the sample documents collected addressed the need for gender-sensitive indicators to assess the situation of women in newsrooms and the representation of women in news content. Nevertheless, parts of some of the other documents thrown up by the search were useful for understanding the nature, purpose and evolution of gender-sensitive indicators.

Perhaps the most useful document among those that the researchers managed to access was *Diversity in Action: Gender Policies in Media Houses - Facilitators Guide & Tools* (Gender Links, 2008), which includes three annexures that are of particular interest and relevance in the process of developing gender-sensitive indicators for media.

A useful definition that the researchers came across in the course of background research clarifies what an indicator is and is not: "An indicator is an instrument which provides information about the status and progress of a specific situation, process or condition. They enable simple, straight-forward and accessible knowledge regarding specific phenomenon. They may be simple or complex, depending on whether they are a set of specific and precise data or the result of a number of simple indicators gathered together." *(Study Assessment Criteria for Media Literacy Levels, Final Report edited by EAVI for the European Commission, 2009).*

In the second phase, Alfaro Moreno and Joseph worked on separate categories of indicators, both relating to news media: one set focused on gender balance in media organisations and the other on gender sensitivity in media content. The two documents prepared were then presented to other gender and media practitioners, activists and scholars from across the world at a consortium held at the IFJ offices in Brussels in April 2011. Based on inputs from all the participants, the documents were redrafted and refined in May 2011.

The Category A document deals with issues of human resources grouped into four themes on gender balance:
[a] at decision-making levels and
[b] in education and training, gender equality
[c] in working conditions and
[d] in unions, associations, clubs and journalists' organisations.

Stakeholders/targeted groups, critical areas of concern, strategic objectives, indicators and means of verification are identified within each of these themes.

For example, for the theme, "Gender balance at decision-making levels," the stakeholder/targeted group is media organisations, the critical area of concern is "Gender equality at decision-making levels in media managements," and the strategic objective is "Gender balance among decision makers within media organisations." The ten indicators for this theme include "number and proportion of women holding leadership positions within media (media owner, editor-in-chief, editor, head of departments, head of desks)" and "existence of affirmative action to increase female presence in media leadership." Among the means of verification are staff interviews, HR records and financial records.

Gerard Telot, Marie-Annick Savripene and Anushka Virahsawmy at the 2010 GEM Summit . *Photo: Trevor Davies*

The Category B document attempts to set out a framework and criteria for the development of indicators to gauge gender awareness and improve gender portrayal in the content of news media. Here, too, the issues are grouped into four areas: news and current affairs, advertising, ethical codes and editorial policies, and journalists' unions, associations and clubs. Critical areas of concern, strategic objectives, indicators and means of verification are identified within each of these themes. The target group for all areas within this second category are media employers, media gender desks, journalists and programme makers.

Many projects examining gender representation in the content of news media focus exclusively on news reports (and in some cases only those reports that appear on the front and general news pages of daily newspapers or prime time news bulletins on broadcast media). Here, however, an attempt has been made to work towards a more holistic picture by covering different forms of news and current affairs media (including periodicals) and different types of coverage (reportage, opinion/comment/analysis, feature articles, documentaries, etc.) in different sections/segments of the media (including special focus pages/ programmes on sports, business, health, civic/ environmental issues, etc.). Accordingly, the outline of possible indicators to measure levels of gender awareness in the editorial content of news media relates to a wider range of news and current affairs media forms and coverage than daily news reports.

Within the news and current affairs theme, the first critical area of concern is: gender parity in editorial content of news media (including print, broadcast and/or online, private, community and/or

public media). The corresponding strategic objective is: fair and balanced presence of men and women, their experiences, actions, views and concerns - reflecting the composition of society - in media coverage.

The New Times for Women, a newsletter at Beijing +15 New York.
Photo: Gender Links Library

Several of the indicators in this category have been derived from international gender/media surveys such as the GMMP, the GMPS and *Gender and Advertising in Southern Africa* (Gender Links, 2007). However, a few new ones have been included.

For example, within news and current affairs, one indicator aims to go beyond just numbers by looking at the number of women and men seen, heard or read about in news and current affairs content who belong to a variety of social, cultural, economic backgrounds, reflecting the composition of society (e.g., class, race/castes/ethnicity, religions, age groups, location [rural/urban, metro/small town, north/south/east/west, etc.], educational levels, health status [ability/disability], etc).

Similarly, another tries to incorporate the notion that women's voices need to be heard on a wide range of topics by seeking the number of women and men seen, heard or read about and/or interviewed/quoted as sources of information/ opinion in news and current affairs content. These content relate to subject areas such as politics and government, economics and business, war and conflict, science and technology, and sports.

The documents are presently with the IFJ and UNESCO. It is expected that they will be further circulated and discussed before being finalised and offered to media organisations as a tool they can consider using to promote gender equality and sensitivity in their policies and practices.

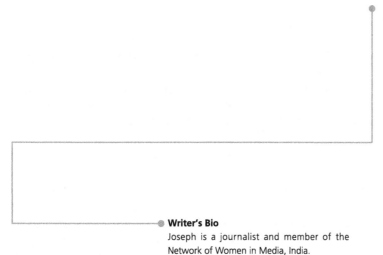

Writer's Bio
Joseph is a journalist and member of the Network of Women in Media, India.

Notes

1 http://www.whomakesthenews.org/
2 http://www.iwmf.org/pioneering-change/international-conference/press-release-032311.aspx
3 http://www.waccglobal.org/

Why there is still a glaring gender gap in Zimbabwe's newsrooms
By Virginia Muwanigwa

Abstract
This article looks at women's representation in the media industry in Zimbabwe. It analyses recent research findings that uncover low representation in all areas - in many instances below regional averages. The article then explores possible reasons why Zimbabwe is underperforming in this area despite strides made in regional and international legislation, including the Windhoek Declaration. It then examines the idea of power imbalances, using a model created to examine different ways power can be withheld from women.

Key words
media freedom, Windhoek Declaration, power, women's representation

As the media in Zimbabwe clamours for more space in which to realise the aspirations of the Windhoek Declaration, and with it, Article XIX of the UN Declaration on Human Rights (UNDHR), this article will analyse the degree to which the media itself is committed to these same aspirations from a gender and good governance perspective.

Just as the media believes that government and other stakeholders have failed to include and respect a free media, so too has the media failed to include and respect the other half of humanity - women.

Low representation of women in media decision-making positions has led to insufficient diversity of perspectives, which is contrary to human rights and other instruments. This is reflected in the lack of gender policies, including on sexual harassment, among media and in media related bodies. This

Leticia Machingura, sub-editor with the *Chronicle* newspaper in Bulawayo, Zimbabwe.   *Photo: Thabani Mpofu*

has resulted in inadequate incorporation of gender and women's rights in organisational composition, products and services by the media and related bodies. Sexual harassment, particularly of women, is rife in newsrooms and media bodies, a manifestation of uneven power distribution.

This is despite Zimbabwe being signatory to the UNDHR principle that states that the "... establishment, maintenance and fostering of an independent, pluralistic and free press is essential to the development and maintenance of democracy in a nation."

Analysis of this principle from a gender perspective means ensuring a diversity of opinions and voices from both men and women. A fundamental human right and indicator of media credibility is ensuring inclusion of women in all media institutions, processes and outcomes. Against this definition, this paper seeks to explore whether the Zimbabwean media is walking the talk.

Another barometer to use in assessing the degree of gender sensitivity and women's empowerment is reference to gender in media instruments. Article XIX of the UNDHR states that "everyone" not one sex, has "same rights" and "equality."

The International Covenant on Civil and Political Rights (ICCPR) and the International Covenant on Economic Social and Cultural Rights (ICESCR) both state that women's rights are interdependent and indivisible. This implies that these rights transcend all sectors, including the media.

The Convention on the Elimination of all forms of Discrimination against Women (CEDAW) says "no to discrimination or any distinction... based on sex... in the political, economic, social, cultural, civil or any other field."

Closer to home, the Southern African Development Community (SADC) Protocol on Gender and Development goes a step further to "encourage media and media related bodies to mainstream gender in their codes of conduct, policies and procedures" and "take measures to promote the equal representation of women in the ownership of, and decision-making structures of the media." Nationally, the Zimbabwe National Gender Policy also calls for "affirmative action for the advancement of female media practitioners."

Against this plethora of instruments, all promising in vain to deliver gender justice and women's integration within the media, as in other sectors, it becomes obvious that the battle to transform society to be inclusive goes beyond the adoption of instruments but requires a sustainable change in people's values, beliefs, attitudes and behaviours.

Activists and scholars state that at a structural level in Zimbabwean society in general, the existence of a dual legal system (customary tradition and statutory law) leads to disparities between aspirations of some progressive laws and traditional practice.

It is against this background that the Zimbabwe Union of Journalists (ZUJ) says it "...has consciously made efforts to address issues of gender imbalances in its structures as well as in media houses." To this end, a gender mainstreaming committee has been incorporated into the ZUJ constitution and "a five member committee is in place to strategise and implement decisions aimed at redressing gender imbalances."

Whether the committee has been effective, however, remains to be seen if findings in a recent Gender Links survey are an indicator. The survey revealed disparities in favour of men in almost all areas of concern within the country's media. Disparities were obvious in division of labour within the industry; access to, and control over, resources and benefits; responsiveness to women's specific needs; and constraints and opportunities for women in relation to men. *Glass Ceilings, Women and Men in Zimbabwe Media* 2009, revealed that there are six times as many men as women in those Zimbabwean media houses surveyed. Men constitute 87% of employees in the Zimbabwe media - almost seven times the 13% women employees.

The study also found that female representation varies among media houses. With 38% women, Radio Dialogue had the highest proportion of women, followed by Zimind Publishers, which has 28% women on its payroll. Zimpapers had the lowest proportion of women at 11%.

Chaka Bosha, the National Coordinator for the ZUJ attributes the low representation of women to the fact that the media has failed to create a working environment which is responsive to women's specific needs. "Most female journalists do not stay in the industry but move on to public relations or the NGO field," he notes.

Women constitute more than a third of boards of directors in the media at 38% compared with 28% in the regional study. However, women barely feature in top management as they occupy a very low 13% proportion of these positions in Zimbabwean media surveyed, lower that the regional average of 23%. Women hold only a tenth of senior management positions in Zimbabwe media houses surveyed; lower than the regional average of 28%.

Although Constantine Chimakure, an editor with the *Zimbabwe Independent*, agrees with Bosha, he believes the main reason is that women find it difficult to cope within the demanding media. He says women do not stay long enough to rise within the ranks and therefore miss out on chances to become prominent. "Female journalists use the media to gain skills in writing but move on to other areas, this is despite the fact that efforts have been increased to recognise women and elevate them," he says.

Some of these efforts include maternity leave, as a form of parental rights, which was found by the survey to be a high priority among Zimbabwean media. Paternity leave, however, is a different story. Of the media houses, 75% indicated they had maternity leave, lower than the regional average of 81%. But none offers paternity leave; perpetuating the stereotype that child-rearing is a female responsibility. The lack of obligation to share parental duties among couples may explain the reason why women working in media find the long hours in the newsroom impossible. They are also expected to be at home, looking after the family in the evenings.

Radio Dialogue, whose operations are currently contested, is the only media house that has a gender policy. Zimpapers and GL have also signed a progressive MOU that will see the media house adopting a gender policy.

The survey found that men at 82% are more likely than 18% women to be employed in full-time, open-ended contracts, compared to 42% women in the rest of the region. In turn, men dominate most departments in Zimbabwean media houses, except for design, where there is parity. According to the study, this male domination was especially pronounced in the editorial department at 83%, while the technical/IT and printing and distribution departments are completely devoid of women at 100% men.

Women are concentrated in the support departments, in areas considered "women's work" such as advertising and marketing (40%) and human resources (58%). Regionally, Zimbabwe topped the list in terms of the least women in editorial departments at just 17%. This is unfortunate considering that over the years many women have gained both prominence and confidence in the field yet struggle to get to leadership positions or simply have this recognised.

Women are grossly under-represented in most newsrooms in Zimbabwe.
Photo: Sikhonzile Ndlovu

Geoff Nyarota, a former editor, notes that it is unfortunate that in the current media environment, women who had risen within the ranks, particularly in the old Daily News, now seem to hold junior positions. The reticence to recognise and elevate

women to top positions appears to be visible in the new Daily News, which has named one of its top reporters, Thelma Chikwanha, as Community Affairs Editor. "I believe the issue is with women journalists as we are not assertive. If we could have the guts to demand our rights, who knows, we may find our concerns addressed,' says Chikwanha, who observed that the lack of a supportive environment for women may be a factor.

The gender division of labour is sharply defined with male journos hogging the hard beats, such as human rights (100%), sustainable development and environment (100%) and sport (92%). Conversely, women predominate in gender equality (100%), gender violence (100%) and religion (100%), so called "women's beats."

Despite these uncomplimentary figures, half of Zimbabwean media houses have gender-parity targets. Carving out career paths for women in Zimbabwean media houses is not a priority and there are no strategies to fast-track women. But half the media houses said they had considered promoting women. No efforts were being made to target good women candidates, which was obvious in that none of the Zimbabwean media houses in the sample indicated they had a database of women candidates. It appears that contrary to usual trends, the best practices in the regional sample have not rubbed off on Zimbabwe, as 40% of the media houses in the region have such a database, while a high proportion of media houses in the region target women specifically for jobs. This may partly be explained by the lack of confidence among women. According to Edna Machirori, once one of the leading women editors in the country, women in media have low self-esteem and believe they are not good enough to lead even when leading.

There have been calls for a paper, run by and for women in the country. Yet two years after a formal call was made by women activists attending a meeting during a 2009 exchange visit involving a delegation of businesswomen from Nordic countries, the call is still to be heeded. Then, prominent Zimbabwean women journalists were challenged to start such a paper. While technically the idea is feasible, the challenge is a lack of the requisite resources. Women, particularly those in marriage, seldom own resources in their own right which would be necessary to run and fully such an enterprise.

Miriam Madziwa, a journalist and commissioner on the newly formed Zimbabwe Media Council, confirms this: "most women do not have the economic muscle to start and maintain newspapers. Those who start initiatives are dependent on their male relatives and this takes away any control one might have."

A media research report commissioned in February 2011 noted that sexual harassment is endemic in the newsrooms and increasingly perpetuated by prominent male figures. This manifestation of male power over female journalists is compounded by the lack of gender policies. Therefore there are no procedures to name, deal with, or prevent sexual harassment. Those female journalists who have sought to defend their rights find themselves alienated, if not out of a job. The situation is so dire that an annual media stakeholder workshop held on 15 September 2011 identified the issue of sexual harassment, victimisation and discrimination against female journalists as needing responsive strategies, including penalties.

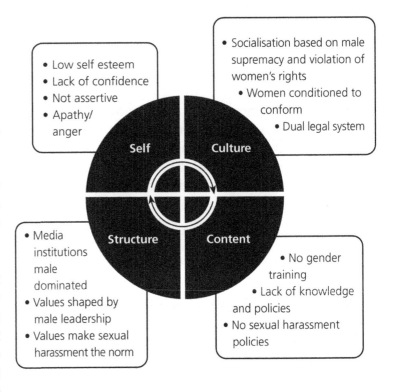

If this happens, this may inspire more confidence among female journalists, who for many years have witnessed insufficient will on the part of male leaders to take action against fellow men. This has also resulted in impunity and secondary trauma experienced by harassed women. At a time when the job market is flooded and opportunities few, fear of losing jobs, including those in senior management, results in further impunity.

In cases of sexual harassment, possible exposure to HIV and AIDS becomes another challenge. Beatrice Tonhodzayi-Ngondo, of SAFAIDS, speaking on Press Freedom Day, noted that lack of negotiating power around condom use exposes female subordinates to HIV.

Sharon Hudson Dean, Counselor for Public Affairs at the US Embassy in Harare, attributes the continued marginalisation of women in the media to patriarchy:

This situation, unfortunately, is found in many countries. Women all over the world face challenges reaching the highest levels of mainstream media. In Zimbabwe, the patriarchal culture is a barrier to change, but developments over the last 40 years in the US and other countries show that this is something that can be overcome through hard work and focused collaboration. Just recently, my office kicked off a women journalists mentoring program for 28 female journalists throughout Zimbabwe. We set up the programme to enable the women to help each other through networking and mentoring and to develop their personal and professional writing and leadership skills. By tapping into networks in Zimbabwe, the region and the US, we want to create a critical mass of talented, highly skilled women journalists who work together on breaking the glass ceiling. After seeing the drive shown by this group of women, it is easy to imagine the tide changing in the next decade.

In her position, Hudson oversees the US govern-ment's cultural, information and education program-ming in Zimbabwe.

At its peak, the Federation of African Media Women - Zimbabwe (FAMWZ) conducted a concerted campaign to fight violence against women. Through regular discussions, including with senior male journalists, the organisation lobbied for better working conditions for women media practitioners. It is for this reason that national research recently recommended, among other things, that a survey about sexual harassment in newsrooms must be conducted by FAMWZ for presentation and discussion within the broad media sector in the country. It noted that FAMWZ should investigate the obstacles men and women face in the newsroom and the reasons why many women leave the media industry.

More recently, the Women in Politics Support Unit (WIPSU) and the Zimbabwe Women's Resource Centre and Network (ZWRCN) have both engaged journalists to facilitate a conductive environment for women, either as leaders or as sources of news. The Media Institute of Southern Africa Zimbabwe has campaigned against sexist advertise-ments that denigrate women and treat them as sex symbols.

Gender and advertising: What has this woman got to do with selling of cigarettes.
Photo: Gender Links Library

In conclusion, this paper has employed a framework for power analysis posited by Lisa Veneklasen and Valerie Miller[1] to summarise why media women remain marginalised despite landmark documents such as the Windhoek Declaration.

"Visible Power," reflected in policies, rules, regulations and codes of conduct is still heavily tipped in favour of men. Women are thus marginalised from making and enforcing rules through biased constitution/laws/policies, discriminatory media newsroom procedures for recruitment, retention, development, protection and separation of staff and generally non representative media structures.

The Zimbabwe Union of Journalists (ZUJ) notes the need for media houses to be more vigorous in the campaign for female journalist's rights while a media stakeholder meeting organised by the Media Alliance of Zimbabwe (MAZ) recently noted that discrimination is still rife in the media profession and newsrooms, prompting a resolution for women's empowerment and gender equality.

Women still largely lack "Hidden Power" - this manifests in determining the agenda priorities in the national media, newsroom/media content; representation in decision-making and negotiations including access to information; responsiveness of media to media women's specific needs; lack of child care facilities; and flexitime.

Finally, women are still in the grip of "Invisible Power" - where socialisation instills values, beliefs and certain behaviours in conformity with agreed standards and norms. The male-dominated culture has subdued women into subordination and powerlessness; alienation; self-blame in cases of sexual harassment; low self esteem. There is need, therefore, for any efforts to increase media women's influence to address four areas of power: power over; power within; power with; and power to.

The sector should recognise that men hold disproportionate "power over" their female counterparts and this should be addressed. There is also need to build media women's "power within" for them to be more confident, assertive and ready to lead if called upon. However, this can only happen if there is a critical mass of media women to provide mutual support and backstopping where necessary and this is referred to as "power with." Finally, it is hoped that when all this is done, success will be seen in the media

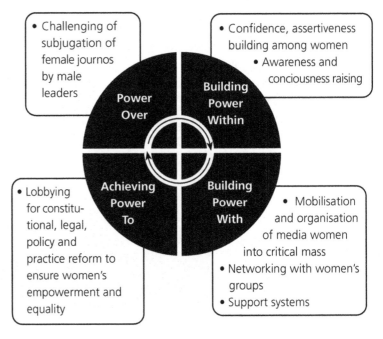

- Challenging of subjugation of female journos by male leaders

Power Over

- Confidence, assertiveness building among women
- Awareness and conciousness raising

Building Power Within

- Lobbying for constitutional, legal, policy and practice reform to ensure women's empowerment and equality

Achieving Power To

Building Power With

- Mobilisation and organisation of media women into critical mass
- Networking with women's groups
- Support systems

women's "power to" demand rights according to the laws, and the various instruments that have been adopted since the Windhoek Declaration.

Writer's Bio
Muwanigwa is a Zimbabwean gender rights advocate.

Notes

1 http://www.powercube.net/resources/handouts/

GENDER IN MEDIA CONTENT

Denisha Seedoyal presenting at the 2008 GEM Summit in Johannesburg, South Africa.

Photo: Trevor Davies

Media reporting of mass sexual violence in war: Unintended consequences or structural flaw?

By Funmi Vogt

Abstract

This paper analyses the issue of media reporting of violence against women in conflicts in Africa. It argues that media over-sensationalisation of the experiences of sexual violence victims has served to further violate the rights of the women it is purporting to help. This invariably violates, even if inadvertently, their rights to privacy and dignity in the face of tragedy; reiterates stereotypical views of women as helpless and victimised; and sends a message to aggressors that their desired objective has been achieve.[1] Over-sensationalisation by the media (understood as news media via online and print newspaper/magazines and books/radio/television) in the context of this paper, is understood as:

1. Instances where victims of sexual violence are made to relive their experiences over and over again either through media interviews or research/fact-finding missions, or through media portrayal via documentaries, movies, articles, etc;
2. Depicting lewd and graphic details of the women's ordeals;
3. Media mongering - using the tragedies of women in conflict situations for self-serving agenda(s), other than that which will change their circumstances for the better or empower them to do it themselves.

In essence, the mass media is considered as a perpetuator because it portrays images and attitudes (many of which are stereotypical) to which policies, programmes, and perhaps even the aggressors of these women, respond. This takes the focus away from deeper structural causes, which lie at the heart of finding lasting solutions to this issue.[2] The paper begins with an overview of existing legal and international policy standards, in an attempt to begin making sense of internationally accepted standards that guide the actions of media actors around the world. This is useful as a lens through which to see how this is played out at the local level in Africa. Section two analyses two case studies which further give context to the premise of this study. Section three concludes by taking a forward-look approach and identifying what can be done to start giving agency back to women affected by conflict in general, and particularly women who are victims of sexual violence during conflict.

Key words

conflict, women's rights, Democratic Republic of the Congo, Rwanda, victimisation

Legal and international policy frameworks

International policies that govern the media

It would be remiss to conduct an analysis of current media/information laws in Africa, without also looking at international policy frameworks and how African media policies engage and intersect with them. The wave of democratisation which has swept across the continent of Africa since the 1990's hearkened a transitioning from the view of human rights issues as solely the domain of the State, toward embracing the view that human rights issues fall under continental and international oversight (Berger, 2007). This view has seen the advent of regional organisations like the African Union, which aims to address social, economic and political challenges on the continent,[3] as well as an increase in United Nations Security Council Resolutions which call for actions to protect human rights worldwide, with a focus on Africa given the proliferation of conflicts and human rights violations on the continent in recent times.

Demanding a platform: a female marcher expresses herself at 2011 Take Back the Night. *Photo: Trevor Davies*

Media legislation, although dynamic and constantly changing, especially given the advent of contemporary phenomena like terrorism, and the electronic and social media explosion (blogging and other online activity), is embedded within the following human rights that are universally held as constant:

- **Freedom of expression:** "freedom to seek, receive and impart information and ideas of all kinds, regardless of frontiers, either orally, in writing, or in print, in the form of art or through any other media of choice."[4]
- **Freedom of information:** Is an extension of freedom of speech/expression, and protects the right to publish and share information, through any medium: print, radio, television, online, etc.
- **Freedom of access to information:** This act, while directly linked to the other two, is also distinct in that it protects the right of an individual to access any information, which is in the public domain.

These three are entrenched in the Universal Declaration of Human Rights (1948), Article 19 which asserts that "Everyone has the right to freedom of opinion and expression; this right includes freedom to hold opinions without interference and to seek, receive and impart information and ideas through any media and regardless of frontiers."

This declaration, although non-binding on state actors, has had a significant impact on the development and implementation of further legislation to protect the rights of groups and individuals to seek, publish and access information. This is directly tied to freedom of media or the press.

Following the UDHR, international instruments like the African Charter on Human and Peoples Rights (1981), the Global Campaign for Free Expression and the International Covenant on Civil and Political Rights (1993) were enacted.[5] These accords, which are more binding on State governments, have formed the basis on which the rights of media agencies and individuals representing the media are protected. Finally, these policy frameworks have become the yardstick by which the international media engages, both in its own immediate contexts and in foreign environments.

Regional Frameworks

In sub-Saharan Africa, legal frameworks, which protect the rights of freedom of expression, freedom of information and freedom to access information, are still undergoing a process of reform at the national level. There are, however, regional policies like the Windhoek Declaration (1991), the Constitutive Act of the African Union (2000), and the model law by the African Union on Access to Information, which is still in draft form.[6] These regional policies are modelled to be

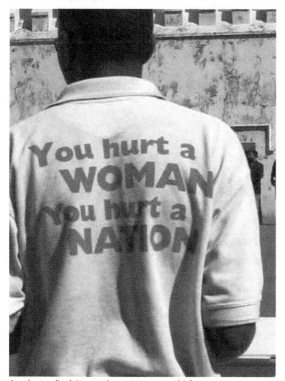

Are the media doing any better to prevent this?

Photo: Colleen Lowe Morna

compatible with international frameworks, and advocate for less repressive state policies that encourage "pluralism" and "diversity" in the media *(Berger, 2007)*.

Across the continent, media legislation remains in a process of reform and advancement as civil society discourse, leadership changes and environmental requirements (conflict, natural resource issues, etc.) continue to advance and shape existing legislation (Berger, 2007). In an analysis of state-level legislation, it was found that more democratic countries (Ghana and South Africa, for example) have greater media freedom and access to information due to advancements in their media reform discourse/legislation. This has led to an explosion in the media industry in these countries, in terms of existence and access. In countries still struggling to embrace democratic values and human rights liberties (Ethiopia, for example), the process is much further behind.

An analysis of existing media/information legislation both at the regional and state levels, revealed the following:

i) Regional legislation (where existent)[7] appears more focused on creating laws that complement the international frameworks, without immediately appearing to put mechanisms in place to monitor how the international media engages at the local level.

ii) Legislation both at the regional and state level - where there is evidence of reform in terms of facilitating pluralism and diversity in the media - show very little evidence of engaging communities in this process. If we move forward on the basic assumption that public information should be the property of all individuals,[8] and spaces should be created for citizens to contribute to, and own, information gathering and dissemination processes, then we find that regional and local legislation on the continent is not living up to universally held standards. Leadership through media education is all the more important in this regard because research has shown that access to education and information impacts how individuals access their rights to expression and information, and how they shape their media environments *(Gigli, 2004)*.

iii) Legislation both at the regional and state levels show little to no gender sensitivity in terms of acknowledging the importance of making spaces for women in the media and ensuring that marginalised groups have the freedoms of expression, information, and access to information. Marginalised groups are particularly vulnerable to media "exclusion," and more focus is needed to create spaces for their voices.

When these three factors are considered collectively a clear theme begins to emerge. International media policy is explicit in its protection of the rights to freedom of expression, information and access to Information, universally. On the other hand, media laws in Africa both at the regional and state levels need to consolidate mechanisms to guide how these international policies (and actors in the form of media) engage at the local level.

Issues like who is permitted to come and gather information, how this information is gathered, how this information will be used, and how much control individuals and communities have over these processes - remain apparent gaps. Furthermore, the most vulnerable people in communities (women and children in unstable and conflict-prone environments) - who are also the most subject to media attention - are left with their rights to privacy and dignity compromised,

because they are not empowered to control how information concerning them is used.

This makes for a fundamental gap between freedoms of speech and expression at the regional or international level, and the basic right of a human being to protect his or her privacy and dignity, and to leverage these same rights (freedom of expression and information) at the local level. Key among those who receive the most exposure as a result of this gap, are those who are socially at the margins of society (women and children especially) whose rights are viewed as secondary to those who have access to power (the elite, and ruling masculinities).[9]

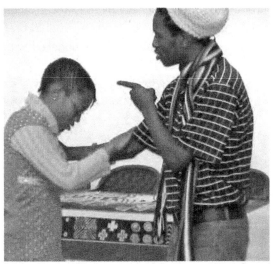

Relationship control factors are associated with perpetration of sexual violence. *Photo: Colleen Lowe Morna*

Portrayals of women affected by violence in the media

Democratic Republic of the Congo

"LUVUNGI, Democratic Republic of Congo - Four armed men barged into Anna Mburano's hut, slapped the children and threw them down. They flipped Mrs. Mburano on her back, she said, and raped her, repeatedly... It did not matter that

dozens of United Nations peacekeepers were based just up the road. Or that Mrs. Mburano is around 80 years old.

"Grandsons!" she yelled. "Get off me!"

As soon as they finished, they moved house to house, along with hundreds of other marauding rebels, gang-raping at least 200 women."
(New York Times, 3 October 2010)

This article's intent appears to be to highlight the failure of the United Nations in protecting civilians in the Democratic Republic of the Congo, yet the actual message goes deeper. Not only is the victim's name used (there was no disclaimer that she was given an alias), but a picture of the victim was displayed along with the article (albeit her face was turned away from the camera). While the intent was to bring a harsh reality to the public and an international audience, the victim in question was further victimised through this portrayal. This article is one of many which have been used to try to bring the issue of sexual violence in the DRC conflict onto the world agenda.

The case of the DRC is unique because it is an ongoing conflict, and there have been recent reports that the Congolese army - who are meant to protect civilians from the rebel forces - has been taking part in these incidents of mass rape.[10] Several studies have shed light on the impact of media images of rape or sexual violation, particularly on a male audience.[11]

These studies all provide empirical evidence which suggest that certain factors like cultural stereotypes, general acceptance of violence, and continuous exposure to violence, have a considerable impact on how marginalised groups are subjugated. Many

of these studies also contend that the media plays a critical role in shaping these attitudes.

Considering the already patriarchal nature of African social systems, a picture begins to emerge of the effects of media representation on commu- nities where there is already a culture of domi- nance over marginalised

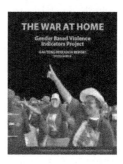

groups. This should by no means lay all the blame on the doorstep of the international media. Evidence of these representations of violence and aggression towards women are also found in local media; not so much in news reporting, but in the entertainment industry - which has an even larger audience. Nigerian Movie Industry (Nollywood) films are widely viewed across the continent, and to a large extent entrench stereotypical views of women as subject to the whims of men, as ordained by God.[12] While some might argue that these are representations of actual social interactions, it is important to start asking questions around what roles the media *should* play in changing some of these attitudes.

Rwanda

In Rwanda, where the genocide of 1994 led to the most rampant and violent incidents of sexual aggression against women in recorded African history, there has been an ongoing outpouring of media reports on the violations suffered by Rwandese women, which have yet to abate. Movies like *100 Days* and *Shake Hands with the Devil*; documentaries like *Valentina's Story* and *Journey into Darkness*, and numerous books, newspaper articles and reports, continue to retell the story of violence against women in the genocide - in many cases very lurid and horrific details. There is no immediate evidence of how much of this media is available to those who actually suffered these atrocities, however, it is widely available to an international audience.[13] Furthermore, there does not appear to be any data in terms of how this media impacts (either positively or negatively) the lives of those women who suffered these atrocities. Some women have been able to tell their stories for financial benefit,[14] however there is still a veil of silence in terms of how these women communicate with each other, their communities and the world about their experiences.

The following excerpt was collected from Denise (not her real name), a rape survivor in the Rwandan genocide:

...they began to beat me on the legs with sticks. Then one of them raped me... When he finished, he took me inside and put me on a bed. He held one leg of mine open and another one held the other leg. He called everyone who was outside and said, 'you come and see how *Tutsikaziare* on the inside.' Then he said, 'You Tutsikazi, you think you are the only beautiful women in the world.' Then he cut out the inside of my vagina. He took the flesh outside, took a small stick and put what he had cut on the top. He stuck the stick in the ground outside the door and was shouting, 'Every-one who comes past here will see how Tutsikazi look.' Then he came back inside and beat me again. Up to today, my legs are swollen. Then they left. I crawled out of the house bleeding. There was blood everywhere. A Hutu neighbour took me and put traditional medicine on me. I stayed for over a month with her until I could walk. During that time, she hid me and helped me. When the militias found out where I was, I had to leave again. I fled to another neighbor. In July 1994, the RPF came. I still have medical problems. I have extreme pain every month during my menstrual period. I have not seen a doctor. I have heard of the International Criminal Tribunal and I would talk to them, but they have never come here. I reported my case to the authorities three times, but nothing has happened.[15]

Excerpts like this bring home the reality of the horror of what happened in Rwanda, however this level of detail in such a horrific experience takes the reader away from the substance of what happened in Rwanda - that rape was used as a weapon in ethnic cleansing and subjugation. Furthermore, it puts a picture in the mind of the reader such that if one day they meet a woman from Rwanda, they are quite likely to almost immediately wonder if that woman was violated like Denise. The image of the victim has been formed.

Gender based violence: mere product of male aggressive behaviour?
Photo: Gender Links Library

These are only two brief case studies, however. In other contexts (Uganda, Liberia, Sierra Leone, Mozambique, for example) similar patterns of reportage (particularly international media) on sexual violence against women in conflict situations are evident. Atrocities occur, and the media swoops in to gather "facts" which are in turn sensationalised on different media platforms around the world (stories like those of Denise can be found on the internet with a simple web-search). Women are almost always reported as helpless victims and men the violent aggressors.

Realities on the ground, however, reveal dynamics which are far more complex than these portrayals suggest, and which beg for nuance and a deeper analysis than re-telling of an act of rape - which is arguably merely a product of deeper (and often male aggressive) social relationships.[16] This failure to provide context and analysis has led to the following consequences, perhaps amongst others:

The "gun in hand" approach
International documents tackling rape or violence against women have not immediately based their policies on sound facts and data, but have rather done so as a reaction to media images.[17] As such these frameworks, as well as policies and programmes, that have been created to respond to events, have responded superficially without addressing structural factors underlying the problem, and have thus been largely ineffective. It is only recently that there has been a growing realisation of a gap in terms of what is being reported, versus actual realities. Lack of adequate information and data on which to ground useful policy, resulted in UNSCR 1960 (2010), which calls for more detailed and systematic monitoring, analysis and reporting on sexual violence in conflict. More will be said about the importance of critical data later.

Reinforcing "aggressive" masculinities
Sexual violence (particularly mass sexual violence) in conflict is rarely random and senseless. UNSCR 1820 and 1888, which describe such acts as "tactics of war," are apt in the acknowledgment that in patriarchal social systems, the ability to control natural resources and women (whose child-bearing abilities make them crucial to community/society growth), is equal to the control of power. There is nothing more damaging to such communities (and the men at their helm) as not knowing if the children born after acts of rape really belong to them, or if they belong to an outsider. It is perhaps for this reason more than any that women from these societies who have suffered as a result of rape are forced to remain silent about the ordeal or ostracised. Their children are often rejected by the community. In addition, taking women as "spoils of war" is tantamount to emasculating the opposing belligerent faction,

Demanding justice: there is no justification for rape.

Photo: Trevor Davies

even though victims are oftentimes brutalised to the point of death to heighten the sense of terror. In conflict, violating women in the most aggressive ways possible is intended to reinforce the image of power and control (an image rooted in aggressive masculinities).[18]

Desensitisation

The act of raping women, whatever the context, is not a construct of modern times. At practically every point in recorded history and regardless of environment, there is evidence of men physically violating women - an act which escalates during periods of warfare. It is arguably the oldest human rights violation on record. Yet to this day, very little strikes fear and remorse more deeply into the psyche of a family/community, than the knowledge that one of its members has been raped - the more violent the act, the more heightened the terror. This is not the space to delve into the reasons for this, however the point should be made that the act of a man (or group of men) raping a woman is an act which has the power to create significant emotional disturbance within a community.

Research has shown that excessive exposure to information and images of rape and violence against women can have the effect of desensitising the audience - particularly a male audience (Malamuth, 1981). Desensitisation may be in the form of dismissing such acts by men as normal male behaviour towards the "weaker" sex, or perhaps worse, people may feel that the women did something to deserve it or want it. Desensitisation can even occur within programmes that advocate against sexual violence, as this may lead to a shift away from stopping the rape from taking place in the first place (perhaps because they feel that nothing can be done in this regard), to treating the victim after the act has occurred.

Further and more detailed research is needed to be able to fully comprehend how media exposure affects victims of sexual violence and their communities, however there is increasing evidence that this is a significant gap which must be closed in order to get closer to addressing the issue of sexual violence against women, particularly during periods of conflict.

Rafeeuddin Ahmed, former UN Under-Secretary General, gave some context to this issue when he stated: "In retrospect, I realise how much of my perception about women in war was influenced by the media. The incessant images of desperation and victimisation tell only part of the story. The other part, the strength, courage and resilience, is rarely captured."[19]

Proudia Mosupi, survivor of gender-based violence.
Photo: Colleen Lowe Morna

Critical and context-specific data is needed in order to get a sense of what type of media information is circulated on sexual violence in conflict, and how this data is used. This will not only form a baseline for creating frameworks to monitor information generation and circulation around this issue, but it will also give a sense of the types of media spaces that need to be created for women to intervene in the issues which impact them the most.

Giving agency back: building a monitoring framework

It is generally agreed that the most effective way of breaking down social structures, which inhibit and victimise women, is to include women in decision-making processes and in positions of leadership.[20] Although useful as a take-off point, more work needs to be done to empower women at the community level to build the leadership skills necessary to usefully participate in processes which impact them and their communities. There is a need for African women to assume agency for themselves, in terms of how they are portrayed in the media. In order for this to be achieved spaces must be created for them to do so and the way forward might include the following:

1. *Data gathering to form a baseline:* It is much easier to fix a problem when the problem is well and truly understood. It is crucial that critical facts and figures are obtained around incidents of violence against women, and given the heightened occurrences of this during conflict, particular attention should be paid to conflict situations. This will then form a baseline on which useful information dissemination (through the media), and policy intervention can occur.

2. *Confront the structural roots of the problem in media portrayal of sexual violence:* Without dealing with the structural causes it is difficult for media reporting, and indeed policy, to transform practice. Johan Galtung's work (1996) looks at "structural violence," i.e. violence which is embedded within social structures (for example class, race and gender-based violence); and juxtaposes it against "structural peace," which can only be attained by tackling repressive social structures. The current practice of media reporting mechanisms (and the policies that result from them) to merely skim the surface is therefore largely ineffective, because sexual violence cannot be prevented or reduced without delving into the roots of these acts.

3. *Including women in information processes:* African regional and state media/information legislation must become more gendered, not only by including more women in the media to advocate for better representation and access to information for African women (Rehn and Sirleaf, 2002) but legislation must also be more inward-focused by understanding the uniqueness of its immediate environment and by shaping its policies to fill internal gaps.

4. *Leadership:* A gap remains to be filled in terms of guaranteeing women inclusion in all processes of reconstruction and development (of which the media is a part). This is the gap that the UNSCR 1325 framework has attempted to fill, but which remains far from realised due to the lack of women who are prepared to fully participate in these processes and to take up positions of leadership. More initiatives which focus on women's leadership (from the grassroots) are needed, as this is one of the surest ways to counteract the exclusion of women (particularly victimised women) in the media.

Conclusion

Universal human rights standards are explicit in their protection of the rights of individuals to free speech, free expression, and freedom to access information. These rights are the raison d'être for media engagement worldwide, and form the basis on which the international media engages at the local level. However, legislation at the regional and national level on the African continent is still trying to catch up with universal standards, in terms of providing citizens with these same rights as well as protecting their rights to privacy and dignity that can be violated by thoughtless media reporting. The media has the power to change social attitudes and beliefs, which put women in a position of vulnerability and victimisation; and the media also has the ability to reinforce these attitudes and to render efforts towards advocacy and intervention useless. It is of vital importance to empower African women at all levels of society, to take control of how they are portrayed in the media. Unless this happens, policy frameworks that protect the rights of women to maintain their privacy and dignity in the media will remain lacking.

References

Abrahams, Naeemah, Jewkes Rachel, and Laubsher, Ria (1999). *"I Do not Believe In Democracy In The Home"* Men`s Relationships With And Abuse of Women. Cape Town: CERSA-Women`s Health Medical Research Council, August.

African Union (2010). *Draft Model Law for AU Member States on Access to Information*, Prepared under the Auspices of the Special Rapporteur on Freedom of Expression and the Right to access to Information in Africa in partnership with the Centre for Human Rights, University of Pretoria: 24 November, 2010. http://www.achpr.org/english/other/MODEL%20LAW%20FINAL.pdf

African Union. *AU in a nutshell*, access date July, 2011. http://www.au.int/en/about/nutshell.

Aguirre, Maria Teresa. "Organisation s in Middle East Monitor Media Images of Violence against Women," WACC- Middle East Regional Association, access date 2nd June, 2011. www.waccglobal.org/fr/cr-updates

Berger, Guy (2007). "Media Registration In Africa: A Comparative Legal Survey.'' Cape Town: School of Journalism & Media Studies, Rhodes University, South Africa.

Berkowitz, Leonard and Frodi, Ann (1977). "Stimulus Characteristics That Can Enhance or Decrease Aggression: Associations with Prior Positive or Negative Reinforcements for Aggression." *Aggressive Behaviour* 3:1-15.

Burt, Martha R (1980). "Cultural Myths and Supports for Rape," *Journal of Personality and Social Psychology* 38, 2: 217-230.

Clarke, Yaliwe (2008). "Security Sector Reform in Africa: A Lost Opportunity to Deconstruct Militarized Masculinities?" *Feminist Africa* 10: 49-66.

Donnerstein, Edward and Linz, Daniel (1986). "Mass Media Sexual Violence and Male Viewers: Current Theory and Research," *American Behavioral Scientist* 29, 5 May/June: 601-618.

Writer's Bio

Vogt has spent the last 12 years working on issues concerning the African continent, with a specific focus on peace and security issues as they relate to women's development.

Notes

1. This paper takes into account some of the work, which has been done on aggressive/ruling masculinities, and of the impact of media images portraying sexual aggression against women, on a male audience. See Linz et al, 1992; Clarke, 2008; Abrahams et al, 1999; Muthien, 2005 amongst others.
2. Johan Galtung's model of structural violence, versus structural peace is a key assertion in this study.
3. The African Union was founded in September 1999 through the Sirte Declaration, with a mandate to move the continent from an insular continent still coming to terms with the legacies of colonialisation and trying to define a common identity; towards a focus on making Africa a player in the global economy. http://www.au.int/en/about/nutshell
4. For further background on the Universal Declaration of Human Rights, see http://www.un.org/en/documents/udhr/
5. More detail on these can be found at http://en.wikipedia.org/wiki/Main_Page.

Gettlemen, Jeffrey (2010). "Mass Rapes in Congo Reveals U.N Weakness." *New York Times*, 3 October.

Gigli, Susan (2004). "Children, Youth and Media Around the World: An Overview of Trends and Issues," *4th World Summit on Media for Children and Adolescents*, Rio de Janeiro: Intermedia Survey Institute for UNICEF, April, 2004.

Ismail, Wale; Olonisakin, 'Funmi; Picciotto, Robert; Wybrow, David (2009). *Youth Vulnerability (YOVEX)* in West Africa: Synthesis Report, CSDG Papers, No. 21.

Malamuth, Neil, Addison, Tamara and Koss, Mary (2000). "Pornography and Sexual Aggression: Are There Reliable Effects and Can We Understand Them?" *Annual Review of Sex Research* 11: 26-91.

Muthien, Bernedette (2005). "Engendering Security." Cape Town: Engender, http://www.engender.org.za/publications/engenderingsecurity.html

Rehn, Elizabeth and Sirleaf, Johnson (2002). "Media Power," in *Women, War, Peace: The Independent Experts Assessment on the Impact of Armed Conflict on Women and Women's Role in Peace-Building. United Nations Development Fund for Women*, pp 103 - 110.
Smith, David (2010). "UN-backed Troops `Murdering and Raping` Villagers in Congo." The Guardian.15 October 2010

http://www.guardian.co.uk/world/2010/oct/15/un-backed-troops-accused-rape-congo
United Nations. *15 Years of The United Nations Special Rapporteur on Violence Against Women, its Causes and Consequences*
United Nations (2010). UN Security Council Resolution 1960, UN Doc.S/RES/1960 (2010), 16 December.

United Nations. *Universal Declaration of Human Rights*, 1949. http://www.un.org/en/documents/udhr/

Valasek, Kristin; Nelson, Kaitlin and Anderson Hilary (2006). "Securing Equality, Engendering Peace: A Guide to Policy and Planning on Women, Peace and Security (UN SCR 1325)," Santo Domingo: United Nations International Research and Training Institute for the Advancement of Women.

"Voices from Rwanda: Rape and Mutilation During Genocide." *clg.portalxm.com*. Center on Law & Globalization, n.d. Web. 2 Apr. 2011.

Wikipedia. *The Global Campaign for Free Expression and the International Covenant on Civil and Political Rights*. Last modified on 14 September 2011 http://en.wikipedia.org/wiki/Freedom_of_speech

Wikipedia. *The African Charter on Human and Peoples Rights*, last modified on 18 November 2010. http://en.wikipedia.org/wiki/African_Charter_on_Human_and_Peoples%27_Rights

[6] A copy of this draft law can be found at http://www.achpr.org/english/other/MODEL%20LAW%20FINAL.pdf
[7] See Berger (2007) for a useful recent analysis of what exists.
[8] See the text of the Universal Declaration of Human Rights for information on Freedom of Access to Information.
[9] The Youth, Vulnerability and Exculusion Project (YOVEX) conducted by the Conflict, Security and Development Group, gives some context to the issue of exclusion and living at the margins of society http://www.securityanddevelopment.org/index.php?option=com_content&view=article&id=60
[10] http://www.guardian.co.uk/world/2010/oct/15/un-backed-troops-accused-rape-congo
[11] See Burt, 1980; Berkowitz and Frodi, 1999; Donnerstein and Linz, 1986.
[12] This paper is not intended to analyse the Nigerian Movie Industry - which will be done in a different paper - however more information on Nollywood can be obtained from this website: http://www.nollywood.com/
[13] The Rwandese government has established a Genocide Memorial as well as an archive to collect media on the genocide, but it remains to be seen how the Rwandese - especially victims of the genocide - can access these resources and what impact it has on them.
[14] This is mostly in the form of selling their stories in novels, for example Jansen, Hanna 2002. *Over a Thousand Hills I Walk With You*, Cox & Wyman, Reading, Berkshire.
[15] http://clg.portalxm.com/library/keytext.cfm?keytext_id=134
[16] Galtung, Muthien, and Ratele, for example, look at structural violence which is in the form of domination and control over the "other," and stress the importance of tackling structural violence to achieve structural peace.
[17] UNSCR 1820 and 1888 specifically address the issues of rape as a weapon of war, and both called for strong, almost zero-tolerance, action against aggressors.
[18] This paper does not aim to delve to deeply into the psychology of rape, however alot of work has been done on the issue of Sexual Violence and the Mass Media. See for example, Linz, et al 1992; Malamuth and Check, 1981; Malamuth et al, 1980.
[19] Media Power article.
[20] The Beijing Declaration and UNSCR 1325 constitute the framework for standpoint.

Missing: Nursing in the South African press
By Greer van Zyl and Nicola Christofides

Abstract

Nurses are the backbone of the health system yet the largely female nursing profession is virtually invisible in the South African press. A content analysis of all newspaper cuttings (242) about nursing over six months in 2010 found a quarter of articles quoted nurses, yet spokespeople featured twice as often. A third of nursing quotes were anonymous, mainly on labour, protest and service delivery issues. Females were quoted first most often and in full articles. Nurses need to speak for themselves and engage the media on healthcare issues; their space in the press is well overdue.

Key words
nursing, content analysis, nurse voices, gender and power

Introduction

Nursing is critical to healthcare delivery, and nurses represent the largest segment of the healthcare workforce. Globally, the status of nurses and their profession is diminishing, partly due to the media image of nursing, which is portrayed as a profession with heavy workloads and poor pay. This impacts nursing recruitment and health service delivery (Bridges 1990; Hall, Angus et al. 2003; Brodie, Andrews et al. 2004). South Africa has 231 086 nurses to serve 49.9 million people, of which 115 244 are registered nurses comprising 8215 (7.6%) male nurses (SANC 2011).

As a largely female profession, nursing has been subjected to gender subordination as nurses are seen as caring, compassionate and the "handmaidens of doctors" (Salvage 1985; Marks 2001). While 92% of South Africa's nurses are women, they are seen either knowingly or unconsciously as "subordinates in patriarchal society, particularly in the male, physician-dominated health care system" (Evans 1997). Male nurses are often perceived as a privileged minority rising rapidly to managerial positions (Salvage 1985; Evans 1997). International research found that physicians (doctors) as a professional group were quoted most often in healthcare articles (Buresh and Gordon 2006), and nurses tended not to be included among spokespersons offered by hospitals (Gordon 2005). When they were featured, their quotes were brief (Schmidt 2001), possibly anonymous, and they were unidentified in photographs (Gordon 2005).

Nursing: a profession largely occupied by women.
Photo: Trevor Davies

How media frames nurses can reinforce or challenge these gender dynamics. The mass media's framing of news and events can affect how consumers of news understand these events (Price, Tewksbury et al. 1995; Scheufele 1999), and plays a key role in shaping public perceptions by focusing attention on an issue and choosing whom to quote. The media can confer status to a quoted individual, help broaden policy dialogue and establish what is "normative" behaviour (Schramm 1964).

When the public is ill-informed about the role of nurses, "neither consumers nor policymakers can be expected to support their work or allocate the required resources to carry out their responsibilities in health care" (Kalisch and Kalisch 1985). However, when the public understands the critical role of nursing in healthcare, nursing's image can move from the stereotype of physician's handmaid, angel of mercy, sex object or dragon-lady (Salvage

1985; Marks 2001; Brodie, Andrews et al. 2004) to one in which nurses are educated in schools of nursing and are "viewed as major contributors to university academic enterprise" (Buresh and Gordon 2006).

This cross-sectional study used a quantitative content analysis to investigate who is quoted in nursing articles in the South African lay press, with attention to gender and power. The research described who, what, when, where and how nursing was portrayed in print articles published in the lay press from 1 January - 30 June 2010.

Methodology

We identified 242 lay press articles in 95 publications featuring the word "nurse/s" or "nursing." These were clipped and sent in PDF format from Monitoring South Africa (MSA), a press cutting agency. Quality was controlled by cross-checking with the web-based agency, Meltwater, to ensure no articles were omitted. Geographical distribution of media was verified through Targetmedia[1].

The first author developed a data coding sheet to capture the dimensions of extent of nursing coverage (publication and article type, geographical coverage, number of articles) and who was quoted in articles, and in which media, for each of six categorical variables of nurse, patient/family member, doctor, union, spokespersons, and sex of persons. Data was numerical or transposed to numerical values and presented as frequencies and proportions for analysis. Since a number of articles featured anonymous quotes, a dichotomous variable was generated for "identity protected" and "identity not protected." Proportions and chi-square analysis were calculated using STATA9.

The second author coded a 10% sample, and inter-rater reliability was assessed for the potentially subjective variable of topic and found almost perfect agreement (Kappa = 0.84). Eleven articles of the total 242 were passing mentions and did not contain sufficient information for categorisation by topic and were dropped from analysis, yielding a total of 231. Regarding voice, not all articles had quotes and it was possible for different categories of people to be quoted in a single article hence the total number of quotes (256) was more than the total number of articles (242).

Let Us Grow careworker: Women shoulder the burden of caring for the needy.
Photo: Trevor Davies

Results

Extent of nursing quotes

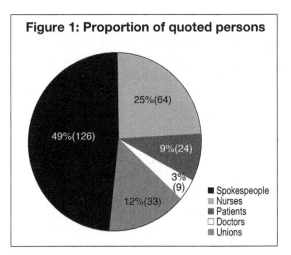

Figure 1: Proportion of quoted persons

25%(64)
49%(126)
9%(24)
3%(9)
12%(33)

■ Spokespeople
▦ Nurses
■ Patients
□ Doctors
▦ Unions

Figure 1 illustrates the extent of quotes about nursing. A quarter of 256 quotes were from nurses while nearly 50% of quotes were from spokespeople. Unions were quoted in 12% of articles, patients in 10% and doctors in 3%. Nurses were quoted once in 15% (37) of articles, twice in 2% (5) of articles, and three or more times in 9% (22) of articles.

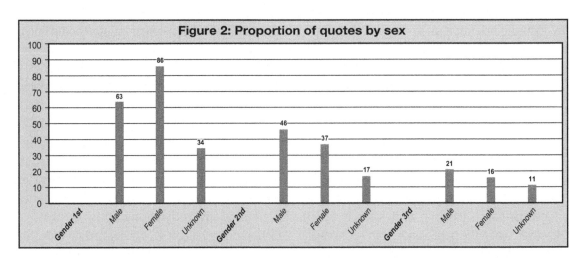

Figure 2: Proportion of quotes by sex

	Male	Female	Unknown
Gender 1st	63	86	34
Gender 2nd	46	37	17
Gender 3rd	21	16	11

In terms of sex[2], **Figure 2** shows that females were quoted first more frequently than males in the first quote in articles, but in second and third quotes, males were quoted more often.

Table 1: Nursing quotes by media characteristics

Publication type	Nurse quote % (n)	Patient quote % (n)	Doctor quote% (n)	Union quote % (n)	Spokesperson quote % (n)	Total
National	20.3% (13)	20.8% (5)	11.1% (1)	24.2% (8)	26.9% (34)	23.8% (61)
Regional	32.8% (21)	33.3% (8)	55.5% (5)	69.7% (23)	37.3% (47)	40%(104)
Community	40.6% (26)	29.1% (7)	0	6% (2)	32.5% (41)	29.6%(76)
Magazine	6.2% (4)	16.6% (4)	33.3% (3)	0	3.1% (4)	5.8% (15)
Total	100% (64)	100% (24)	100% (9)	100% (33)	100% (126)	100% (256)
P-value	0.145	0.000	i	0.000	0.000	
Frequency						
Daily	46.8% (30)	50% (12)	22.2% (2)	75.7% (25)	57.9% (73)	55.4%(142)
Weekly	51.5% (33)	41.6% (10)	66.6% (6)	24.2% (8)	40.4% (51)	42.1%(108)
Fortnightly	0	4.1% (1)	0	0	0	0.3%(1)
Monthly	1.5% (1)	4.1% (1)	11.1% (1)	0	1.5% (2)	1.9%(5)
Total	100% (64)	100% (24)	100% (9)	100% (33)	100% (126)	100% (256)
P-value ii	0.190	0.991	i	0.009	0. 172	
Geographic distribution						
National	25% (16)	37.5% (9)	44.4% (4)	24.2% (8)	6.9% (34)	27.7%(71)
Gauteng	12.5% (8)	8.3% (2)	33.3% (3)	27.2% (9)	19.8%% (25)	18.3%(47)
KwaZulu-Natal	3.1% (2)	16.6% (4)	11.1% (1)	12.1% (4)	10.3% (13)	9.3%(24)
Western Cape	32.8% (21)	12.5% (3)	0	12.1% (4)	15.8% (20)	18.7%(48)
Eastern Cape	14% (9)	16.6% (4)	11.1% (1)	21.1% (7)	13.4% (17)	14.8%(38)
Others	12.5% (8)	8.3% (2)	0	3% (1)	13.4% (17)	10.9%(28)
Total	100% (64)	100% (24)	100% (9)	100% (33)	100% (126)	100%(256)
P-value	0.149	0.158	i	0.091	0.087	
Ownership						
Caxton	9.3% (6)	4.1% (1)	0	3% (1)	11.1% (14)	8.59%(22)
Independent	23.4% (15)	25% (6)	44.4% (4)	51.5% (17)	22.2% (28)	27.3%(70)
Avusa	17.1% (11)	16.6% (4)	11.1% (1)	36.6% (12)	23% (29)	22.5%(57)
CTP	1.5% (1)	4.1% (1)	0	3% (1)	2.3% (3)	2.3%(6)
Media24	29.6% (19)	37.9% (9)	22.2% (2)	3% (1)	23% (29)	23.4%(60)
Other	18.7% (12)	12.5% (3)	22.2% (2)	3% (1)	18.2% (23)	16%(41)
Total	100% (64)	100% (24)	100% (9)	100% (33)	100% (126)	100% (256)
P-value	0.349	0.425		0.000	0.556	
Topic	**Nurse quote % (n)**	**Patient quote % (n)**	**Doctor quote % (n)**	**Union quote % (n)**	**Spokesperson quote % (n)**	**Total**
Professionalism	15.6% (10)	0	11.1% (1)	12.1% (4)	12.8% (16)	12.1%(31)
Neglect	6.2% (4)	75% (18)	22.2% (2)	3% (1)	20% (25)	19.6%(50)
Training	9.3% (6)	4.1% (1)	0	3% (1)	12% (15)	9%(23)
Strikes	29.6% (19)	8.3% (2)	0	60.6% (20)	24.8% (31)	28.2%(72)
Labour	15.6% (10)	12.5% (3)	66.6% (6)	21.2% (7)	16.8% (21)	18.4%(47)
IND	23.4% (15)	0	0	0	13.6% (17)	12.5%(32)
Total	100% (64)	100% (24)	100% (9)	100% (33)	100% (125)	100%(255) vi
P-value	0.014	0.000 iii	iv	0.000 v	0.239	

(i) Too few observations to calculate Chi-square for doctor quotes
(ii) Small cell sizes precluded Chi-square analysis for "Fortnightly" and "Monthly" categories
(iii) All topics except "neglect" were collapsed into "other" for patient quotes for Chi-square analysis
(iv) Small cell sizes precluded Chi-square analysis
(v) All topics except "strikes" were collapsed into "other" for union quotes for Chi-square analysis
(vi) One of the 11 articles excluded from thematic analysis quoted a spokesperson; the total is thus reduced by one

In terms of quotes by media characteristics, **Table 1** shows nurses were quoted more often in community[3] (40%) and weekly (51.5%) publications. The majority of total quotes appeared in the regional press (40%) which featured 70% of quotes by spokespeople. Over half of all quotes - and the majority of patient, union and spokesperson quotes - featured in the daily press.

The Western Cape press featured more nurse quotes than any other region (32%) while only 3% of KwaZulu-Natal publications quoted nurses. The Independent Newspapers group featured the majority of all quotes and more than 50% of union quotes, although most nurse (30%) and patient quotes (38%) appeared in Media24 publications. Most quotes were about strikes. Significantly, nurses were quoted most often in relation to strikes (30%; p=0.014) followed by International Nurses Day (IND). Nurse quotes featured equally in articles on professionalism and labour (15.6%), but only 6% of articles on neglect featured nurse quotes. Patients were quoted in 75% of articles on neglect, while unions were quoted most often in relation to strikes, which was significant (p=0.000).

Table 2: Nursing quotes by sex and selected media and article characteristics

Person quoted	Sex of 1st quote% (n)			Total	p-value
	M	F	U		
Nurse	9.3% (6)	64% (41)	26.5% (17)	100% (64)	0.000
Patient	8.3% (2)	87.5% (21)	4.1% (1)	100% (24)	0.000
Doctor	66.6% (6)	22.2% (2)	11.1% (1)	100% (9)	0.123
Union	57.5% (19)	27.2% (9)	15.1% (5)	100% (33)	0.010
Spokesperson	40.4% (51)	43.6% (55)	15.8% (20)	100% (126)	0.046
Topic					
Professionalism	32% (8)	60% (15)	8% (2)	100% (25)	0.000
Neglect	26.3% (10)	57.8% (22)	15.7% (6)	100% (38)	
Training	57.8% (11)	15.7% (3)	26.3% (5)	100% (19)	
Strikes	35% (14)	32.5% (13)	32.5% (13	100% (40)	
Labour	51.6% (16)	22.5% (7)	25.8% (8)	100% (31)	
IND	11.5% (3)	88.4% (23)	0	100% (26)	
Total	34.6% (62)	46.3% (83)	18.9% (34)	100% (179)	
Prominence					
Full article	29.3% (37)	54.7% (69)	15.8% (20)	100% (126)	0.002
<3 sentences	42.2% (19)	28.8% (13)	28.8% (13)	100% (45)	
<1 sentence	77.7% (7)	11.1% (1)	11.1% (1)	100% (9)	
Total	35% (63)	46.1% (83)	18.8% (34)	100% (180)	
Anonymity					
Anonymous	9.7% (4)	36.5% (15)	53.6% (22)	100% (139)	0.000
Not anonymous	42.5% (59)	48.9% (68)	8.6% 12)	100% (41)	
Total	35% (63)	46.1% (83)	18.8% (34)	100% (180)	

Legend: M=male; F=Female; U = Unknown

Table 2 illustrates that most nurse and patient quotes were female (p<0.001), while quotes by unions were male (p=0.01). Females were quoted first significantly more often in articles on professionalism (60%), neglect (58%) and IND (88%), while males were quoted more often in relation to training (58%), labour (52%) and strikes (35%) (p=0.000). Gender and prominence of articles were associated with females being quoted more often in prominent articles (55%), while men were quoted most frequently in articles of passing mention (78%) or of one sentence (42%) (p=0.002). Significantly, the sex of those quoted anonymously in more than half of articles was unknown, while over a third of anonymous quotes (37%) were female, compared to 10% of anonymous male quotes.

Discussion

Overall, nurses were quoted in about a quarter of articles on nursing. In 9% of articles, nurses were quoted extensively i.e. three or more times. Nurses were quoted more often in community papers which appeared weekly, reflecting an opportunity for them to raise their profile in regional and national newspapers. The Western-Cape featured nurse quotes in a third of all articles quoting nurses (n=21), compared to KwaZulu-Natal's 3% (n=2).

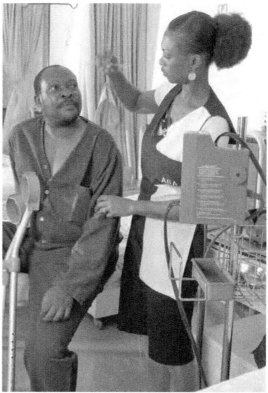

A medical practitioner treating a patient.   Photo: Trevor Davies

As found internationally, South African nurses were anonymous in more than a third of articles quoting nurses, while more than half of the quotes by doctors were anonymous. Many institutions place limitations on staff regarding media engagement, which may explain their fear to be attributed. Nurses spoke anonymously on topics dealing with labour, protest and service delivery, with several articles showing nurses as anonymous whistleblowers on failing health systems: "When courageous nurses take controversial positions to protect their patients and the public, this sends a powerful message about the value of professional nursing" (Buresh and Gordon 2006). Most nurse quotes were about strikes, mainly related to wage issues such as unpaid Occupational Specific Dispensation or increases, and in relation to poor working conditions.

Nurse voices were largely absent from articles dealing with unprofessional behaviour, signifying either that journalists had not sought their comments, or that in line with Banja's normalisation of deviance (2010), nurses preferred not to speak out about colleagues, a missed opportunity to have their voices heard to protect patients and the public. Very few articles on training featured nurse quotes.

In contrast to international literature, which finds nurses' voices drowned by the views of physicians, most of whom are male (Salvage 1985; Bridges 1990; Sieber, Powers et al. 1998; Bridge, Dickenson-Hazard et al. 1999; Schmidt 2001; Gordon 2005; Buresh and Gordon 2006), this study found that spokespeople's voices, fairly balanced between male and female, dominated in more than half of the articles. Spokespeople were quoted on nursing neglect, shortages and strike action, and remarkably, more often on IND than nurses. Doctors were quoted in only 4% (n=9) of articles.

Unlike international findings which note that male nurses are seldom quoted, this study found that proportionately, male nurses were quoted more often (9.3%) than their nursing numbers (7.6%). Women were quoted first more often on professionalism and IND, while males were quoted more often on strikes and labour. The finding that women were quoted first more often than men in relation to neglect was somewhat surprising but is likely due to the fact that most patients quoted were women. That most first quotes in relation to training were from men was also an unusual finding, but could be ascribed to articles where males were quoted in favour of females at graduation ceremonies, illustrating the media's regard of male nurses as newsworthy, and thereby conferring status on them. Women were more likely to remain anonymous than men, which could reflect their fear of reprisal or social norms which associate women with non-aggression and compliance.

Limitations

The six-month period conveys a general idea of the voice of nursing in the mainstream press, but may not be representative of the entire year. Some articles not dispatched by MSA or sourced through Meltwater may have been excluded. The choice of the term "community press" was convenient to allow differentiation from regional and national publications.

Conclusion

While the voice of nursing is not silent - over a quarter of articles featured nurse quotes - their voices are drowned by spokespeople who were quoted twice as often. Nurse voices were strident on strikes and labour issues, and were quoted anonymously in a third of articles. Nurses' voices are virtually silent on academic nursing and training. Female nurses should be cautious about "fronting" their male colleagues when engaging with the press for the associated power and status which will be conferred on them. Buresh and Gordon assert that nurses will acquire power "when they articulate the skill and knowledge embedded in their practice" (2006). Capacity development through media training will assist nurses to claim their space in the media and status in society as the backbone of healthcare delivery. The South African press has a key role to play in helping the public to understand the vital role of nurses by framing them as intelligent professionals and critical contributors to quality and equitable healthcare for all South Africans.

Writer's Bio

Van Zyl is a freelance writer and communications consultant of the niche health communications consultancy, Healthwrite. Christofides is a senior lecturer in the School of Public Health at the University of the Witwatersrand, where she heads up the Masters in Public Health Programme.

References

Banja, J. (2010). "The normalization of deviance in healthcare delivery." Business *Horizons* **53**: 139-148.

Bridge, J., N. Dickenson-Hazard, et al. (1999). The Woodhull Study on Nursing and the Media: healthcare's invisible partner.

Bridges, J. M. (1990). "Literature review on the image of the nurse and nursing in the media." *Journal of Advanced Nursing* **15**: 850-854.

Brodie, D. A., G. J. Andrews, et al. (2004). "Perceptions of nursing: confirmation, change and the student experience." *International Journal of Nursing Studies* **41**: 721-733.

Buresh, B. and S. Gordon (2006). *From Silence to Voice: what nurses know and must communicate to the public.* New York, Cornell University Press.

Evans, J. (1997). "Men in nursing: issues of gender segregation and hidden advantage." *Journal of Advanced Nursing* **26**: 226-231.

Gordon, S. (2005). *Nursing against the odds: how healthcare cost cutting, media stereotypes and medical hubris undermine nurses and patient care.* New York, Cornell University Press.

Hall, L. M., J. Angus, et al. (2003). "Media portrayal of nurses'perspectives and concerns in the SARS crisis in Toronto." *Journal of Nursing Scholarship* **35**(3): 211-216.

Kalisch, B. J. and P. A. Kalisch (1985). "Good News, Bad News, or No News: improving radio and TV coverage of nursing issues." *Nursing and Healthcare* **May 6**(5): 255-260.

Marks, S. (2001). *Divided sisterhood: Race, class and gender in the South African nursing profession* Johannesburg, Witwatersrand University Press.

Price, V., D. Tewksbury, et al. (1995). Switching trains of thought: the impact of news frames on readers' cognitive responses. *Annual conference of the Midwest Association for Public Opinion Research.* Chicago.

Salvage, J. (1985). *The Politics of Nursing.* London, Heinemann Nursing.

SANC (2011). "S A Nursing Council: Growth in the Registers." Retrieved 20 January 2011, from http://www.sanc.org.za/stats/stat2010/Distribution%202010xls.htm

Scheufele, D. A. (1999). "Framing as a Theory of Media Effects." *Journal of Communication* **Winter 1999**.

Schmidt, K. (2001). "A Sharper Image: nurses strive to garner more - and more accurate - media coverage." *Nurse Week* **December 10**.

Schramm, W. (1964). What mass communication can do and what it can help to do in national development. *Mass Media and National Development: The role of information in the developing countries in Communication for Social Change Anthology: Historical and Contemporary Readings.* A. Gumucio-Dagron and T. Tufte. South Orange, New Jersey, Communication for Social Change Consortium: 26-36.

Sieber, J. R., C. A. Powers, et al. (1998). "Missing in Action: Nurses in the media." *American Journal of Nursing* **98**(12): 55-56.

Notes

1 www.targetmedia.co.za
2 Here, "sex" categorises quotes between men and women, while "gender" is used to interpret the construct in the context of nursing quotes.
3 Free distribution publications and those sold in small towns.

The role of community media in fostering the inclusion of the rural voice in national debate
By Bruce Chooma

Abstract
This article looks at the role of community media in rural Zambia. It is noted that while for many years rural Zambians were cut off from the decision-making structures in larger centres, community media has given many rural citizens a voice for the first time. With the advent of local radio stations, rural Zambians are able to access information that allows them to hold their leaders to account.

Key words
community media, rural, community radio, print, broadcast

G one are the days when the voice on radio was so distant and detached from its audience," Mike Daka, proprietor of Breeze FM, told media trainers in Chipata, the administrative centre of Zambia's Eastern Province. "Today, one listens to a voice of a person next door and hears a story of what is happening in a street they walk on every day. That enriches the relevance of our work to our audiences."

Even after many years of independence in Zambia, for those in rural regions, news and information was not easily available. Newspapers and television continued to be unaffordable for most people. Radio was the only hope for many because of its affordability and ease of use.

Radio remains the most widespread mass communication medium in Zambia, with community radio being the largest form of community media. Today, with many community radio stations dotted around the country, many problems associated with early broadcasting, such as language difficulties and localisation of content, have now been addressed through locally-owned and controlled media.

"Radio One was the only radio station catering for us in local language for many years, the problem was that it had to broadcast in the seven main languages and one had to master its schedule to know what time programmes in their language would be aired," said Mirriam Kaulule a resident of rural Kasama in Zambia's Northern Province.

Kaulule, a mother of four, is glad that today a new voice broadcasts in Kasama: Radio Mano. Its programmes are tailored to the lifestyles of the rural community it serves with local language programmes and an opportunity for the community to contribute through various feedback mechanisms.

"Our radio station is very good because a lot of issues in our communities are covered and sometimes the people working there come into the villages to record us and they ask us to tell them which programmes we like the most and it is always good to hear our own voices on radio," said Kaulule.

On 20 September 2011, Zambia held presidential, parliamentary and local government elections and community media once again proved very handy in providing a platform for all aspiring candidates to tell constituents what they would do if elected.

In general, community media draws its existence from widespread realisation of the mainstream media's weakness at communicating localised development-focused information. There is also discontentment with how the mainstream media tackles these topics.

People in rural areas realised that programming of news and information from much further away meant they were being denied access to information about what was going on in their communities, and from hearing local voices on local concerns.

In Zambia, despite the liberalisation of the airwaves, the growth of community media was for many years not backed by clear policy.

Because of this scenario, community media has often come under attack from government when it provides a platform for opposition parties to discuss national issues. The minister of information and broadcasting services has often threatened

to close community radio stations that aired programmes perceived as anti-government. These stations have been accused of operating outside the provisions of their licenses.

This development has, however, only worked to make community radio more popular as a platform for the discussion of issues of public interest. It continues to be a battleground for politicians during election campaigns.

Journalists and community volunteers working in community media have a passion for what they do and communities not only believe in their work but also shape it.

Broadcasters have a role to play in shaping their society.
Photo: Colleen Lowe Morna

Whether broadcast or print, community media works on a relatively small scale and is modelled in such a way that it is owned by the community for coverage of the community, using participatory, democratic governance structures.

Residents of Mongu, in Zambia's Western Province, took to the streets in January 2011 to protest against the escalating poverty in their province and the failure by government to revisit the Barotse Agreement that provided for greater decentralisation of powers and access to productive resources for people in the region.

The government singled out Radio Lyambai, a local community radio station, and accused it of inciting people to riot and rise against government; the police visited the station and confiscated its studio and broadcasting equipment. Police accused the station of playing songs that encouraged locals to rise against the government. These allegations were not substantiated and the government later bowed to public pressure and returned the equipment to the station.

Radio Lyambai and Radio Liseli have been torchbearers for the people of Western Province and have been consistent in providing a platform for the community to receive education and entertainment.

In Zambia, despite some of the abovementioned challenges, community broadcasting enjoys special promotion given that it expands access to information for poor and rural communities and provides a platform for communities to discuss issues that pertain to their own development, thus enabling them to hold their leaders accountable.

Community members often contribute to local community radio stations because they believe in the value of the station and its potential to enrich their lives and their community. However, another challenge for community radio is access to resources to meet operational costs and train volunteers.

This author was one of the media trainers from the Zambia Institute of Mass Communication (ZAMCOM) that joined with experts from the University of Kentucky to design a model for training community radio volunteers using a citizen journalism approach dubbed "Zambia Community Correspondents Corps."

Colleen Lowe Morna, GL CEO, being interviewed by a Zambian journalist. *Photo: Frank Windeck*

The trainings were delivered across the country and built a cadre of volunteers and journalists that specifically tackled the issue of HIV and AIDS in the community. The community members identified individuals who served as models in their communities and they shared stories and testimonies about how they succeeded in bringing about behavioral change. The community volunteers worked with radio station producers to design interactive radio programmes with limited resources.

The model is working well, considering most radio stations rely on volunteers to produce content for talk programmes and news. This is a welcome model for community radio stations because volunteers have an opportunity to receive training in exchange for their time and effort.

The ultimate goal of community radio is to provide listeners with information and entertainment that is non-commercially supported. The realisation of such a goal takes the efforts of many dedicated people, often volunteers, who believe in the power of local radio.

The work of community radio journalists is increasingly playing a crucial role in the entrenchment of democracy in Zambia, as well as in communicating messages on health matters. The growth of community media in Zambia proves that if communities are empowered with the means to tell their own stories, and a platform to share real experiences, they reach a point where knowledge transforms into action.

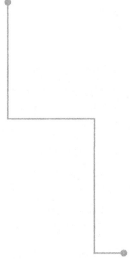

Writer's Bio

Chooma is a Zambian journalist, communication consultant and media trainer. He has written extensively in the print and online media and spent a couple of years working as an assistant HIV / AIDS and Gender Media Specialist at the Zambia Institute of Mass Communication Educational Trust (ZAMCOM).

GENDER AND (ICTs)

Making IT work for gender justice: Cyber dialogue participants in Johannesburg, South Africa.
Photo: Colleen Lowe Morna

Can ICTs enhance access and provide an alternative for women to be heard?
By Fanisa Masia

Abstract
This paper provides an overview of how women can use information and communication tools to improve their lives and provide an alternative outlet for expression. Cellphones have been identified as the most popular technological tool to help open doors for women to either access information or voice their views. ICT trends such as social networking, mobile phone services and digital story-telling have given women a platform to express themselves while also receiving information on relevant issues. However, opportunities created by ICTs also come with challenges, including access, affordability and availability.

Key words
ICTs, women, cell phones, computer technology

Introduction

Information and communication technologies (ICT) provide a great development opportunity for several reasons, especially in that they contribute to information dissemination, provide diverse communication capabilities and boost access to technology and knowledge *(Jorge, 2002)*.

The remarkable growth in the use of ICTs has shifted the way we share and access information, communicate with each other and do research. One particular ICT tool that has become tremendously popular in Africa is the mobile phone. "Access to mobile networks is now available to 90% of the world population and 80% of the population living in rural areas," noted the 2010 International Telecommunication Union Report.

Arun, Heeks and Morgan (2004) noted that considering one of the eight UN Millennium Development Goals includes gender equality and empowerment, this should be seen both as an end and means to achieving social and economic development. For this reason there is growing interest in the ways ICTs may be used to help deliver on this goal. It is therefore imperative to encourage women and girls to use ICT tools to address their needs.

ICT barriers for women

Existing gender relations in patriarchal societies continue to influence how women use ICTs. Men have long been seen as the users of technology, as well as gaming consoles, which are considered "boys' toys." These perceptions hinder women from using ICT tools effectively. Elnaggar (2007) cites factual findings related to a traditionally male-dominated ICT sector, unequal access to training, lack of internet content and training, high internet connectivity costs, and lack of awareness and policy, as some of the challenges women face in accessing ICTs.

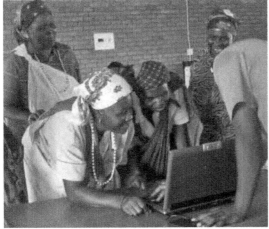

Women rarely have access to ICT facilities like computers.
Photo: Women's Net

So long as these challenges are not addressed, women will not have the opportunity to enjoy the benefits that come with ICTs. Infrastructure alone is not enough. Social, economic and technical factors continue to impact women's access to ICTs.

Among others, illiteracy is another barrier preventing access. A pilot Women's Net research project in three provinces in South Africa found that cellphone ownership among women crafters is very high but women are not able to use the tool effectively. In most cases, the cellphone was used to make and receive calls with the help of children.

In addition, Jorge (2002) outlines two key factors that challenge women's use of ICTs for economic empowerment. These are:

1. ***Affordable access and availability of infrastructure***
   - Access to telecommunications infrastructure.
   - Access to ICT.
   - Cost of access and lack of affordable solutions.
   - Lack of gender awareness in telecommunications and ICT policy.
2. ***Social, cultural and economic factors***
   - Language and content limitations.
   - Education and skills.
   - Addressing women in the informal sector.

Opportunities for women using ICTs

To a certain extent, one can argue that ICTs provide an alternative for women to be heard. Initiatives such as the use of digital storytelling have provided a tool for women to tell their stories while taking control of an ICT tool used to do it. Partnered with photo journalism, this has given women an amplified voice and platform.

The cellphone is the most relevant ICT tool for African women. The opportunities that come with access to a mobile phone means women are able

Do ICTs offer women an alternative platform to be heard?
Photo: Trevor Davies

to access and share information which helps in advocating for their rights and also in social and economic development. In a Cherie Blair Foundation study, women surveyed across low- and middle-income countries on three continents cited that mobile ownership provides distinct benefits, including improved access to education, health, business and employment opportunities, and a more secure, connected and productive life (2010).

Others have stated that ICTs increase women's participation in a variety of productive fields and give them an avenue to express their personalities and capacities (Huyer and Sikoska, 2003;

Gurumurthy, 2004; Copper and Weaver, 2003; Rainer, Loasethkul & Astone, 2003 as quoted in Elnaggar, 2007). ICTs also enable women to participate in numerous development fields, including planning and decision-making at the level of the family, institutions and society.

Source: Women's Net

Therefore, ensuring equal gender access to ICTs has become an essential core objective and integral element in many extensive research and development initiatives at the global level. As a result, more and more women have begun to utilise technology through initiatives that promote their access to, and understanding of, ICTs.

Conclusion

There are numerous opportunities for women to use ICT tools to their advantage. As Gillian Marcelle (as cited in Jorge 2002) said, the question is "how ICT can adjust to the needs of women rather than women having to adjust to the ICT sector." ICT tools need to be accessible, affordable, and available to women.

Writer's Bio
Masia works as a project officer at Women's Net.

References

Arun, S., Heeks, R. & MORGAN, S. (2004) *ICT Initiatives, Women and Work in Developing Countries: Reinforcing or Changing Gender Inequalities in South India?* Manchester: Institute for Development Policy and Management http://e-space.openrepository.com/e-space/bitstream/2173/97901/1/di_wp20.pdf site accessed on 14 September 2011

International Telecommunication Union *The world in 2010: ICT facts and figures* http://www.itu.int/ITU-D/ict/material/FactsFigures2010.pdf site accessed 14 September 2011

Cherie Blair Foundation for Women February 2010. *Women & Mobile; A Global Opportunity- A study on the mobile phone gender gap in low and middle-income countries.* http://www.cherieblairfoundation.org/uploads/pdf/women_and_mobile_a_global_opportunity.pdf site accessed 16 September 2011

Elnaggar, A. (2007) 'The status of Omani women in the ICT sector', *International Journal of Education and Development using Information and Communication Technology.* Vol. 3, Issue 3, pp. 4-15 http://www.google.co.za/#sclient=psy-ab&hl=en&source=hp&q=The+status+of+Omani+women+in+the+ICT+sector&pbx=1&oq=The+status+of+Omani+women+in+the+ICT+sector&aq=f&aqi=&aql=1&gs_sm=s&gs_upl=17697l23220l0l2404 2l3l3l0l0l0l0l1784l1784l8-1l2l0&bav=on.2,or.r_gc.r_pw.&fp=72329923ee36947c&biw=1024&bih=677 site accessed 16 September 2011

Jorge, S. N (2002) "Information and communication technologies and their impact on and use as an instrument for the advancement and empowerment of women', Expert Group Meeting on The Economics of ICT: Challenges and Practical strategies of ICT use for Women's Economic Empowerment Seoul, Republic of Korea 11 -14 November 2002

United Nations: Division for the Advancement of Women (DAW) http://www.un.org/womenwatch/daw/egm/ict2002/reports/Paper%20by%20Sonia%20Jorge.pdf site accessed 19 September 2011

Cyberqueer SA: Reflections on Internet usage by some transgender and lesbian South Africans

By Jeanne Prinsloo, Relebohile Moletsane and Nicolene McClean

Abstract

In this article we briefly describe the research undertaken that investigates certain usage of the internet in South Africa[1] (sm Kee 2011). It explored whether and how the internet can enhance access to information and provide an alternative platform for expression by focusing on two sets of voices generally excluded as a consequence of the dominant gender order, namely lesbian and transgender. It considered the nature of regulatory policy in South Africa in relation to its potential impact on the freedom of sexual expression and the ways in which transgender and lesbian people use the internet to negotiate and perform their sexuality. In this article, we briefly establish the theoretical understanding of gender that informs the research and the limitations of the regulation policy context before considering two ways in which the internet serves the project of freedom of expression and access to information; we argue that it can potentially enable virtual community formation as well as (but not necessarily) an alternative public sphere that can serve social movements.

The researchers were mindful that as few as just over 10% of South Africans had internet access in 2009 (Goldstuck 2010), but recognized many South Africans who do not use the internet at all presently will increasingly have access to this form of expression and access to information particularly as a result of mobile telephone and its significance will develop accordingly. It is important then to monitor the form of regulation of the internet, whether by the state or corporate interests.

Key words
cyber queer, sexuality, freedom of expression

Introduction

In South Africa the laws and policies regulating the media and the internet and those that pertain to sexuality are informed by the Constitution, internationally lauded for its progressive Bill of Rights. Sections refer to freedom of expression, access to information, equality and lack of discrimination on lines of gender and sexual

orientation, and privacy. In spite of a Constitution that guarantees freedom of expression, deep tensions exist between these values and those espoused by certain public figures and parliamentarians. Recent attempts by the state have included the proposed Media Appeals Tribunal, the Protection of Information Bill and the threat of withdrawal of state advertising on the basis of content unsympathetic to the government (Daniels 2011).

Similarly, censorious behaviours have been most evident when it comes to issues of sexuality. For example, Deputy Home Affairs Minister Malusi Gigaba called for a complete ban on digitally distributed pornography[2]. Additionally, Arts and Culture Minister Lulu Xingwana was so affronted by photographs of lesbian couples at an exhibition by black women artists in Johannesburg, that she walked out declaring the photographs 'immoral' and 'against nation-building'[3]. Hers is not an exceptional response, for homosexuality and other non-heteronormative positions are frequently met with intolerance and violence. Such positions are cause for concern as such individuals presume to stand in some kind of moral guardianship, deciding what counts as appropriate forms of sensual and erotic representations.

These attempts at definition of appropriate morality occur in a context of hostility. Homosexuality is constructed as a Western import and this belief is reinforced by the lack of visibility of women in same-sex relationships. The policing of lesbian women, apart from the kind of exclusionary practice cited above, has taken the form of extreme physical abuse including 'corrective rape' and murder. Matebeni argues 'fear and "forced" silence among many black lesbians has led to many remaining voiceless about their sexuality' (2009: 102/3). Life for transgender people is

similarly challenging. Muholi, lesbian activist, co-founder of Federation for the Empowerment of Women (FEW) and photographer, notes that:

As black women, lesbians and transmen, we continue to live on the margins of society, still struggling to claim our sexual citizenship, visibility and safety in the public sphere (Undated:7)

Gender framing

Within the patriarchal gender order there are two genders only and they correspond with the two sexes (Gilbert, 2009). Particular forms of masculinities and femininities are naturalised (Connell, 1987) and femininity and masculinity are viewed as dichotomous. Dominant masculinities are validated as powerful, rational, active, less communicative, and in control. Emphasised femininities are similarly validated as slight, physically weak, emotional, communicative and nurturing and passive. Moreover, the dominant gender order is heteronormative as it assumes heterosexuality as the norm. Any gender fluidity is considered deviant and therefore includes contesting gender identities whether lesbian, gay, bisexual, transgender or intersex (LGBTI). Central to this framework is Judith Butler's conceptualisation of gender performativity. Rather than being or having a gender, she proposes that we 'do' gender. 'Doing' gender does not result from singular acts, but through repeated performances and expression the gendered subject comes into being.

The idea of sex/gender performance has become central to queer theory which rejects the expectation of stability and insists on fluidity in identity discourses (Talburt, 2000). It has led to considering not only doing, but also undoing or rather redoing gender (West and Zimmerman, 2009; Connell, 2010). The transgender figure is central in these debates for transpeople reject their original gender assignment and actively seek to redo their sex/gender. The internet becomes an obvious space then for performing gendered and sexual identities, perhaps especially for those outside of the patriarchal and heteronormative frame.

Policy context

This section briefly focuses on the limitations of the media regulatory framework within which lesbian and transgender identities are/ may be constructed and performed, particularly through the internet in South Africa. The South African policy framework generally and the policies which regulate the internet, informed by their links to the principles of human rights and social justice espoused in the Constitution, should be enabling. However, our analysis suggests that these policies have tended to focus mainly on regulating what is/is not acceptable for public consumption (through censorship) in the electronic and other media, and on punishing those who commit infringements.

To illustrate, in 2008 one of the regulatory bodies, the Film and Publication Board, established a website (www.fpbprochild.org.za) to alert internet service providers of criminal activities relating to child pornograph or images of sexual abuse hosted on their services or through their infrastructure and to enable members of the public to report incidences of pornography[4]. In a related move, in 2009, the Department of Home Affairs announced that it was working with other government departments, the South African Police Service and the National Prosecuting Authority to develop a protocol on the protection of children against child pornography, with a focus on advocacy and law enforcement[5].

More recently, the popular social networking website MXit announced a zero-tolerance policy against offenders who abuse its online community. The chief executive officer of the Film and Publication Board, Yoliswa Makhasi, commended MXit, stating that "the move came at a crucial time since children would be most likely drawn into social networking platforms during and after the 2010 World Cup" (sm Kee 2011:145).

It is always difficult to define and agree on what is harmful and for/to whom, particularly in a country as diverse as South Africa. However, rather than enabling access as is intended by the Bill of Rights, the focus of these policies is on constraint for the "moral good" and their inherent heteronormativity may function to curtail any expressions of sexualities, particularly those which segments of society deem un-African, ungodly or unnatural, such as transgender and lesbian sexualities.

This article argues that in a democracy, regulating access to and content on the internet is counterproductive. In particular, the interests of sexual minorities in an arguably homophobic, sexist and racist country are not served if the few safe spaces for exploring sexual identities available to them, including virtual spaces of the internet, are regulated and their freedom of expression curtailed by censorship. Instead, a policy trajectory informed by an understanding of the internet as potentially a space that provides opportunities for expressing ideas and opinions freely and engaging in debate in ways that are not always possible in other public spaces is needed. Most importantly, as our analysis suggests, the internet should be viewed as a space where groups can meet to forge relationships and develop alternative communities, including those defined by sexual orientation and cultural politics.

Internet usage - a transgender community

Transgender people engage deliberately in reconstituting their identities and they face particular challenges that require them to disown the practices prescribed for their sex and which they have had to conform to for many years, and take on those that are socially disapproved of for their sex. To do this, they might undertake surgical and medical procedures at the physical level, but they also need to perform their gender through bodily deportment and clothing, gestures, ways of speaking and ways of being in the world. For many who are, in transgender terms, "stealth", it requires a safe space to do this. The internet can serve as a space where like-minded people meet and forge bonds, whether political, social or cultural, as virtual 'communities' (Campbell, 2007; Watson, 1998). In deciding what would constitute a community, three aspects are considered fundamental to a community by Campbell (2007:199), namely emotional investment, social interaction and open channels of communication. These aspects of community were drawn on when considering the internet use by South African transgender users.

The research focuses on the postings on a single transgender site in order to look at how transgender people, both male to female and female to male use a single site, namely *Gender DynamiX* (GDX), over a period of three and a half months (9 October 2009 to 21 January 2010). It involved a critical textual analysis of the various threads in order to look for patterns and themes, as well as subsequent interviews with a sample of members of GDX.

The GDX site has two community forums that take the sex/gender binary as their structuring device and are called Girl Talk and Boy Talk and it is these postings that were considered. Particular themes did emerge. In both Boy Talk and Girl Talk concerns with aspects of transitioning were the central concerns and included the challenges and stages of physical transitioning, social issues such as 'passing', and bureaucratic issues, particularly identity documentation. The discussions of hormonal supplementation and surgery occurred in slightly different ways across the two forums. Stages of transitioning were greeted in a celebratory way in Boy Talk (e.g. 'congrats, dude'). The language was arguably masculine, both in its brevity and the words used that are synonymous with 'man' and markers of being masculine. This ranges from ' dudes', ' guys', ' brother ', 'bra' and '*ou*', suggesting a streetwise masculinity and warmth. Other ways that masculinity was signalled related to leisure activities. While sometimes humorous, they are clearly not gender neutral but laddish, e.g. comparing belly hairs, having a 'braai'[6], playing pool, 'lur[ing] them with porn' - performances and attitudes are associated with dominant masculinity.

The transwomen also focused on physical transitioning but rather than a celebratory tone, they disclosed their anxieties around feminine physical appearance much in line with the way women tend to again in relation to the dominant gender order. Their style of communication was markedly different from those of Boy Talk. They addressed each other as 'hon', 'sweetie' and 'girl'. In contrast to Boy Talk's abrupt communications, they discuss their transitioning progress in detail, with greater self-disclosure and lengthy advice. The interviews conducted with some GDX members confirmed the sense of the value of the internet in enabling expression and identity formation. For transgender people the process of transitioning responds to a discomfort with their assigned sex.

The interviewees spoke of how transgender is generally constructed as deviant or 'freaky' in mainstream media and society with little access to information about transgender issues. For them, the internet offered access to information, to the experiences of others, and to support from an affinity group. Several respondents spoke of having reached a point of real despair and one interviewee viewed the internet as having literally saved her life at a very low point. Its value also lay in the global scope of the internet and in its transcending space and national boundaries.

Trevor Davies speaks to a group of young men.
Photo: Gender Links Library

Significantly, the research found that GDX site provides for a virtual community for transpeople in line with the three requirements of community identified above. First, there is an emotional investment in the shared issues and challenges of being transgender; second, members interact socially and with a degree of generosity; and, third, GDX enables open channels of communication where members shared experiences as well

as directed each other to information relating to transgender concerns. In this fairly safe space transpeople can perform their sexual identities and engage with an affinity group. However, their interactions relate to the personal. While arguably the personal is also political, the users were more concerned with the immediate challenges of transitioning and GDX enabled a community concerned with their personal identity formation, rather than engagement with identity politics in the public realm.

Internet usage - lesbian usage and the public sphere

If the research into transgender internet usage revealed an engaged virtual community, this was not apparent among lesbian internet users. In the first instance, the online lesbian network was more fragmented and complex with many internet sites. To understand it better we constructed a lesbian web sphere or map of the various South African sites. The different sites were further categorised as dating, lifestyle or political sites and our observations showed that the internet usage was very different from that of GDX, at least during the research period.

The dating sites are confined to relationship issues for individuals, rather than invoking a community. They do offer a space for the users to enact their sexual identity, to potentially come out and develop a personal lesbian social network. These sites are significant for many lesbians as a virtual space, especially if they find it necessary to be secretive about their sexual orientation.

Lifestyle sites are hybrid sites with strands of dating and politics, often in the form of soft news stories about gay celebrities. They are the products of niche marketing with a strong consumerist impulse.

Like the dating sites, they do not meet the community criterion of open channels of communication as the interaction is limited to comments on postings rather than initiating discussions. Certainly they have value for lesbian users' sense of an affinity group and access to related ideas and news.

Political sites would be those with postings relating to lesbian rights and struggles. It was here that we as researchers anticipated encountering a greater sense of community interaction. However, during the research period, there was little evidence of engagement. Some sites (e.g. *Behind the Mask*) had been hit by spammers and members had migrated to other platforms such as Facebook. The *Federation for the Empowerment of Women* (FEW) site played a valuable authoritative and informative role. However, we found no sites that suggested that South African lesbians were participating in discussions around identity or issues impacting the LGBTI community. The sites did presume an emotional investment by the members of the site, but the other criteria for a virtual community of social interaction and open channels of communication were not met during the research period.

To understand this situation better, a questionnaire was used to get responses from lesbian internet users about their sense of the value of the internet for lesbians. We experienced difficulty obtaining a large number of responses and analysed 28 responses[7]. Interestingly though, the respondents identified the internet as valuable because of their marginalisation and sense of being discriminated against. They considered the internet valuable in terms of access to information and dialogue about gay issues including 'useful information on the best ways to come out to friends and family, how to deal with other people's reactions'. The internet was perceived as both personally valuable and relevant to gay and lesbian politics and activism.

Curiously, there was an emphasis on social networking that was articulated in terms of a "community". As noted, a community is premised on emotional investment, social interaction and open channels of communication are vital elements in the formation of online communities (Campbell 2007:199). The interviewees' perceptions of community flies in the face of our more sceptical account. Rather than concluding that an online lesbian community does not exist, we would argue that it was not visible during the research period. To conclude that it does not exist would be to confuse a lack of visibility at a particular moment with absence. Instead we suggest, a community, virtual or otherwise, can be latent and come into being in response to particular moments.

The internet and Protest Action across South Africa.

One such moment did occur shortly after the completion of the research and it catalysed a lesbian community into action and protest. On this occasion, the internet served as both a virtual community and a counter public to be reckoned with. Dahlberg describes the internet as 'a space of struggle, supporting both the reproduction of dominant social relations and their contestation by excluded groups' (2007: 48). Marginalised groups are able to constitute themselves not merely as a community but as a 'counter public' (Dahlberg 2007: 48) and the internet becomes central to rallying numbers and support for protests, petitions and discussions.

The issue which served as the catalyst for the lesbian community on and offline was the protest action around hate crimes against lesbian women.

These crimes often involve 'corrective rape' and murder of lesbian women[8]. Protest Action across South Africa was organized as a series of protests against hate crimes in general and the murder of Nqobile Khumalo in a township near Durban on 12 May 2011 in particular. A call for action across South Africa was posted on Facebook for the following Sunday, 15 May 2011, in line with the International Day against Homophobia and Transphobia on 17 May. The call read as follows:

We cannot stand another rape of a lesbian, or a gay, bisexual, transgender, intersex, asexual, queer or genderqueer person. We cannot have another one of our own murdered. It has to stop now (www.facebook.com/event.php?eid =215079295187417).

The internet was used to call for action in cities across South Africa including Durban, Grahamstown, Cape Town, Pretoria and Johannesburg, and for people to document the protests so that 'this moment in history is remembered'. It also encouraged the use of Twitter to record the action through the use of the particular hashtags. After these protest actions, Facebook and Twitter were used again to call a successful protest outside of Parliament in Cape Town on 15 May 2011.

In these instances the internet served to invoke a virtual lesbian community and counter public in response to particular issues that arose at that specific time. As Dahlberg proposed, the internet served to provide spaces for marginalised groups to develop counter-publics and to engage in debate and develop arguments to counter the mainstream public sphere. Additionally, as he argued, it assisted 'geographically dispersed counter-publics in finding shared points of identity'; it also supported 'online and offline counter-

public contestation of dominant discourses' (Dahlberg 2007: 56).

Security - a cautionary note

The argument presented here has been reasonably celebratory of the potential of the internet in terms of community formation and counter publics. Yet, hand in hand with the freedom and opportunities the internet offers are particular security risks. There exists the very real threat that a person can be 'outed' online without their consent on a platform such as Facebook. It is easy to assume that Facebook postings are private. Many are not necessarily aware that all content that they upload onto a platform such as Facebook belongs to that platform, including all images uploaded during the 'Protest Action across South Africa'.

A potential risk lies in the possible sale of information about users of a platform, such as Facebook, for 'state and corporate control and surveillance' (Dahlberg 2007: 52) and Facebook has allegedly sold sexuality information to advertisers (Deane 2010). In recognition of this possibility there are a range of security precautions that can be taken. A useful source exists in the online publications by Tactical Tech (www.tacticaltech.org) that addresses the security of websites and how the data which can be accessed and used against users.[9]

Conclusion

The research undertaken points to the importance of the internet in not only allowing access to information, but in its potential for the formation of communities that are marginalised whether on grounds of sexual identity and orientation or other premises, and for enabling counter publics to exist and contest dominant power relations. Regulation is however predominantly undertaken to constrain access and argued on grounds of moral rectitude. Little is done to ensure access and to nurture freedom of expression and the recent state interventions are additional reasons for concern. The comments of parliamentarians noted in the introduction that run counter to the values enshrined in the Constitution and flagged in Article 19 of the Universal Declaration of Human Rights (UDHR) must ring warning bells about the conservative attitudes of people in positions of power. Rather than increasing censorship to

address some of the concerns around children concerted media education programmes as protective strategies would provide a proactive rather than a reactive strategy. As the rights we have need to be fiercely guarded and legislation actively monitored, it remains vital for a concerned citizenry to engage in policy processes to ensure their survival.

Writer's Bio

Nicolene McLean is the Head of Print and Mobile at the New loveLife Trust, and editor of UNCUT, loveLife's youth publication. She holds a Master's Degree from Rhodes University. Her areas of interest are: gender, sexuality, identity, media for social change, social media and youth development.

Relebohile Moletsane is Professor and JL Dube Chair in Rural Education in the Faculty of Education, the University of KwaZulu-Natal. Her teaching and research experience is in the areas of curriculum studies, teacher education and professional development, rural education and development, gender and education, including gender-based violence and its links to HIV and AIDS and AIDS-related stigma, body politics, as well as on girlhood studies in Southern African contexts.

Professor Jeanne Prinsloo teaches Media and Texts at Honours and Masters level at Rhodes University and University of Kwazulu Natal. Jeanne Prinsloo's current research focus relates to children's media, and news coverage surrounding Jacob Zuma.

References

Campbell, J. E. (2007) 'Virtual citizens or dream consumers: looking for civic community on Gay.com', *Queer online. Media technology and sexuality* in O'Riordan, K. and D. J. Phillips(eds), *Queer online. Media technology and sexuality*,New York: Peter Lang.

Comins, L. (2010) "Offenders Beware, MXit Warns" *IOLnews* 30 March 2010 www.iol.co.za/news/south-africa/offenders-beware-mxit-warns-1.477967

Connell, R. (1987) *Gender and power*, Cambridge: Polity Press.

Dahlberg, L. (2007) 'The internet, deliberative democracy, an power: radicalizing the public sphere', *International journal of media and cultural politics* 3(1): 47-64.

Deane, A. (2010) 'Facebook sells sexuality information to advertisers.' Big brother watch Retrieved 25 08 2011, 2011, from http://www.bigbrotherwatch.org.uk/home/2010/10/facebook-sells-sexuality-information-to-advertisers.html.

Gilbert, M. A. (2009) 'Defeating bigenderism: changing gender assumptions in the twenty first century', Hypatia 24(3): 93-112.

Goldstuck, A. (2010) *Internet access In South Africa 2010*, Johannesburg: World Wide Worx.

Matebeni, Z. (2009) 'Young black lesbians' reflections on sex and responses to safe(r) sex', in V. Reddy, T. Sandfort and L. Rispel (eds.) *From social silence to social science: same-sex sexuality, HIV & AIDS and gender in South Africa*, Pretoria: HSRC Press.

Muholi, Z. 'Mapping our histories: a visual history of black lesbians in post-apartheid South Africa.' Retrieved 15 May 2010, 2010, from http://www.zanelemuholi.com/ZM%20moh_final_230609.pdf.

sm Kee, J. (ed.) (2011) *EROTICS: Sex, rights and the internet. An exploratory research study*. Association of Progressive Communications (APC). http://www.apc.org/en/system/files/EROTICS.pdf

Talburt, S. (ed.) (2000) *Thinking Queer: sexuality, culture and education*, New York: Peter Lang.

West, C. and D. H. Zimmerman (1987) 'Doing gender.' *Gender & society* 1(2): 125-151.

Notes

[1] EROticS refers to research into the internet and sexuality undertaken by the Association of Progressive Communication in five different countries (smKee (ed.) 2011).

[2] 'Internet porn ban in SA on the cards?' http://mybroadband.co.za/news/internet/12711-Internet-porn-ban-the-cards.html, 28 May, 2010.

[3] 'Lulu Xingwana describes lesbian photos as immoral' http://www.mg.co.za/article/2010-03-03-lulu-xingwana-describes-lesbian-photos-as-immoral, Mar 03 2010.

[4] Lyse Comins "Offenders Beware, MXit Warns" IOLnews 30 March 2010 www.iol.co.za/news/south-africa/offenders-beware-mxit-warns-1.477967

[5] Ibid.

[6] A 'braai' is the South African word, originally Afrikaans, for a barbecue.

[7] The EROticS report (smKee 2011) describes the research process in greater detail.

[8] The frequency of hate crimes has increased and according to the Luleki Sizwe website 'more than 10 lesbians a week are raped or gang raped in Cape Town alone' (www.lulekisizwe.com).

[9] Security in-a-box: tools and tactics for your digital security addresses the security of a website. For instance Gmail) has the following address: https://gmail.com. The 's' after 'http' signals that the connection is secure. However, Facebook has the following address: http://facebook.com. The 's' missing after 'http' indicates that the connection is not secure and means someone could find a way to access the data on that site.

Blogging: My journey to expression
By Fungai Machirori

When I began blogging on a hot and slow October day back in 2009, I could scarcely have imagined what a story I would have to tell about my journey just two short years later. Fungai Neni, which translates in English to mean "Think With Me" is a virtual space that would equate, in the physical, to my dragging a big wooden platform to the centre of Harare's Africa Unity Square, standing on top of that block and sharing my thoughts through a powerful megaphone. It is my voice. And people are listening to it!

There were various motivations for why I started the blog, but a few stand out more prominently. One is that oftentimes, the newspapers that I contributed articles to censored so much of my language that a lot of what I was saying and meant to say was lost in shrouds of conservatism and political correctness. So, in writing about male circumcision, all references to the word "penis" were changed to terms like "the male member." "Sex" was omitted from many pieces, even if it was being discussed as one of the main modes of HIV transmission and ah yes, the worst word of them all - that scandalous "vagina"- had the editors cringing to the point that they almost always spiked any of my articles that mentioned the word.

My journalism is political - isn't all journalism? But I must quickly dismiss any ideas that I am a political reporter in that "accompanying ministers on official state visits" or "unearthing potentially divisive political party grime" kind of way. The personal is political, so goes the saying. And this is the politics that I discuss: the politics of body, spirit, mind, society, culture and gender. So while I might never have intelligence officials hounding me about my writings, or face the same sort of struggles that many Zimbabwean journalists face in gaining access to heavily guarded public information and officials, I have faced the challenge of constant censorship of my work because of its intimate nature and brutal forthrightness.

It is true, Zimbabwe is a conservative country - a country where discussing the things that matter most is often cast in a scandalous light to the point where silence is often the safest option. Talk about sex work and you must be a sex worker; write about abortion and you must have had one yourself; say something about homosexuality and yes, you must be a lesbian too. It is this linear train of thinking that a fair portion of society holds around taboo issues, which is why they never get the fair hearing they deserve in the local media, or in many other arenas beyond Zimbabwe for that matter. Sadly, it is also why a great number of journalists refuse to report on some important but taboo beats.

And that's why blogging has been a godsend for me. When I blog, no one can censor my thoughts. I can say what needs saying and say it loud! And what I am finding is that more people are willing to take the arguments that I make than leave them, even if they do have different opinions - this is what makes for critical awareness-building within society, after all.

With almost 50 000 page visits in the last 22 months - an average of more than 2000 visits per month - it's safe to assume that people out there are doing exactly as my blog implores: they are thinking with me! No, not idly accepting what I think or say; but rather, engaging with the range of debates and bringing in their own perspectives. Below are just two examples.

Giving the vagina a voice
Posted: October 2010
Views: 5 363
Comments: 46

With the pointed opening sentence, "What does a 'normal' vagina look like?", this piece prompts discussion around how comfortable women are with exploring their own bodies amid the cultural disapproval of this. It also raises issues around body image and women's constant pursuit of the "ideal," which can lead women to extreme measures such as vaginoplasty (plastic surgery carried out on the vagina).

Some of the more interesting comments:

Funny that you should mention it, I for one, clearly wouldn't be able to spot my vagina were it put in a line up; I find it rather embarrassing to engage in the awkward acrobatics just to get a sight of it... sadly because society taught to feel this way. Regardless of my thoughts, however, despite this fact I am so proud of my vagina because it's mine, whatever shape, size or colour... it's mine and I love it! It is sad that once again women find themselves having to alter the way they are in order to fit in with in a society dominated by patriarchal mindsets, attitudes and beliefs. Women need to know that we are enough, adequate as we are, hate it or love it, take it or leave it!

Women have always looked at their vaginas relative to what men think and feel hence there has not been need to intimately know it. As long as the man is happy then the woman is happy. Fungai you have adequately challenged women to look at their vaginas in a different way and to accept them as part of who they are; the uniqueness and diversity that makes the world go round.

Condoms in our schools
Posted: July 2011
Views: 662
Comments: 11

Following on from news that Zimbabwe's National AIDS Council was considering introducing a programme that would see condoms distributed within high schools, I wrote this article as a prompt to get people discussing whether or not Zimbabwe was ready for such a policy move. I argued for the introduction of condoms to teenagers and stated that it was high time that sexual and reproductive health and rights (SRHR) policy became more responsive to the plight of young girls and women, many of whom either drop out of high school or college because of unwanted pregnancy, or resort to unsafe abortions.

Some of the most interesting comments included the following:

Well, this is indeed a hot topic and I think it would be interesting to take note of how things have changed over the years including how we view sex, sexuality, relationships, etc. As a parent myself, I think the idea of giving condoms in schools is noble but only after rigorous educational conditioning on the other issues... condoms are not what makes people want to have sex, people have sex because they want to or are forced to (in this case its rape) and at the end of the day I feel that yes, there should be education on the proper use of condoms because even now I have friends who really do not know that for condoms to be effective you need correct and consistent usage and if you're gonna go rough, you need to change it after every turn/style. Of course, I am digressing but at the end of the day this debate was the same as the one about condoms being given out in church etc. I think as Zimbabweans and as Africans, its high time we stop the "righteous than thou" mentality where we hold on to pseudo-beliefs and values that add to the spread of HIV and AIDS... as HIV mutates, we need our interventions to also mutate to meet the new challenges it poses to our nation... one of those is to say, yes let's try this and see if it does not decrease the teenage pregnancies and new HIV infections among the youth.

I strongly disagree! I've tried to see your point of view but as far as I'm concerned condoms have never been a solution! Look at South Africa; they have all these freedoms including abortion and condoms in schools for teenagers but the HIV infection rate is still high, teenage pregnancy is worse there than in Zimbabwe! Clearly condoms aren't helping. Sometimes these human rights people want to foist rights upon us that will only

harm our society and legalise immorality all in the name of AIDS activism. I strongly oppose condoms in our schools. I went through high school and survived without a condom. The younger generation should. If they can't they need to go pick their self-control from wherever they left it and put it to use. AIDS is not controlled by condoms and safe sex but by abstinence and faithfulness.

Freedom of expression through ICTs. *Photo: Trevor Davies*

Upholding the right to access to information goes hand in hand with respecting freedom of expression. Why, I wonder, can Zimbabwe's mainstream media not understand the great importance of discussing issues just as they are? Frank talk needs to get out there more, because ultimately, beyond whatever beliefs we may hold morally or religiously, the facts remain - people continue to suffer unnecessarily for lack of access to diverse information on issues that affect their lives. A blog can only reach so many people, and furthermore, it can only reach those with access to the internet (which remains a minority in Zimbabwe and much of Southern Africa). This is why it's high time media practitioners and owners stop playing the safe game and dare to reflect the many faces of society.

In so doing, we might all finally get the chance to have our stories heard.

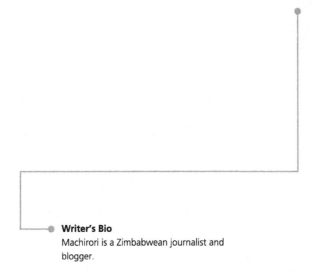

Writer's Bio
Machirori is a Zimbabwean journalist and blogger.

What about tweeting for gender justice?
By Saeanna Chingamuka

There was recently a revolution in Tunisia. Some sources say the revolution was not televised, but rather twitterised. On 14 January 2011, Tunisian President Zine El Abidine Ben Ali dissolved his government, called for legislative elections in six months and promised not to run in 2014. But this late decision did not quiet public anger on social media platforms, in particular Facebook and Twitter. Later that evening, the president fled Tunis.

Over the past months we've seen the power of social media as it helped facilitate the organisation of protests so Egyptians, Yemenis, Serbians, Algerians and others could take to the streets in their numbers and demand political change.

Closer to home, in September 2010, there was unrest and deadly riots in Mozambique after the release of a simple anonymous text message: "Mozambicans, prepare yourself to enjoy the great day of the strike. Let's protest the increase in energy, water, mini-bus taxi and bread prices. Send to other Mozambicans."

The power of new technology should not be underestimated.The Mail and Guardian's Chris Roper recently said the internet will be Africa's next battleground.

"The true worth of social media lies not in its ability to make time pass in a blur, but in its disruptive potential politically," he noted. "All over the world, social media practitioners are using the power of the internet to fight despots, dictators, corrupt politicians, evil regimes and cellphone companies."

So why don't we add patriarchal structures, violence against women and gender disparity to that list?

Social media is on the verge of taking over in the absence of traditional media, especially in African countries where governments have created repressive media laws, and where the imprisonment of journalists is the order of the day.

It is important to note that 2011 marked the 20th anniversary of the Windhoek Declaration, a statement for press freedom principles signed by African journalists at a UNESCO seminar in Windhoek in 1991. Considering press freedom has yet to be realised in many African countries, citizens are turning to cell phones and social media to protest societal injustices. These tools become an instrument of empowerment which can also motivate marginalised citizens and communities to voice their concerns.

In 2010 I attended the World Journalism Educators Congress (WJEC) in Grahamstown, South Africa. I remember my surprise when a young man walked up to me, introduced himself and said he was working for a Grahamstown youth newspaper called Upstart. He requested an interview and I remember thinking he didn't look like a journalist. He wasn't even carrying a notebook - and what is a journalist without a notebook?

But he then removed an ordinary cell phone from his pocket and began to ask me questions. Just as I was trying to figure out what was happening, he clicked a key on his phone and said "we start." He was recording me on his phone. In a minute and a half we were done and seconds later the clip was posted to his website.

As I recalled this incident, I realised how empowering it was for me to be interviewed at this conference, attended by more than 700 participants.

In 2010 Gender Links released the Gender and Media Progress Study (GMPS), which found that women sources constitute just 19% of the total number of sources in Southern African media, a very slight increase from 17% in 2003.

But although women's voices only increased two percentage points in seven years, maybe things are only changing now. If my voice could be heard at this conference, in a non-traditional format, it was a score for women.

And social media in Africa is on the rise. Writing in Africa Renewal magazine last year, André-Michel Essoungou found that Facebook has seen incredible growth on the continent, with more than 17 million users, an increase of seven million from 2009.

"More than 15% of people online in Africa are currently using the platform, compared to 11% in Asia," he wrote. "Two other social networking websites, Twitter and YouTube, rank among the most visited websites in most African countries."

Just as social media is reshaping politics in Africa and beyond, it holds the same potential to challenge gender inequalities in society. From preventing violence against women to profiling the successes of ordinary women, cell phones and social media can enhance women's empowerment in Africa's communities. Maybe rather than using cell phones for "sexting," we should begin to cultivate a culture of employing technology for social change. What about cell phone messages or "tweets" that castigate rape and sexual harassment in educational institutions? Or why don't we use technology to hold leaders accountable when it comes to changing the lives of women for the better?

The lesson here is that technology can be controlled by us, the users, and women can produce their own content to assist in the fight for gender equality. How we choose to use this technology and the social media tools available to challenge patriarchy and unequal power relations will definitely be something to watch in the months ahead.

Using social media to empower women: a case study from Southern Africa
By Danny Glenwright

Abstract
This paper describes the political and societal impact of social media on Southern Africa, discussing the increase of social media technologies in the region as a tool for development. Further, it presents the case study of Gender Links, a regional organisation working in the media, and its history of social media, from online dialogues to the incorporation of Facebook and Twitter into its work.

Key words
cyber dialogues, gender, women's empowerment

Introduction

In the middle of the 2010 16 Days of Activism Campaign to end gender-based violence, Gender Links hosted a discussion around sexuality and gender-based violence. The session was held on World AIDS Day in Johannesburg and brought together HIV and AIDS activists who were attending a World AIDS Day event. The session began with a discussion around the link between sexual orientation and gender-based violence, and was moderated by Jennifer Elle Lewis, the then Gender and Media Diversity Centre Manager at Gender Links. The panel consisted of the author of this report, Danny Glenwright, on behalf of Gender Links, and Fikile Vilakazi, Programme Director at the Coalition of African Lesbians.

Lewis hosted a robust discussion around several pertinent issues, including the recent outing of scores of gay men and women in Uganda by a Kampala newspaper. The publication, *The Rolling Stone*, had called for all 100 of Uganda's "Top homos" to be hunted down and hanged.[1] I argued that African media is often responsible for stirring up hatred and encouraging witch hunts against gays and lesbians, noting several regional examples where such hate-mongering had been on display. I then asked the question of the audience, which was made up of about 50 activists (mostly women with a handful of men), whether they knew anyone who was gay or lesbian. Most responded that they did. There followed an active discussion

on some of the key issues, although it was mostly myself, Vilakazi, Lewis, along with one or two of the participants, who took part - the rest remained silent yet attentive.

At one point in the discussion I felt safe enough to disclose my sexuality and come out as gay, revealing that I am also happily married. Several members of the group applauded and there was an overall positive atmosphere. There was a sense that some of the participants may have had a "eureka" moment, internalising our arguments against homophobia and changing their opinions about homosexuality.

The group discussion was followed by a Gender Links cyber dialogue[2]. This paper will discuss cyber dialogues in greater detail below. The dialogue is an online chat bringing together participants from across southern Africa and the world to touch base and anonymously discuss hot-button issues in the region. Gender Links hosts a cyber dialogue for every day of the 16 Days Campaign[3] and on this particular day the topic of the dialogue was also around sexuality and gender-based violence. The participants in the talk were able to turn their chairs, find a laptop in the same room, log in

Discussing hot-button issues through cyber dialogues.
Photo: Zotonantenaina Razanadratefa

under a username of their choice, and take part in an anonymous moderated discussion on the same issues we'd been discussing as a group, face-to-face.

Surprisingly, once everyone was unidentified, the discussion became much more interesting and the variety of views (and homophobic opinions) which had been absent in the verbal group discussion were on full display on the computer screens. The group was also joined online by participants from elsewhere in the region, including Tanzania, Namibia and Mauritius. Where the verbal discussion had been dominated by one or two voices and views, the online discussion came alive and percolated into a very real debate on the issues. Where participants had tiptoed around potentially embarrassing or controversial subjects in the face-to-face group, there were no holds barred in the online chat, which featured heated debates on everything from anal sex to the bible to paedophilia. Although the cyber dialogue revealed much more homophobia than the verbal discussion had, it also opened a space for some of the substantive issues to be addressed and discussed, honestly and without hesitation or fear. It was an organic, meaningful and sincere dialogue about the issue of sexual orientation that brought in all participants, compared to the verbal discussion where the opinions of one or two were dominant.

This anecdote suggests the power of social media as a tool for dialogue, discussion, change and possibly much more.

Cyber dialogues

Gender Links' first foray into social media came with its successful cyber dialogues, which were first spearheaded in 2004 during the 16 Days of

Activism Campaign. Since then, the dialogues have grown to become a major part of Gender Links' work in the region, both during 16 Days and also at other times of the year. The cyber dialogues seek to maximise the exchange of information, bringing together politicians and decision-makers with average citizens, all online. The dialogues involve facilitated, interactive online chatting with central hubs at national level where experts can answer questions from users throughout the region. The model also involves a bulletin board, where users can post questions and messages and daily exchanges, sometimes using video links. Through the cyber dialogues, citizens throughout the SADC region have been able to learn how to use online chatting to discuss issues from gender-based violence to polygamy, religion, homosexuality and politics. A 2004 Gender Links report notes the rationale for the dialogues:

The idea behind the cyber dialogues is to harness an increasingly important mode of communication that is relatively cheap and has tremendous reach in the campaign against gender violence. Such a campaign, if well planned and accompanied by the necessary capacity building strategies has the potential to:
- Empower citizens, and especially women, in the use of new technologies.
- Encourage all citizens to air their views and speak out against violence and abuse.
- Claim the freedom that can be found in cyber-space and demand that the same apply at home.
- Serve as an accountability forum, by providing direct access by citizens to decision-makers.
- Link people across provinces and across borders in a common cause and in sharing ideas about what works in the fight against gender violence (p.1).

Gender Links has been using cyber dialogues as a tool for empowerment and discussion since they were first launched in 2004. Each year they have become more successful and widespread, reaching more citizens in more remote parts of Southern Africa. For this study I conducted phone and online interviews with several gender campaigners throughout the SADC region. Each woman interviewed has taken part in Gender Links cyber dialogues as a facilitator, some over several years. The interviews shed some light on the impact of using cyber dialogues and social media as a tool to empower women:

Loga Virahsawmy (Mauritius): Women in general feel empowered when they can connect, contact and contribute with women of the region. Some of them went on the internet for the first time in their lives and have never seen a keyboard before. Through cyber dialogues they have been able to share quite a lot of their personal experiences and learn a lot of what is happening in the region. The cyber dialogues encouraged them to have their own email address.

Perpetual Sichikwenkwe (Zambia): Cyber dialogues have empowered more than 100 women in Zambia since I got involved. The women have been empowered in many ways such as being able to use internet to express themselves on issues that affect them. The women are also educated on several topics that they did not understand. For example, there are times after discussions on a certain topic that women have opened up to say that before the discussion they did not understand that their rights were being abused... Furthermore, some women before the cyber dialogues have no courage to speak out on their experiences with other people but after they are even able to speak to the media. Most women that have participated in the cyber dialogues always look forward to another opportunity as they find it very educative... they also get to share information they gain with other people in their communities. The women also begin to understand that they have the right to take their leaders to task or make them accountable on issues that affect them.

Ntombentsha Mbadlanyana (South Africa):
The cyber dialogues have empowered women in my country because it has given them the opportunity to network with other people from around the globe, exchanging ideas. Women feel that the cyber dialogues have also given them the opportunity to voice their thoughts freely, and to also have a space where they are not judged for expressing their own feelings, thoughts and fear relating to a variety of topics.

It is important to note the many positive benefits mentioned by Sichikwenkwe, Mbadlanyana and Virahsawmy. Not only have the cyber dialogues opened Southern African women to the internet and new technologies, but these facilitators note it has allowed women to better understand their basic human rights and to share this knowledge with others in their community. Through the cyber dialogues and women's ability to connect across borders and countries on the internet, women throughout the SADC region have become empowered on issues where they have traditionally been kept in the dark. Respondents noted that some topics have been more memorable or empowering than others:

Priscilla Maposa (Zimbabwe): Topics
addressing issues of culture, religion, tradition and gender-based violence were very interesting.

Everyone, regardless of background, would contribute something since these are experiences people go through every time. People felt so much relaxed as they debated on certain practices that are bad and coming up with solutions to end those bad practices in their workplaces, homes and communities.

Cyber dialogues networking empower more women through exchange of ideas. *Photo: Mary-Jane Piang-Nee*

Abigail Jacobs-Williams (South Africa): The
one I remember most was the one I facilitated. Having people online immediately respond to issues around my field of work makes it very refreshing and real. Often you do not get that kind of feedback or questions in that kind of way. So you have to think on your toes and you really get a genuine feel as to what the challenges and victories are in other countries.

Loga Virahsawmy (Mauritius): My most
compelling cyber dialogue was when I organised a group of former sex workers to chat with the region. Their experiences were heartbreaking. They spoke of the violence they went through with clients; they started doing sex work because they had to get money so that their partners could buy drugs and they themselves became injecting drug users. They could not type and

did not understand a word of English. I translated the questions for them and got three volunteers to type what they had to say.

The interviews clarify that not only have cyber dialogues been used to empower women on their rights, but also as a platform to catapult taboo or controversial topics into the discussion. In a region where conservative, traditional attitudes still hamper development, it is important for such discussions to take place in such organic, local, accessible ways.

The cyber dialogues have grown annually, bringing key stakeholders and government figures into the discussion. During the 2005 16 Days of Activism campaign, 703 users participated in cyber dialogues, and IT training in advance of the dialogues also saw 369 people trained in 18 sites (71% were women). The dialogues that year were hosted in eight languages and in 12 countries in Southern Africa. The dialogues consisted of a co-ordinating committee of members from key regional institutions, including the Network on Violence Against Women; sub-committees made of technical, media and content experts; daily facilitators on each topic; identified satellite points throughout South Africa and the region; a central hub from which the dialogues were managed; a media centre where media was briefed on themes and outcomes; a bulletin board where members of the public could post comments or questions and a website with the chatroom where anyone could log on between 13.00 to 14.00 each day and join the cyber discussion live.

The 2005 Gender Links cyber dialogue report "How IT worked for gender justice" (2005) noted that the South African government was prompted into action after taking part in discussions around Post Exposure Prophylaxis (PEP), a course of drugs

that can be taken within 72 hours after intercourse to reduce chances of transmission of HIV - something vital for those who have been raped in a country with some of the highest numbers of rape and HIV infection in the world. The report noted: "During the cyber dialogues Esther Maluleke of the Ministry of Health said that her ministry will be conducting an audit in 2005 on the availability of Post Exposure Prophylaxis to reduce the possibility of HIV infection for the survivors of sexual assault (pg. 4)."

The report also noted several other commitments made by the government during the 2005 dialogues, including a commitment by the South African Police Services to launch an inter-sectoral training programme on domestic violence and a commitment by the Department of Justice and Constitutional Development to launch a hotline for complaints that survivors of sexual assault are experiencing with the country's court system. From around 200 participants in 2004 to several hundred participants in subsequent years, the cyber dialogues have continued to grow[4] to become one of the most successful ways of empowering southern African women in computer skills and around basic human rights.

The cyber dialogues and other social media initiatives have also increased Gender Links' web traffic. In 2003 Gender Links had a total of 210 visits to its 16 Days homepage between November 18 and December 10. This number in 2010 was 3360 - a 1500% increase.

Enter Facebook and Twitter

In July 2010 Gender Links began a process of implementing and incorporating social media platforms Facebook and Twitter into its work. Gender Links approached Creative Spark, a Cape

Town-based web, mobile and application development company, to help make the organisation more social media-friendly in order to reach a new and larger audience. One staff member commented on its use in relation to cyber dialogues during the 2010 16 Days of Activism.

Ntombentsha Mbadlanyana (South Africa):
The most compelling cyber dialogue was related to social media and technology and the fact that social media can be a useful tool, but at the same time it can also be rather harmful to women and children. The discussion centred on the Jules High School rape saga, and the fact that it exposed how social media can pose as a problem. There were young women in the cyber dialogue sharing their stories on how men preyed on them asking them for nude pictures and also shared how violated they often felt when they would enter various chat rooms. The response that came from some of the male participants was often rather very shocking: one participant even stated that

Online social media could be harmful to women and children.
Photo: Gender Links Library

young women go into these chat rooms knowingly, flirting openly with men. Yet they will turn around and cry that they have been violated and this is not the case, women know what they are exposing themselves to.

Mbadlanyana's comments underscore the need for organisations like Gender Links to continue working in, and expanding the discussion on, social media. By providing a safe platform for women and men in Southern Africa to engage on human rights issues, Gender Links has helped grow the social media space in the region, thus furthering women's empowerment as noted earlier.

Other Gender Links partners and staff were asked if women in their countries had become more empowered because of the work of Gender Links.

Perpetual Sichikwenkwe (Zambia): Yes.
Most women have been empowered in the use of internet with a step further of knowing how to use chat rooms. Some women who have never had email addresses the first time they participated in Gender Links activities now have email addresses and are able to communicate with friends and family. Some of the participants did not even know how to use a mouse the first day they participated but now they are able to do so. One example is of a marriage counsellor and community school owner who was part of the training that was offered by Gender Links. The woman had no idea how to use the computer and did not even have an email address. By the end of the training, the woman had been assisted to create an email address and was also able to use the computer to type... She is now able to type proposals on her own to seek funding for her school.

Sichikwenke was also asked about how the incorporation of social media such as Facebook and Twitter on Gender Links might help the women of Zambia:

Women in my country will benefit in that they will be able to be educated on a lot of gender issues on Facebook and be able to take part in the discussions that Gender Links posts on different issues that affect them. Since this is an election year for Zambia, women can use Facebook to hold their leaders accountable on many unfulfilled promises on women's issues and also to campaign for fellow women to be in decision making through the use of Facebook. Gender Links can play a role generating debates on such topics for the benefit of Zambian women. The good thing about Facebook is that even those people in leadership or in key decision making positions are on Facebook and they are able to respond or take note of the issues discussed. For example, if a woman joins a group on the campaign against GBV on face book, she will be able to share experiences and learn a lot of things. Women will also be empowered in that they will be able to know the kind of services that Gender Links offers through the use of Facebook.

Social media has been one of the easiest and safest ways of fighting human rights violation against women. Usually when you use the social media such as cyber dialogues, Twitter, you can freely express yourself without fearing to be known by perpetrators or any other person. Social media can be used to debate different issues that affect women such as reproductive health rights by posting to friends that would react to your comments thus educating other people. You can also use messages to campaign or air views on an issue that you think should

be shared and discussed. For example, I have read several touching stories on how women are beaten or abused by their husbands through Facebook. Friends on Facebook are able to offer solutions or advice on such issues especially to victims. This has or will continue helping a lot of women.

What these testaments show is that although Gender Links' experiments with social media have yet to yield macro results, these interventions are bringing about change on the micro level, one person at a time. As research has shown, the digital divide does exist but it is narrowing. In order for it to continue to narrow, the work of organisations like Gender Links around issues of IT and social media skills will be vital. Once Southern Africans are able to access the world of social media, much of the rest of the world is then opened to them:

Abigail Jacobs-Williams (South Africa): Social media gives people access to resources and information. Having a Facebook page on a human rights issue, following a human rights cause on Twitter and having a platform to engage and debate human rights issues through cyber dialogues makes it easy for people to get messages. Social media is a powerful tool that can push human rights agendas if used correctly. Now all you need is a cell phone or a laptop to influence people's thoughts and offer them alternatives through advocating and educating.

By incorporating social media into its work through a partnership with Creative Spark, Gender Links has been able to reach new audiences, deliver new messages while continuing to educate and empower its traditional audience. Its website hits have increased every month since the partnership was created, which means the social media is also acting as a link to the Gender Links website, bringing new people who will hopefully take away the vast amounts of information contained there.

Links to Facebook and Twitter also mean commentaries and other media outputs are being shared more widely and the comments section on the Gender Links website is more active than ever before, with ongoing discussions and fluid, organic cyber dialogues happening all the time rather than at set times. Although Gender Links still continues to intervene in traditional ways: research, publications, workshops and training, etc., it is apparent that social media is now playing an increasingly important role in publicising this work.

Conclusion

There is no longer much question around the issue of the power of social media to effect change, even if it is only the original catalyst. In March 2011 Gender Links celebrated its tenth year of existence and those same ten years have been some of the most transformational in terms of internet and social media. From NEPAD's first discussion of ICTs in 2001 up until Africa's first Twitter revolution in 2011, the transformational power of new media technologies has only grown.

This article looked at some of the ways social media is being harnessed and found that it is widely responsible for empowering women and the previously disadvantaged. From educating people about their human rights to allowing Southern Africans the ability to tap into global movements and networks, the vast potential for social media as a tool for transformation, education and empowerment in Southern Africa and beyond is clear. The case study of Gender Links has shown how social media can be used to empower women, providing them with IT skills and knowledge about pertinent issues from HIV and AIDS to gender-based violence. Finally, the example of Gender Links has also shown how the incorporation of social media can be used to grow an organisation. Through its incorporation of social media, Gender Links was able to reach new audiences, ensuring its important and educational work and research is seen by hundreds (and possibly thousands) more people than ever before. The era of social media has enveloped Southern Africa and we have only just begun to see where it may lead.

Writer's Bio
Glenwright is a Canadian journalist.

References
Gender Links Sixteen Days of Activism Summary, 2003. *Summary.* Gender Links,Johannesburg.

Gender Links Sixteen Days of Activism: The Cyber Dialogues, 2004. *How IT worked for gender justice.* Gender Links, Johannesburg.

Gender Links cyber dialogue proposal, 2004. *Making IT work for gender justice.* Gender Links, Johannesburg.

Gender Links, 2005. *IT for advocacy training.* Gender Links, Johannesburg.

Gender Links Sixteen Days of Peace Report, 2005. *Peace begins at home.* Gender Links, Johannesburg.

Gender Links Sixteen Days of Activism Report, 2007. *16 Days for life.* Gender Links, Johannesburg.

Notes

[1] The Ugandan article was originally published in early October and was widely discussed at the 2010 Gender and Media Summit, with Gender Links and partners putting out a press release to condemn the type of reporting on display in *The Rolling Stone.* That release is available from the Gender Links website: http://www.genderlinks.org.za/article/activists-condemn-ugandan-tabloids-homophobic-violence-2010-10-15

[2] This study uses the term cyber dialogue in reference to the online chat initiative spearheaded by Gender Links in 2002.

[3] For more on the Gender Links 2010 16 Days of Activism see here: http://www.genderlinks.org.za/page/16-days-of-activism-2010

[4] Cyber dialogues summaries for most years are available on the Gender Links website: http://www.genderlinks.org.za/page/gender-justice-past-campaigns

Cyber abuse and women in Southern Africa: Is there cause for caution?
By Glory Mushinge

Abstract

Information and Communication Technologies (ICTs) have no doubt created a level of dynamism in the way the world does business today. Like never before, innovators find themselves constantly on their feet in pursuit of new ways to improve the technologies of the day. As much as these trends are evidently commercially driven, it can also be agreed that they are equally intended to make life easier and more modern for consumers. However, some segments of society choose to use them selfishly, in a way that ends up hurting others. An example is cyber abuse, especially the kind tailored against women. This article is a factual opinion piece that examines the extent to which women are affected by cyber abuse and how some online resources are used to perpetuate this trend. Using examples of some cyber abuse cases to drive the point home, the article is intended to offer insights on how women in Southern Africa can identify cyber abuse and protect themselves from it. The feature endeavours to address the question: Should women in Southern Africa be concerned about cyber abuse?

Key words
cyber abuse, cyber crime, ICTs, social media, cyber stalking

The dynamic nature of internet technology

Internet technology is fast advancing and activity around it is becoming the order of the day in many parts of the world. Citizens increasingly use online resources for different aspects of their lives. For many communities, the internet has become a panacea for emotional and social issues, while some find it a means to address financial needs, such as looking for paid assignments.

Social networks are some of the most popular sites, with many people accessing sites like Facebook, Myspace, Twitter, hi5 and a host of dating sites, among others[1]. No doubt people have found love on dating sites, solutions to personal problems through discussion fora and jobs through professional networks, to name but a few positives.

But as much as many agree that the founders of these sorts of programmes had the best intentions when they set them up, these technologies have sometimes fallen in the wrong hands. We now see and hear of people using these information tools with bad intent, to destroy others or help themselves to resources they do not deserve, or have not worked for. For example, identity theft is an increasingly common problem. In his paper "The battle against identity theft," Sal Perri, an Authority Research analyst, fears that as technology continues to evolve, the stealing of a person's identity will become a more common occurrence.[2]

Recent statistics indicate that identity theft is already occurring at epidemic proportions in the United States, and many criminologists are calling it the fastest growing crime in America. It is estimated that identity theft is affecting 500 000 new victims per year at an annual cost of between $700 million and $3 billion. *(Perri 2011)*

Some of these selfish acts have even stretched to matters of the heart and women in search of love have had their money stolen by thieves masquerading as potential soulmates.

The BBC recently produced a documentary about women who had been ripped off online by people

The internet exposes women to numerous crimes.
Photo: Colleen Lowe Morna

purporting to be in search of love. In it, most of the women who fell for this trick had unquestioningly given huge sums of money to these men, some of whom were from developing countries. One or two of these men had expressed intentions of visiting the women and said they were going to return the money when they finally met. The victims of these lies realised too late that not only had their dreams of finding love turned into a mirage, but they had also been scammed.[3]

After BBC South's *Inside Out* programme featured a woman who lost £80,000 pounds in an internet dating scam, others realised they too were being scammed by fake internet partners. One victim believed she had an online relationship with an American soldier, but ended up transferring thousands of dollars to Nigeria. *(BBC, 2011)*

Invasion of privacy is another of internet problem. In some cases women have discovered personal photos have been used on sites they did not know existed. In the worst cases, women's photos have been shared on pornography sites.

Facebook, a popular social networking site.

Chris Bruno, a retired police officer and contributing author to Safety Products Depot,[4] warns women to be careful of hidden cameras which are used to take video of people without their knowledge. "It has become way too easy to snap a picture of someone without their knowledge. Many women have been horrified to find out they were the victim of a voyeurism attack when they find nude or other compromising pictures of themselves posted on the internet," writes Bruno.

Voyeurism isn't new, but the methods these individuals use are. For years all we had to do to protect our privacy was close the blinds or pull down the shades and the "Peeping Tom" was forced to look elsewhere for his cheap thrills. These days cameras come in all shapes and sizes. Both still and video cameras can be hidden in anything. Not to mention that just about every cellphone is equipped with a quality digital camera. (Bruno, 2011)

Then there are those who use websites to recruit women from poor countries under the pretext of offering them work in developed countries. They either use websites or direct email communication to entice unsuspecting ambitious girls, and once they have convinced them, force them into sex work or forced labour.[5]

The internet has created another disturbing problem around sex trafficking because the greatest demand for internet pornography is in the US. Before the age of the internet, traffickers had to travel through the US and abroad to sell and purchase sex slaves, and business was conducted in person and in the streets. However, with the increasing use of the internet as a marketplace, sex trafficking has gone further underground (Icha, 2010).

Another form of cyber abuse is bullying. It can have deadly consequences. In the developed world, some young people have committed suicide after they were bullied online.

In November 2007, The Mail Online reported the case of a 13-year-old girl who hanged herself after she was cyber bullied by her neighbour.[6] The story titled "Girl, 13, commits suicide after being cyber-bullied by neighbour posing as teenage boy," noted that Megan Meier believed she had been instant messaging with a "cute" boy she had met over the social networking site Myspace.

The story noted: "She struck up a friendship with 'Josh' and the pair exchanged dozens of messages... But what she didn't know was Josh was the fake name used by a female neighbour who lived in the same street in the town of Dardenne Praire, Missouri. When Josh told her he didn't want to be her friend and called her a 'liar and slut' she became depressed. Her father Ron found her hanging by a cord inside her wardrobe the day after her online friendship ended. Police who later examined Megan's computer found a message in which 'Josh' told her the world would be a better place without her."

One might wonder how these cases are relevant somewhere like Southern Africa when the internet culture is still nascent here. Yet in a region which faces issues around access to ICTs, the digital gap often means women in Africa are placed at an even higher risk of cyber abuse.[7] One who is exposed to the internet, especially when surrounded by other users, can never be too careful about falling prey to such abuse.

Take the scenario of women who travel to meet in person men they have met online. In some cases women travel to other countries only to discover the man they thought was their soulmate is abusive. Situations like this continue despite legal protections and court cases. A recent example is a case in which a man admitted to stalking his girlfriend online.

In a story published by *The Guardian* "Man admits to elaborate stalking campaign against girlfriend"[8] the man in question harassed his girlfriend for three years before he was caught. His abuse caused his girlfriend to become "withdrawn and depressed." The man impersonated his girlfriend online and sent naked photos of her to her friends and family. She eventually became frightened to leave the house.

As internet usage grows and spreads around the world, cyber abuse knows no boundaries. Therefore women need to be cyber smart and protect themselves.

Women can do this in several ways:

• ***Protecting images and being alert:*** When dealing with invasion of privacy, it is important that women think twice about what type of images or information we share. Bruno (2011) advises that it is very imperative for one to be aware of what is going on around them: this includes being alert if someone is trying to stand very close, especially if he/she moves towards you when you move away. When in a changing room in a clothing store, look carefully at any object that appears as if it doesn't belong. Keep in mind that cameras can be hidden in common, everyday items like smoke detectors, electrical outlets, tissue boxes, etc. Take a close look at these items. When carefully examined, the camera lens does become visible. If you find a hidden camera in a location where it obviously shouldn't be, remain calm. Cover the lens if possible and notify the police immediately.

• ***Research:*** There are many ways women can get information about a person or organisation online before deciding whether to trust them. For example, if a job offer is received via email, ask for a physical address and verify if it is genuine. If the job is not in your country, try calling the embassy of the country it is in and ask for information about the company. Women can also contact their embassy in that country for further information. When entering into a personal relationship, ask potential mates for their social media information in order to assess them better.

Facebook rapist.   *Daily Sun newspaper*

- **Report the perpetrator:** In cases where women are bullied, they should kindly tell the perpetrator to stop. If he/she does not stop, it is advisable to report them. Other solutions include de-activating your online account or changing your online identity. Be wary of friendship invitations you are not sure about.
- **Get help online:** Look for other ways of getting help online. There are people and online experts who are able to offer free advice and insight.

Online help can be found through such organisations as WiredSafety,[9] which describes itself as "The world's first internet safety and help group." The organisation consists of thousands of volunteers working together online, including people of all ages and walks of life. VAOnline[10] is another resource that can provide support and relevant information about cyber abuse.

Welsh Ant Bullying Network screenshot.

Its website states:

This organisation has four goals:
(1) To unite police officers worldwide and educate them on cybercrime, cyberlaw, investigative techniques and how they interact.
(2) To provide investigative assistance to police departments when requested.
(3) To provide online help and education for victims of cyber stalking, cyber harassment, paedo-philes, hacking, and virus attacks as well as access to support groups and online coun-selling.
(4) To standardise relations and communications between police departments, Internet Service Providers, legal system contacts and victim advocacy groups worldwide.

The Anti-Bullying Network also has further infor-mation for professionals working with young people against cyber abuse. It provides advice about how professionals should conduct them-selves when working with young people.

Regardless of the issue, it is wise never to take anything online at face value. If it sounds dodgy, it likely is. Cyber abuse should not be taken lightly as it has dire consequences.

References
BBC News (2011) Victims of web dating scams lose thousands of pounds [Accessed online on 28th September 2011] at: http://www.bbc.co.uk/news/uk-12442415

Bruno C. (2011) Protecting yourself from hidden cameras. [Accessed online on 28th September 2011] at: http://ezinearticles.com/?Protecting-Yourself-From-Hidden-Cameras&id=6465060

Fewster S (2010) .'Smearing Internet' Cop Darren James Clohesy does deal. [Accessed online on 28th September 2011] at :http://www.adelaidenow.com.au/smearing-internet-cop-darren-james-clohesy-does-deal/story-e6frea6u-1225900045218

Writer's Bio
Mushinge is a Zambian freelance journalist currently based in the UK.

Icha (2010) Sex trafficking and prostituttion:Craigslist: Gateway to Internet Sex Trafficking [Accessed online on 28th September 2011] at : http://stanford.edu/group/womenscourage/cgi-bin/blogs/sextraffickingandprostitution/2010/05/06/craigslist-gateway-to-internet-sex-trafficking/

Mail Online (2007) Girl 13 commits suicide after being cyber bullied by neighbour posing as teenage boy. [Accessed online on 28th September 2011] at: http://www.dailymail.co.uk/news/article-494809/Girl-13-commits-suicide-cyber-bullied-neighbour-posing-teenage-boy.html

Moran K (2009). Information Ignorance and the Digital Divide. [Accessed online on 28th September 2011] at: http://airdalebarks.blogspot.com/2009/07/information-ignorance-and-digital.htmlreview.toptenreviews.com/

Perri S (2011) The battle against Identity Theft. [Accessed online on 28th September 2011] at: Battlehttp://www.icjia.state.il.us/public/pdf/identitytheft.pdf (Social networking website review (2011): Why Social Network? [Accessed online on 28th September 2011] at: http://social-networking-websites-

The Guardian (2011). Man admits to elaborate online stalking campaign against girlfriend. [Accessed online on 28th September 2011] at : http://www.guardian.co.uk/uk/2011/sep/21/man-online-stalking-girlfriend-nottingham

Notes

1   Social networking website review 2011: Why Social Network? http://social-networking-websites-review.toptenreviews.com/
2   http://www.icjia.state.il.us/public/pdf/identitytheft.pdf
3   http://www.bbc.co.uk/news/uk-12442415
4   http://EzineArticles.com/6465060
    http://stanford.edu/group/womenscourage/cgibin/blogs/sextraffickingandprostitution/2010/05/06/craigslist-gateway-to-internet-sex-trafficking
5   http://www.dailymail.co.uk/news/article-494809/Girl-13-commits-suicide-cyber-bullied-neighbour-posing-teenage-boy.html
6   http://airdalebarks.blogspot.com/2009/07/information-ignorance-and-digital.html
7   http://www.guardian.co.uk/uk/2011/sep/21/man-online-stalking-girlfriend-nottingham,
8   http://www.wiredsafety.org/
9   http://www.vaonline.org/internet_reporting.html

An analysis of gender differentiation in Zimbabwe's ICT legislation
By Angela Shoko

Abstract
Although Zimbabwe currently has five pieces of legislation governing the information and communication technology arena, this article confines itself to an analysis of two related documents: Zimbabwe's Draft Information Communication Technology (ICT) Bill and the Strategic Plan 2010-2014 for the Ministry of Information Communication Technology (MICT). (Ministry of Information Communication Technology 2008; 2010). This article looks at the gaps in the draft ICT bill, especially in connection to gender equality and women's empowerment in this sector.

Key words
Information Communication Technology, gender, technology, legislation

Zimbabwe's Draft Information Communication Technology (ICT) Bill was officially launched in 2008 but is still in draft format, despite steps taken in June 2009 to bring it before cabinet. The decision to compile a separate ICT bill despite the existence of existing legislation is a recognition of the fragmentation of the Ministry of Information Communication Technology's (MICT) Strategic Plan 2010-2014. These laws are sector-specific and also certain aspects of ICT are not addressed in any of them. The strategic plan and, particularly, the draft ICT bill, acknowledge the convergence of technologies and attempt to bring Zimbabwe's ICT laws under one umbrella.

Any assessment of the differential impact of ICTs on men and women implies an acknowledgement of gender-awareness in the formulation and the implementation of the legislation. This paper contends that Zimbabwe's ICT legislation makes a negligible attempt to integrate the effects of ICTs on different genders. The words "gender," "women," or "girls" appear a total of 14 times in these documents, with a combined 160 pages, representing some 0.02% of the content of Zimbabwe's ICT legislation. Let us analyse it in greater detail based on Hafkin and Taggart's gender concerns in ICT policy (2001).

Ownership, control and pricing

The draft bill provides for the establishment of a national authority whose mandate is the administration of every aspect of the ICT bill specifically and regulation of the ICT industry in its entirety. In listing qualifications and desirable

criteria for councillors to serve on this authority, the draft bill makes a passing reference to gender. No provision is made in terms of a quota for women councillors. Yet it would be desirable to include ICT women professionals who have been exposed to gender training in the highest echelons of the ICT decision-making body so that the gender agenda remains at the forefront of all its decisions. Clause 29 states that the authority shall establish regulations and procedures that govern the granting of licences, but lists only a few of these in clause 30. Although every licensee is required to subscribe to a social corporate investment programme, no mention is made of the specific beneficiaries of these programmes, such as the aged, women, the disabled or girls. In addition, it is silent on licensing procedures that may promote women-owned businesses or businesses with a majority of female managers.

Some differentiation is evident through clauses 34 and 60. Clause 34 empowers the authority to publish regulations for the use of radio and satellite frequency spectrum, taking socio-economic imbalances into account. Women and girls may be considered to belong to this category. Clause 60 addresses broadcasting and empowers the authority to license broadcasters of programmes that promote gender equality.

The draft ICT bill calls on licensees to submit proposals for tariffs and charges which must then be published to allow comments from the public. In the event no such comments are forthcoming, the authority will likely approve these tariffs. Save for a requirement for the licensee to disclose all costs that led to the proposed tariffs and charges, the legislation does not offer any guidelines or incentives relating to discounted tariffs for the provision of services to previously under-served areas such as rural areas and farming commu-

nities, both of which are largely populated by impoverished woman-headed households (International Fund for Agricultural Development 2010).

Access and appropriate technology

The MICT strategic plan lists the Zimbabwe government's vision for ICT as that it "... act[s] as a catalyst for national socio-economic growth thereby propelling Zimbabwe into a knowledge society with ubiquitous connectivity by 2015."

A key step in the attainment of such a laudable vision is the active participation in the ICT legislative process of stakeholders such as civil society organisations, the general public, including rural women and other disadvantaged groups, related government ministries and regulatory bodies, relevant sectoral and special interest non-government organisations (NGOs), private sector players, academia and multi-sectoral professional bodies. There is scant evidence of an inclusive approach in the formulation of this legislation. During the 2009 validation workshop on the draft ICT bill, which was attended by the writer, most of these groups were absent. In addition, a report

Women need to be trained to fully utilise ICTs.

Photo: Gender Links Library

subsequently published by EKOWISA, the NGO which sponsored this workshop, recommends steps that must be taken in order to render the ICT bill process transparent and inclusive, to ensure access to the process by every citizen and other interested parties (Zunguze 2009).

Telecentres like this need to be built in rural areas as well.
Photo: Loga Virahsawmy

Clause 39 of the draft ICT bill provides for the establishment of a Universal Access Fund. It concentrates on facilitating ICT access to disabled persons. Clauses 82 and 83 exhort the MICT minister to outline an e-strategy that ensures universal access to ICTs by previously disadvantaged communities. Indeed, the ICT strategic plan explicitly lists ICT utilisation by women, girls, the aged and rural folk as one of its key result areas (KRAs) but fails to follow through on this as the documented specific objectives do not in any way address the needs of these groups (Ministry of Information Communication Technology 2010).

The ICT legislation does not address the deployment of ICT infrastructure in areas with a majority of women or ensure its accessibility by them and other marginalised groups. One research study conducted by woman professionals at the University of Zimbabwe (Mbambo-Thata, Mlambo and Mwatsiya 2009) established that student access to computer rooms, which is based on a first-come-first-served basis, showed that male students accessed the resources 87% of the time and females a mere 13%.

This study found that there were two major factors attributable to this anomaly: 1) Female students would not access the computer-rooms in the evenings due to family commitments and cultural norms that frown upon women being in public at night and 2) As ICT resources were scarce, male students used their physical superiority to prevail, for the women, understandably, shrank from the prospect of tussling with their male colleagues. Such sex disaggregated statistics on computer resource access and use reinforce the importance of gender-sensitive allocation of ICT resources and of creating women-only ICT access sites.

This legislation makes no of alternative and, usually, cheaper, technology such as solar-powered infrastructure, internet telephony (VoIP) or wireless technology. The strategic plan, however, lists one of MICT's services as the development of ICT products for the disabled, the old, women and children but does not give any details on action steps that will achieve this goal.

Diversification of technology would allow more players and greater competition in the provision of ICT services, driving down prices and tariffs and consequently allowing remote farmers, rural people, widows, single mothers and other disadvantaged users, access to ICTs. Zimbabwe's regulator, the Postal and Communications Regulatory Authority of Zimbabwe (POTRAZ), announced in early 2010 the release of part of the US$24 million from the Universal Services Fund for eight projects in the rural areas. In an article commenting on this development, an ICT consultant, Robert Ndlovu (2010) proposes the construction of telecentres in remote farming and rural areas, providing solar-powered wireless access services. Ndlovu points out that it is crucial to involve targeted communities in such projects so as to facilitate early adaptation of the technology and eventual ownership of the system. Over a year down the line, it was reported that this same project would provide only basic infrastructure such as equipment rooms and that POTRAZ was awaiting the completion of the tender process for the selection of vendors (Balancing Act 2011).

The strategic plan lists one of its objectives as the provision of a national cyber-security framework. One volunteer organisation, Working to Halt Online Abuse (WHOA), is fighting against ICT-related crimes such as cyber-stalking and reports that between the years 2000 and 2010, a total of 2226 cases of cyber-stalking against women were reported to them, representing 72% of all reported case (WHOA 2010). A separate article quotes the Association for Progressive Communications as placing the number of cyber-stalking victims at more than one million annually (Mugoni 2010). In addition, cyber-crime itself is on the rise, usually for monetary gain to the perpetrator or to spread terrorism. It is imperative that MICT's noble objective be translated into action in order to protect women and girls as well as to safeguard citizens from financial losses.

Capacity-building

The draft ICT bill recognises the need for developing human resources through clause 84 and proposes a capacity-building programme be crafted by the MICT in consultation with ministers responsible for labour, youth and education. Conspicuous by absence is the requirement to consult with the ministry responsible for gender and women's affairs.

The strategic plan explicitly cites women, girls, the aged and rural communities for training and development in ICT skills, as a KRA. The accompanying list of objectives, however, refers to road shows, exhibitions and the publication of an ICT magazine. Given that the aged and rural people may have low literacy levels and the further hindrance of being unable to travel to exhibition halls, these may not necessarily be the best communication channels for these groups. Furthermore, although the KRA declares the inclusion of languages in the capacity-building programme, none of the objectives informs the reader about the creation of training materials in local languages, materials suitable for the sight or hearing impaired or the provision of locally relevant content.

In order to effectively build capacity for girls and women in ICTs, Zimbabwe's legislation must ensure equal access to technical training programmes for girls, boys, women and men. Mechanisms are also essential to encourage girls to opt for scientific or technological careers and to support them while they undergo training. Training opportunities must also be offered to technical women professionals who are already in the field so that they keep up with current trends and also gain enough confidence to found their own ICT companies or to secure promotion into management in established ICT-related organisations. As the United Nations eloquently expressed it:

Science curricula in particular are gender-biased. Science textbooks do not relate to women's and girls' daily experience and fail to give recognition to women scientists. Girls are often deprived of basic education in mathematics and science and technical training, which provide knowledge they could apply to improve their daily lives and enhance their employment opportunities. Advanced study in science and technology prepares women to take an active role in the technological and industrial development of their countries, thus necessitating a diverse approach to vocational and technical training. Technology is rapidly changing the world and has also affected the developing countries. It is essential that women not only benefit from technology, but also participate in the process from the design to the application, monitoring and evaluation stages (UN 1995 paragraph 75).

Clause 85 of the draft bill, which provides for the capacitating of small to medium enterprises (SMEs) for e-business, is also supported by clear objectives in the strategic plan. There is a definite drive to encourage the use of ICTs in growing these SMEs both locally and beyond our borders, and also for establishing ICT-related businesses. The glaring omission is the obligation that a certain portion of the funding granted for training go to rural women farmers, woman-headed SMEs and women's clubs involved in commercial activities.

In line with the Zimbabwe government's mission to transform the country into a knowledge-based society through the systematic application and

Zimbabwe: Government's mission is to transform the country into a knowledge-based society through ICTs. *Photo: Nhlanhla Ngwenya*

innovative use of ICTs, the draft bill has several clauses that endorse the development of emerging ICT-based services and of research into diverse areas of ICT. Here, too, the ICT policy should provide for incentives, scholarships and internships for women to encourage innovation through research among women and also to increase the number and levels of responsibility of women in the ICT industry (UNCSTD 2001). This is bound to create positive woman role-models for the girl child. Topics clamouring for research and development include technologies for the illiterate or semi-literate, tools and software in local languages and technologies for the handicapped. The language component must not be relegated as the International Telecommunication Union reports that 80% of content on the internet is in English, yet rural women, women farmers and other disadvantaged groups may not be that proficient in this language (ITU Task Force on Gender Issues 2001). The MICT decided to lead by example by stating, in the strategic plan, their goal to improve gender balance by 5% annually within this ministry.

Also missing from this legislation, yet equally vital, is the promotion of gender awareness and gender-analysis training for all male and female employees in all the stakeholder organisations that are involved in the ICT policy formulation and implementation (International Telecommunication Union, Task Force on Gender Issues 1998).

Conclusion

It is apparent that the government of Zimbabwe has taken modest steps to integrate social considerations as well as gender perspectives into the ICT legislation. There is evidently room for improvement so it is imperative that interventions be introduced in order to attain the third

Millennium Development Goal, namely, Promote Gender Equality and Empower Women.

Recommendations on engendering Zimbabwe's ICT policy

The E-nable Project Initiative that ran from 2005 to 2007 was implemented jointly by E-knowledge for Women in Southern Africa (EKOWISA) and Connect Africa and preceded the legislation under discussion. E-nable's purpose was to ensure the organisation of civil society organisations and communities in Zimbabwe and to fortify them through joint networking focused on ICT initiatives concerned with ICT policy, capacity-building in the use of ICTs and knowledge-sharing (E-nable Project Initiative 2007). As noted elsewhere, ICT policy formulation and implementation is multi-sectoral and must, necessarily, have the active involvement of each of these assorted actors (see figure) (United Nations Commission on Science and Technology for Development 1997). Since the draft ICT bill has already been formulated, it

is highly recommended for the MICT to insist on the participation of other stakeholders in subsequent phases of its formulation and implementation. ICT policy-makers will need to create consultative and collaborative methods to make this a reality as well as to interface with ICT experts in academia, the private sector and research organisations.

Sonia Jorge's engendered approach will be useful here (2000). Every stakeholder must also carry out a gender awareness-raising campaign and gender sensitisation so the needs and aspirations of women and girls are incorporated in the ICT policy.

Gender experts and NGOs could assist with gender analysis. In its gender-aware guidelines for policy-making, the ITU Task Force on Gender Issues proposes the establishment of a gender unit within the ICT ministry and/or as an inter-ministerial effort (International Telecommunication Union, Task Force on Gender Issues 1998).

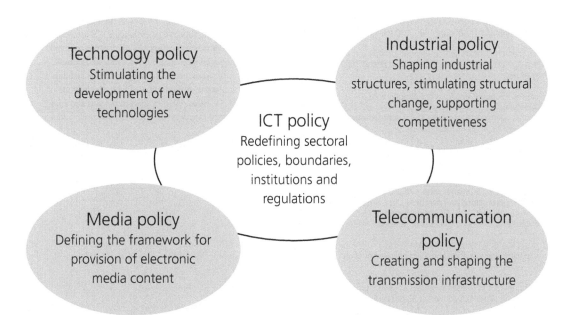

As Zimbabwe already has a ministry for gender, its officers could be permanently seconded to each ministry with a mandate to keep a "gender-sensitive" eye on policies in order that they advise on, and lobby for, gender-aware policies. Balance and efficiency will be achieved if gender and development policymakers are simultaneously trained on ICT matters. The engendered approach to ICT policy evaluation and monitoring should be premised on sex-disaggregated statistics and goals, to make known not only if women are benefiting but also which women by age, race, ethnic group, educational level and location. Both qualitative and quantitative indicators may be utilised for best results.

The African Information Society Initiative Framework (AISI) and the Acacia Initiatives are both credited with the gains in ICT policy implementation in Senegal, Uganda, Mozambique and South Africa, respectively (Marcelle 1998). There may be some value in Zimbabwe's assessing each of these frameworks in order to extract that which may be relevant to Zimbabwe's ICT policy operationalisation.

ICTs continue to play a positive role in bolstering women's empowerment in the entrepreneurial, educational, economic, political and human rights spheres. The Zimbabwe government would do well to conclude the ICT policy formulation and implementation process so that men, women, boys and girls do, indeed, become members of the knowledge society by 2015.

Writer's Bio

Shoko is head of the Information Technology Audit section at the City of Harare, Zimbabwe. Her professional interests cover ICTs for women's empowerment, anti-fraud, risk management, digital forensics, IT governance and IT audit. Shoko is a regular presenter for the Institute of Internal Auditors (Zimbabwe), the Institute of Forensic Auditors (Zimbabwe) and also a part-time lecturer at the Women's University in Africa.

References

Ministry of Information Communication Technology (2008), *Information and Communication Technology Bill* , http://www.ictministry.gov.zw/

Hafkin, N and N. Taggart (2001), *Gender, Information Technology and Developing Countries: An Analytic Study*, Academy for Educational Development

International Fund for Agricultural Development (2010), Rural Poverty in Zimbabwe, www.ruralpovertyportal.org/web/guest/country/home/tags/zimbabwe (Last checked by writer October 2011)

Zunguze, M (2009). 'Zimbabwe Report - Access to Online Information and Knowledge', http://www.giswatch.org/country-report/2009/zimbabwe, (Last checked by writer October 2011)

Mbambo-Thata, B., E. Mlambo and P. Mwatsiya (2009), **'Female-only ICT spaces: perceptions and practices', in I. Buskens and A. Webb (ed.)**, African Women and ICTs - Investigating Technology, Gender and Empowerment, London: International Development Research Centre

Ndlovu, R (2010)'When Solar Meets Wireless', www.thezimbabwesituation.com (Last checked by writer October 2011)

Balancing Act (2011) 'Potraz Launches Rural Telecommunication Project', www.balancingact-africa.com/news. (Last checked by writer October 2011)

Working to Halt Online Abuse (2011) 'Statistics on Cyber-stalking', http://www.haltabuse.org/resources/stats/index.shtml). (Last checked by writer October 2011)

Mugoni, P (2011). 'Southern Africa: We must Protect Women from Cyber-violence', www.genderlinks.com. (Last checked by writer October 2011)

UN Fourth World Conference on Women (1995), 'Beijing Declaration and Platform for Action', http://www.un.org/womenwatch/daw/beijing/platform/ (Last checked by writer October 2011)

United Nations Conference on Trade and Development, Report Of The Expert Meeting On Mainstreaming Gender In Order To Promote Opportunities, Geneva 2001.

International Telecommunication Union's Task Force on Gender Issues (2002), 'Gender and the Digital Divide', www.itu.int/ITU-D/Gender (Last checked by writer October 2011)

International Telecommunication Union's Task Force on Gender Issues (2002), 'Gender-Aware Guidelines for Policy-making and Regulatory Agencies', www.itu.int/ITU-D/Gender (Last checked by writer October 2011)

The E-nable Project Initiative (2007). 'Research Primers On ICT Policy Frameworks and Recommended E-Strategies For Zimbabwe', www.ekowisa.org.zw (Last checked by writer October 2011)

United Nations Commission on Science and Technology for Development (1997), 'Substantive Theme:Information and Communication Technologies for Development'. http://www.unctad.org/en/docs/ecn16_97d4.en.pdf (Last checked by writer October 2011)

S. Jorge (2000). 'Gender Perspectives in Telecommunications Policy: A Curriculum Report', www7.itu.int/treg/Events/Seminars/2000/Symposium/English/document26.pdf

G. Marcelle (1999). , 'Getting Gender into ICT Policy - A Strategic View' in E. Rathgeber and E. Adera (ed.), *Gender and the Information Revolution in Africa*, Ottawa: The International Development Research Centre.

MEDIA WATCH

Media monitoring during the 16 Days of Activism campaign at Municipal Council of Beau Bassin/Rose-Hill in Mauritius.
Photo: Loga Virahsawmy

Media as a tool for gender mainstreaming
By Kudzai Kwangwari

Abstract
This article uses the example of Zimbabwe to illustrate the importance of freedom of expression and freedom of the media to democracy. It is noted that African governments are not prepared to play an active role to promote media freedom because the media is a key tool for accountability and transparency. The author also notes that media freedom and other human rights are only realised when women play an equal role, both in a country's democracy and in its media.

Key words
democracy, freedom of expression, media freedom

Most countries in the world are now advocating for democracy as an effective governance system for development and a better world. Often times, whenever democracy is deficient, it is the media that becomes the greatest casualty because freedoms such as expression, speech, movement, association and thought are clearly conditioned by the extent to which that society is open and free.

By this token, therefore, if one would want to gauge the level of democratic deficit in a country, they have to check the extent to which the media is free. The lower the media freedom indexes in a country, the higher the democratic kwashiorkor. And quite obviously, the media plays a telling role in the promotion of freedom of expression and access to information. It is only when these two are present that one can talk of a functioning democracy. In most parts of Africa, women are usually the most-affected when it comes to access to information and right to freedom of expression.

This is especially so for the following reasons, but not limited to these; media ownership is still in favour of men in Africa and Southern Africa in particular, less women's voices are heard and represented in the media, and in some cases, the cultural set up encourages and reinforces the notion that women must be passive participants in issues including politics, economics, media, and development.

African governments are not prepared to play an active deliberate role to promote media freedom because the media is a key tool for accountability and transparency. Through media, citizens are able to engage their governments on different topical issues that affect them, including women. Because most governments are afraid of being put under pressure by their own people, they would rather ensure that there is no media freedom and people have to fight for it.

Oftentimes people from countries with limited media freedom have to rely on alternative media for access to information and freedom of expression. Countries such as Swaziland, Malawi and Zimbabwe in Southern Africa are clear examples where governments are not engaging in deliberate efforts to ensure media freedom. As a result, citizens from these countries are involved in perennial wars with their governments, fighting for media space and freedom of expression. What is disappointing is that this is happening 20 years after the Windhoek Declaration when we expect the situation to have improved significantly.

Lack of media freedom is the greatest stumbling block for democracy since the active participation of citizens is normally conditioned by levels of awareness and access to information. I argue that if media freedom is improved in Africa, the participation of citizens, especially women, will be enhanced just as democratic deficit will be reduced.

Nothando Mpofu, Radio Dialogue presenter at work. *Photo: Fungai Foto*

Women's contribution is clearly more than what men can and are contributing, though the greater portion of their (women's) contribution is not economically quantifiable. A greater part of the world's 52% women are based in rural communities where access to information and freedom of expression is limited. Here women engage in most of the farming and child development work. It is my argument that once alternative sources of information are provided in these communities, women will have more say in democratic struggles and development, since their participation and social inclusiveness will improve.

In Zimbabwe for instance, Radio Dialogue a community radio initiative which has been fighting for a broadcasting license for the past decade, is creatively using alternative legal means to promote access to information to both rural and urban communities, including production of radio programmes that are put on CDs and tapes for distribution, a cellphone SMS system, and distributing newspaper returns. This, by and large, has enhanced both the participation and general social inclusiveness of women in the communities Radio Dialogue serves. Women in these communities have been able to take an active role in developmental projects in their respective constituencies.

So even in countries where there is limited media freedom, citizens will do well to explore alternative platforms that can be used effectively to advance access to information and freedom of expression. This is especially so with regards to rural women who should have an important voice which shapes the developmental agenda of a nation. If women's voices are given more prominence in the media, the real social issues that affect our communities will be more clearly defined and will be given the attention they deserve.

Women entrepreneurs must also be encouraged to venture into media business so that media coverage of women's issues will be given more prominence and space. Oftentimes prominence is given to male voices and males are accessed as authorities on different topical issues. There should be a deliberate policy in these countries to develop women experts who then become authorities in different fields and their voices accessed in mainstream and alternative media. More women media practitioners must be developed and empowered to tackle women's issues.

The media should also play a very critical role in the promotion of women into not only leadership positions, but all sectors of society so that the issue of gender is mainstreamed to all levels and all spheres of life. While training institution enrolment and intake of female trainees continues to increase in numbers, especially in Zimbabwe, there has not been a corresponding development in roles, including media managers, media owners, and media policy makers. Efforts must be made to create an engendered plan to ensure this does not continue.

This media should not, however, be a preserve of women and "their cause," but it should be all-inclusive so that men don't feel like the intention is to invert the system but to improve it. Male counterparts should play an active role in both gender-friendly policy formulation and improving portrayal of women in the media. On the other hand, women must also do more in terms of advocating and demanding access to information and freedom of expression as they say "Nothing for us without us." This advocacy work must be targeted not only at governments, but also international NGOs that advocate for general women's empowerment.

The participation of women in democratic processes cannot be taken for granted given the fact that they are virtually "passive kingmakers" as most politicians (men), turn to them for political support. It is then mindboggling that when it comes to policy formulation, women are found uninvolved, passive, and at best they only react to bad policy already in place. So women must be given a platform through the use of both equity and equality approaches to ensure their maximum participation.

However, the media also has to play a very critical role in the promotion of women's issues and governments must ensure the mainstreaming of gender issues in all areas so that the full and active participation of women can be realised. It is ill-advised to mourn the negative portrayal of women in the media, or their poor representation in the media, or their lack of access to information, when they (women) are not empowered in other sectors such as education, health, economic and political. The media can then play a very important role not only to sustain the acquired empowering position, but also watchdogging the acquired state of affairs.

Writer's Bio
Kwangwari is the Project Manager at Radio Dialogue FM Trust in Zimbabwe.

Election violence limits freedom of expression amongst journalists
By Perpetual Sichikwenkwe

Freedom of information and access to information are both important to ensure proper functioning of a democratic country like Zambia. The two cannot entirely do without the presence of the other. When there is freedom of information and access to information, government avails a fora for it to be questioned on governance issues by its citizens, while on the other hand, citizens are able to participate because they have information readily available for them to use. It enhances accountability and provides a tool for government to analyse itself.

Media is one way government disseminates information to the public. The media needs access to information and also freedom of expression to be able to distribute information and educate citizens. It is for this reason that the media and civil society have been pushing the Zambian government to create a freedom of information law. The enactment of such a law would keep Zambia on par with other African countries and ensure it meets its obligations under the Windhoek Declaration.

The Zambian media, as in many African countries, does not enjoy or have full access to information as it should. In instances where media personnel have attempted to access certain information, they often put their lives at risk.

It is often during elections when journalists struggle to access information. While it is the duty of journalists to educate and inform members of the public on various national issues, politicians prevent them from doing so by ensuring they do not have the ability to access relevant political information.

Cadres within political parties frequently threaten journalists. It is even worse for female journalists, who fear harassment or worse while in the field. During the past several elections journalists have been threatened while carrying out their duties. They have been denied access to information and in turn had their freedom of expression limited. Elections in Zambia have proven to be a dangerous beat for female journalists, who have sometimes been threatened with rape.

A female voter casts her vote during Zambia's 2011 Presidential election.
Photo: Reuters

The media have a duty to inform and educate members of the public about the electoral process and it is a requirement that they have free access to information so they can report objectively. However, political parties, NGOs, civil society and other stakeholders have often accused the media of biased election coverage. This perception has prompted political actors to vent their anger at journalists.

Zambia is still fighting for a freedom of information bill and the Zambia National Broadcasting Services Act, which would seek to transform ZNBC into a media broadcaster. This has been stalled since 2002 when it was withdrawn from parliament on the pretext that government needed to have more time for consulations. This move threatens the achieve-ment of freedom of expression that citizens in the country have been hoping for.

These bills would hopefully end the frequent assaults on journalists. In the most recent case a television crew was assaulted by more than 100 political operatives because it was going after information a party did not want it to have. Such acts are a direct infringement of freedom of expression and hence, a failure on Zambia's part to uphold its commitments under the Windhoek Declaration.

Another case is that of a private TV station reporter who was beaten during the 2008 presidential elections. On 18 October 2008, political cadres attacked a television crew, which included two women, from Muvi TV, accusing the station of biased reporting against their candidate, acting President Rupiah Banda.

Dainess Nyirenda was one of two female journalists who was also beaten and harassed while she and her colleagues were working. Some of the perpetrators attempted to unbutton her shirt. The crew was forced to run away before they could finish gathering the information they wanted for the story.

Dainess Nyirenda was beaten and harassed while doing her job.
Photo: Nyirenda's facebook photo gallery

Further, law enforcement officers often subject journalists to physical harassment, including at political meetings.

This kind of behaviour has hindered many journalists, stopping them from enjoying full access to information and freedom of expression.

International instruments such as the United Nations Covenant on Civil and Political Rights (ICCPR) set out that freedom of expression and access to information are closely linked. The African Charter on Human and Peoples Rights also protects the right to information. Unfortunately, many African countries like Zambia do not yet have local laws that enforce these vital human rights.

Writer's Bio
Sichikwenkwe is a Zambian journalist and advocate for women's rights.

Creating a new citizen, gender-focused SABC - what is to be done?
By Kate Skinner

Public broadcasting is central to a functioning democracy, being the source of much of the news and information that is consumed by millions of citizens. As such it has an ability to create the frame of reference for many public debates, be these about economic policy or gender issues. As a result, a national public broadcaster that is without sufficient safeguards is often a tempting and vulnerable target for political interference.

The South African Broadcasting Corporation (SABC) has experienced significant governance instability and turmoil since 2007. In 2007, in the dying days of the Mbeki presidency, there was direct political interference in the selection of its board. The board thus started its tenure as illegitimate and politically isolated. Power had shifted to new incoming president, Jacob Zuma. Weak and ineffective, the board found it difficult to hold management to account. Management although originally close to Mbeki, had by then started to realign itself to Zuma. By the end of the 2008/2009 financial year this poorly managed SABC had posted pre-tax losses of R784 million.

After public outcries about these losses, there were strident calls for the SABC board to resign or be removed. Eventually an amendment was passed to the Broadcasting Act, 1999, giving parliament the power to remove the board. The

board was thus removed mid-2009 and an interim board put in its place.

The interim board's tenure ensured a brief period of stability. Chief Executive Dali Mpofu was removed and the interim board moved to secure a R1.47 billion government guarantee to allow the SABC to raise funds from commercial banks to pay back its debts to independent producers (who produce the majority of SABC's local programming) and others. It was also during this period that a new "permanent" board was nominated. An unprecedented 200 nominations were received by parliament.

The year 2010 thus opened on a cautiously optimistic note with a new publically-supported board in place. Sadly, however, things soon went awry. The new chair of the SABC board, Ben Ngubane, created fresh governance crises by unilaterally appointing a new head of news, contrary to the Broadcasting Act, good corporate governance practices and the board's own processes. Allegedly he was acting on instructions from President Zuma, who wanted a particular candidate, Phil Molefe, appointed. Initially board members stood united in their opposition to these governance breaches but when parliament refused to intervene, the board's resolve eventually crumbled. Four members resigned and the remaining members finally ratified the appointment.

Simultaneously, new battles started to emerge between the board and the new CEO appointed by the interim board, Solly Mokoetle. Mokoetle supported the board chair's unilateral appointment of the head of news. Further, Mokoetle failed to deliver on a detailed turn around strategy to ensure the repayment of the SABC's loans secured against the government guarantee.

Reflecting the political flux of the times, a number of further crises then engulfed the SABC. The Board fired Mokoetle, who was replaced by acting CEO Robin Nicholson. Nicholson's contract expired without a new CEO being employed. Court battles and further controversies ensued when Nicholson's contract was not renewed. A new acting CEO, Phil Molefe, was then employed.

In the midst of these crises the "Save our SABC" campaign, later renamed the "SOS: Support Public Broadcasting" Coalition - comprised of unions, NGOs, CBOs, independent film makers etc. - was launched to give civil society a voice in these crises. During this time, Gender Links and Gender and Media Southern Africa (GEMSA) joined the working group.

The Coalition fought for a strong, independent, publically accountable SABC committed to the broadcasting of quality citizen-orientated public programming committed to the furthering of the principles of our constitution, including our bill of rights and socio-economic rights.

The Coalition played a key role in the appointment of the 2010 SABC board, putting forward a number of strong candidates. Further, it played an important role in lobbying for the removal of the controversial Draft Public Service Broadcasting Bill introduced in 2009, ostensibly to stabilise the SABC. The bill called for a new broadcasting tax of up to 1% of personal income to fund public broadcasting and further called for significant new powers for the minister to intervene in management crises.

The Coalition - while welcoming government's commitment to public funding - argued that the funding model needed to be further debated and researched as part of a comprehensive review of the outdated Broadcasting White Paper, 1998. The Coalition argued that this review was long overdue particularly since the SABC was moving into a new digital multi-channel environment.

The SOS Coalition thus called for a comprehensive economic modelling exercise leading to the adopting a new funding model that while still including a percentage of advertising would significantly increase public funding. (The SABC is presently funded by 80% advertising.) And clearly, over and above these technical changes to the public broadcasting model, the SABC needs to be guaranteed the political space to live up to its requirement of being a source of independent and citizen-orientated public programming. Therefore the Coalition put forward a set of detailed proposals to ensure the independence of the SABC including calls for the SABC to be transformed into a constitutionally-protected Chapter 9 institution.

The Coalition has argued that these proposals will go some way to ensure the SABC produces quality citizen-orientated public programming. The Ministry has agreed to a broadcasting policy review process.

Writer's Bio
Skinner is the Coordinator of the civil society SOS: Support Public Broadcasting Coalition.

The War at Home - GBV Indicators Project

Machisa, Rachel Jewkes, Colleen Lowe Morna and Kubi Rama (Editors)

This report shows that over half (51.3%) of women in Gauteng province have experienced some form of violence (emotional, economic, physical or sexual) in their lifetime. Sadly, 75.5% of men in the province admit to perpetrating some form of violence against women. The report further indicate that emotional violence - a form of violence not well defined in domestic violence legislation and thus not well reflected in police data - is the most commonly reported form of violence with 43.7% women experiencing and 65.2% men admitting to its perpetration.

To order: http://www.genderlinks.org.za/page/shop

The Gender Based Violence Indicators Study - Botswana

Colleen Lowe Morna and Kubi Rama (Editors)

This report shows that over two thirds of women in Botswana (67%) have experienced some form of gender violence in their lifetime including partner and non-partner violence. A smaller, but still high, proportion of men (44%) admit to perpetrating violence against women. Nearly one third of women (29%) experienced Intimate Partner Violence (IPV) in the 12 months to the prevalence survey that formed the flagship research tool in this study. In contrast, only 1.2% of Batswana women reported cases of GBV to the police in the same period.

To order: http://www.genderlinks.org.za/page/shop

African Theatre: Media and performance

David Kerr (Guest Editor)

This book focuses on ways African theatre and performance relate to various kinds of media. Several of the articles deal with popular video, with an emphasis on video drama and soaps from Eastern and Southern Africa, though the Nigerian "Nollywood" phenomenon is not completely neglected. One article addresses the interface between live performance and video (or still photography) and the way popular live or recorded music in South Africa creates layers of theatrical and ideological expression and links the on-line social networking phenomenon to new performance identities.

We love to Hate Each Other: mediated football fan culture

By Roy Krovel & Thore Roksvold (Editors)

Football fans are often portrayed as enthusiastic, loyal, critical, and sometimes violent. But what is about football that appeals to them? How do the media - newspapers, radio, TV, blogs and we forums - accommodate the needs of fans and what connection - if any - is there between the imagined community of football fans and the broader society? These are the questions explored by 20 well-known and merited researchers from eight countries in this anthology about the mediation of football.

To order visit:
http://www.nordicom.gu.se/eng.php?portal=publ&main=info_publ2.php&ex=347&me=13

SADC Gender Protocol 2011 Barometer

By Colleen Lowe Morna and Loveness Njambaya Nyakujara (Editors)

This report moves into high gear with the introduction of the SADC Gender and Development Index (SGDI) that complements the Citizen Score Card (CSC) that has been running for three years. With empirical data on 23 indicators in six sectors, the SGDI puts SADC countries at 64% of where they need to be by 2015: the target date for meeting the 28 targets of the Protocol. Seychelles, South Africa and Lesotho lead the way with Mozambique, Angola, Malawi and DRC in the bottom four. Citizens rate their governments at a mere 55% (one percent up from last year).

To order, visit: http://www.genderlinks.org.za/page/shop

So This Is Democracy?

By Media Institute of Southern Africa

The publication documents numerous media freedom and freedom of expression violations that MISA recorded in Southern African during the course of the year. This publication represents joint effort and in particular a collective input from various diverse specialists, media professionals and researchers in the SADC region. In the first instance we are deeply grateful to all the individual authors of the country media freedom and freedom of expression overviews for their thorough and insightful analyses.

To read online:
http://www.misa.org/researchandpublication/democracy/democracy.html

Making Every Voice Count: Gender in the Media Centres of Excellence

By Patricia A. Made and Sikhonzile Ndlovu

The manual maps out the Media Centres of Excellence process, including the manage-ment, monitoring and evaluation tools. Reporting Southern Africa is like a concertina that opens out at the critical Stage 7: Backstopping.The manual facilities stage 7 of the COEs process that will involve on the job training for participating media houses. Individual country contexts will determine the schedule of modules and activities. The training is designed using the ten focus areas in the SADC Gender Protocol.

To order, visit: http://www.genderlinks.org.za/page/shop

Gender Mainstreaming in Local Government: Centres of Excellence Training manual

By Colleen Lowe Morna and Abigail Jacobs Williams

The Gender Mainstreaming in Local Government Centres of Excellence training manual guides local government trainers as they work with local government stakeholders in mainstreaming gender in local council institutions and communities. The manual draws from several GL gender mainstreaming training manuals developed over a number of years for the region. The different training modules in the manual also link closely with SADC Protocol on Gender and Development thematic provisions.

To view the soft copy visit:
http://www.genderlinks.org.za/article/gender-mainstreaming-in-local-government-coe-training-manual-2012-02-29

The Gender and Media Diversity Journal (GMDJ)

The Gender and Media Diversity Journal is the biennial journal of the Gender and Media Diversity Centre (GMDC). The journal is intellectual but not academic. It provides up-to-date and cutting edge information on media diversity in Southern Africa and the space for the dissemination of research findings and projects; case studies; campaigns, policy developments; and opinion and debate on media practice in the region. Each journal focuses on a different thematic areas identified in consultation with the GMDC advisory group. Inaugural issues (before the establishment of the GMDC) focused on the Global Gender Media Monitoring Project and the second on the Gender and Media Summit held in September 2006 under the banner Media Diversity: Good For Business, Good for Democracy. Other issues have looked at tabloidisation of the media, media activism, and case studies based on the 2008 GEM Summit, under the theme Critical Citizens, responsive media.

Why?
Despite its mission of "giving voice to the voiceless," the media worldwide is heavily biased towards covering the views of those in power, an elite group often defined according to race, ethnicity, class and gender. In Southern Africa, where democracy is a relatively new and fragile phenomenon, the media are still largely state dominated. The concept of a public media is weak. Albeit to different degrees, private and community media face political, organisational and financial challenges.

Overall, whether in the public or private sphere, media ownership is concentrated in a few hands. The voices of those most affected by policies and unequal power relations in society are seldom heard even though they constitute the majority of news consumer population. Failure to understand and respond to audiences in all their diversity is also bad for business.

The journal aims to:

- Develop and share a body of knowledge on media diversity in Southern Africa.
- Promote more probing, analytical and contextual journalism.
- Share best practices on how to achieve greater diversity in media content, ownership and market share.
- Contribute to greater media literacy and responsiveness among ordinary citizens - women and men - in Southern Africa.

Each journal will contain:
- Introduction - editorial and news briefs.
- Thematic focus - insights from experts in the regional and around the world.
- Media watch - reviews and reports of programmes, projects, research, policy and development related to gender and diversity in the media.
- Opinion and letters.

The Southern Africa Media Diversity Journal targets media workers and owners, policy-makers, researchers, lecturers, student journalists, activists and those individuals and organisations working towards media diversity in the region. Contributions are invited and solicited from groups and individuals such as these and commissioned by the editor.

How to contribute:
For further information and to request full contributors' guidelines please contact:
Gender Links -
gmdcmanager@genderlinks.org.za
Tel: + 27 11 622 2877